PLOESTI

Books by James Dugan

THE GREAT IRON SHIP

MAN UNDER THE SEA

UNDERSEA EXPLORER

CAPTAIN COUSTEAU'S UNDERWATER TREASURY
(co-editor with Jacques-Yves Cousteau)

PLOESTI

THE GREAT GROUND-AIR

BATTLE OF 1 AUGUST 1943

JAMES DUGAN AND CARROLL STEWART

Editorial Offices:
22883 Quicksilver Drive
Dulles, VA 20166

Order Department:
P.O. Box 960
Herndon, VA 20172

Brassey's books are available at special discounts for bulk purchases
for sales promotions, premiums, fund-raising, or educational use.

Library of Congress Cataloging-in-Publication Data
Dugan, James, 1912–1967.
Ploesti : the great ground-air battle of 1 August, 1943 / James
Dugan and Carroll Stewart. —1st ed.
p. cm.
Includes bibliographical references and index.
ISBN 1-57488-144-2 (pbk.)
1. Ploesti, Battles of, 1943–1944. 2. World War, 1939–1945—
Aerial operations, American. 3. World War, 1939–1945—Campaigns—
Romania. I. Stewart, Carroll. II. Title.
D766.4.D8 1998
940.54'2198—dc21   97-31258
CIP

The quotations beginning Chapters 6, 8 and 10 are from W. H. D. Rouse's
translation of *The Iliad*, published by New American Library of World
Literature, Inc.

The quotation beginning Chapter 12 is from E. V. Rieu's translation of
The Odyssey, published by Penguin Books.

PUBLISHER'S NOTE TO THE ORIGINAL EDITION

During the events described herein James Dugan was with the Photo & Newsreel Section of the Eighth Air Force, which provided three bomb groups for Tidal Wave. Carroll Stewart was the public relations officer of one of them, the Traveling Circus. The authors knew many men who did not return and, shortly after the mission, interviewed scores who did. This material was only used in a 32-page airdrop booklet in French, *Le Bombardement de Ploesti*. Since then the authors have corresponded with about half the living U. S. participants in Tidal Wave, as well as with the ground staff and relatives of the fallen. A questionnaire was circulated among the veterans, and the pilots and navigators were furnished additional target area charts in which to draw their courses over Ploesti. The two forms were also printed in German and distributed among the small percentage of Luftwaffe fliers and flak men who survived the war. The authors found the five surviving German pilots who fought in Tidal Wave, the four top fighter controllers, and a number of Gerstenberg's staff officers.

The authors personally interviewed 164 U. S. combat men of 1 August 1943 and dozens of ground (and grounded) men, widows, and relatives. Dugan and Stewart consulted 28 unpublished personal narratives and diaries of U. S. Tidal Wave men, plus a prison camp chronicle by the inimitable Douglas Collins. The spate of narratives indicated that the men regarded the low raid as the greatest event in their lives. A hundred men wrote shorter recollections of the day. Very few of them had previously told their stories for publication, so that the accounts were relatively fresh, even after the passage of years. Quite a few questionnaires furnished cross checks on what happened in a single aircraft and among squadrons and groups. The percentage of corroboration among these individual accounts was extremely high, notwithstanding the fact that men had been separated for a long time. A handful had improved their memories over the years, and some of these accounts could be checked against earlier versions by the same men.

By compiling the first complete mission roster of Tidal Wave, the authors believe they were able to avoid the sort of evidence on Ploesti that Colonel Kane encountered some time after the raid. Kane was in an air terminal and overheard a U.S.A.F. sergeant telling some new acquaintances, "I was Killer Kane's tail gunner at Ploesti." Kane stepped over and said, "Pardon me, but did I hear my name mentioned?" The sergeant shot out his hand and said, "Colonel, meet the biggest liar west of the Mississippi."

Five or six of the outstanding men of the mission had deliberately or subconsciously put the awful details out of mind, and their stories had to be gathered from others. One of the shining heroes of Ploesti had not spoken a word about it in seventeen years. After a preliminary interview he became upset, refused to say anything more, and would not even furnish a photograph of himself.

The research entailed two trips to Europe and about 50,000 miles of travel in the United States. The U. S. Air Force coöperated wholeheartedly, although this is not an official history. The U.S.A.F. declassified every known document and picture on Tidal Wave. Several former officers provided documents that were not in the official archives because of the primitive record-keeping in the desert.

The U.S.A.F. read the manuscript for security. However, this surveillance did not involve censorship or approval or disapproval of the treatment. The sole remaining security consideration was to protect the real names of certain Europeans who helped the Ploesti men and who may be living today under governments that resent such activity.

CONTENTS

Bibliography and Credits

Maps

PLOESTI

In Tsarist times a game of courage called Kukushka was played late at night in garrisons in Caucasia and Siberia. Two officers stood in adjoining rooms with an open door between. One had a pistol, the other had not. At a signal the lights were extinguished. The unarmed player opened the contest by dashing toward the door, yelling "Kukushka!" The rules permitted him to go through it straight or diagonally, left or right, crouching or leaping. His opponent's problem was to shoot him as he came through the door.

Othmar Gurtner, *The Myth of the Eigerwald*

He who owns the oil will own the world, for he will rule the sea by means of the heavy oils, the air by means of the ultra-refined oils, and the land by means of petrol and the illuminating oils. And, in addition to these, he will rule his fellow men in an economic sense, by reason of the fantastic wealth he will derive from oil.   HENRI BÉRENGER, 1921

1

THE HIDDEN MISSION

During the middle years of World War II the United States Army Air Forces carried on a determined and bloody bombing offensive against one of the most vital, distant and deadly industrial targets in Hitler's Europe, the oil refineries at a city called Ploesti, in the kingdom of Romania. The campaign against Ploesti, which Winston Churchill called "the taproot of German might," opened with a quixotic attempt to avenge the Japanese assault on Pearl Harbor.

In May 1942 a secret, hastily assembled band of American free-booters known as Halverson Project No. 63 took off from Florida in 23 new Consolidated Liberator (B-24) bombers with orders that rivaled science fiction. They were sent to do nothing less than bomb Tokyo.

The planned route from Florida to Tokyo was not the direct 8,200-mile line to the northwest; instead, it equaled a circumnavigation of the globe. The course, south and east, called for a series of formation flights to Brazil, across the equatorial Atlantic, and over the bulge of Africa, without ground navigational aids or bases that could service the new-model bomber. There were no air charts of the route. The navigators used National Geographic Society members' maps and scattered sections of African geological surveys.

The Liberators carried everything needed for the extravaganza except bombs and further installments of gasoline. They were overloaded with three months' food for 231 men and a double issue of anything that could be scrounged. Each navigator had two sextants, each man two mess kits, each plane a spare nosewheel. The Halverson Detachment, or "Halpro" as the outlandish expedition was dubbed, carried its own intelligence echelon, including a stockbroker named Paul Zuckerman; Wilfred J. Smith, Professor of History at Ohio State University; Floyd N. Shumaker, a Mandarin-speaking airplane salesman, whose son, Thomas, was a navigator with the mission; Dr. Lauchlin Currie, President Franklin D. Roosevelt's adviser on China; and General P. H. Wang of the Chinese Air Force. The combat men were also exotic. One of the pilots was a full-blooded Oklahoma Indian, Meech Tahsequah. There was also a war analyst from the Pittsburgh *Post-Gazette*, a former actor in *Our Gang* movie comedies, a Royal Dutch Airlines pilot, and Richard Sanders of Salt Lake City, Utah, who was to become, at the age of twenty-eight, the youngest U. S. general officer since the Civil War. Even a skeleton ground echelon was aboard. Each plane carried two mechanics who were expected to do the work of the usual seven-man ground crew.

The cutting-out party was named for its leader, a dark, impetuous pilot, Colonel Harry A. ("Hurry-Up") Halverson.* His expedition was the product of the shocked, frantic days after Pearl Harbor, when the Japanese almost obliterated the U. S. air forces in Hawaii and the Far East. Halpro came from vengeful councils of veteran American airmen with their chief, General Henry

* Born Halvor A. Halvorsen.

("Hap") Arnold. Colonel James A. Doolittle's carrier-based raid on Japan a month earlier came from the same fiery moots.

At Chengtu, in interior China, Halverson's Liberators were to fuel from buried caches, sling Italian bombs, and move up to operational fields around Chekiang within return range of Japan. The forward bases were primitive earthen fighter strips, hardly capable of handling spotter planes, and the Liberator was a 60,000-pound four-engined bomber with a 110-foot wingspread. Indeed, Doolittle's raid had drawn attention to the likelihood of further attacks on Japan, and the Japanese army was marching rapidly toward the Chekiang bases.

As they headed out from Florida on the chimerical adventure, Halverson's outfit did not know the Japanese strike was impossible and that, instead, they were to be sent to Romania on the longest bombing mission ever to be attempted until the long-range Super-fortress came into action two years later.

Halpro island-hopped to Natal, Brazil, with one ship unable to keep up with the formation because its right wheel would not retract. It was the flagship carrying the furious Halverson and his executive officer, Colonel George F. ("Mickey") McGuire, piloted by a thirty-four-year-old ex-KLM pilot from Indiana, Alfred Kalberer, who had been flying since he was seventeen. Kalberer's flight engineer was a newly recruited garage mechanic, who could not find anyone able to fix the hanging wheel on the Caribbean stops. The flagship barely made 135 miles an hour and its stalling speed was 110.

Without waiting for their commander the other pilots took off from Natal and completed the first formation flight across the South Atlantic to Africa. They landed on the Pan-American passenger base at Accra—there were no military airdromes available. The pilots intended to lay over a few days to service their over-worked craft and wait for Halverson, but the airport manager was nervous about German air raids, so they gassed up and took off directly on the 2,400-mile flight to the Anglo-Egyptian Sudan. They ran into an evening cyclone which scattered the formation. Each plane continued on its own in the howling rain, unable to take starsights, and, of course, without ground radio-direction.

As they groped across Africa in the stormy night, Kalberer took off from Brazil to fly his overburdened bus across the Atlantic with the wheels down.

In the morning the forward element gazed down on solid African jungle without landmarks. The navigators pored over the geological survey charts, unable to relate them to anything below. The navigator of *Babe the Big Blue Ox* was Lieutenant Walter L. Shea of the Bronx, New York, who had been washed out of pilot training by the discovery that he was nearly blind in the left eye from an air rifle accident as a boy. He had concealed this handicap from pilot John Wilkinson. The pilot said, "Come on, Shea boy, give us a fix." Shea handed up a chart with a position vaguely outlined. John Wilcox, the co-pilot, said, "I can't make out where we are from this." Shea said, "All right, *you* guys tell me where we are." Wilcox cried, "I think I got it!" Shea said, "Okay, see that you mark my chart correctly."

Further along in the voyage another Liberator was flying through cloud when the pilot, Captain Robert Paullin, noticed dark patches passing below his wings. "What's the highest mountain around here?" he phoned his navigator, Thomas A. Shumaker. "Mount Marra," came the reply. "Three thousand seventy." Paullin said, "Three thousand seventy what?" Shumaker said, "This damn French map . . . Hey, it's three thousand *meters!*" That was more than ten thousand feet. Paullin pushed up full throttle and barely cleared the peak.

The fliers looked down at giraffes and elephants on the savannah. A few weeks before, many of them had been sitting in humdrum offices, with no more thought of traveling in Africa than of rocketing to the moon. In the fuselage the sergeants breached canned peaches, played poker, and wondered what the women would be like in China.

The main element landed intact at the Pan-American base at Wadi Seidna, Khartoum. An R.A.F. officer asked Shea, "How close did you come to your ETA [Estimated Time of Arrival]?" The one-eyed navigator replied nonchalantly, "Two miles off the heading and one minute early"—improving his plotting by 75 minutes. The Briton pointed his handle-bar mustaches in sheer admiration.

Indeed, it was an extraordinary flight. Halpro had come eight thousand miles on uncharted ways over sea, jungle and desert, through storms and starless night, freighted with the contents of a food warehouse, a supply depot and its ground personnel. A British lorry driver gave Shea a lift, noting that the navigator was packing a .45 automatic on each hip. "Where do you blokes think you are—Africa?" asked the driver.

In the meantime Kalberer completed his precarious trudge across the ocean and landed at Abidjan on the Ivory Coast with zero on his gas gauges. He refueled and started across Africa, still dragging his wheels, and was forced down at an R.A.F. base at El Fasher in the Sudanese desert. He asked the station commander for 500 gallons of gas. Tears welled into the Briton's eyes. "Lieutenant," he said, "every pint of petrol we've got has to be carried here on camel back, eight hundred miles across the desert." Nevertheless he gave Kalberer the gas, and the flagship went on to Khartoum.

Meeting U. S. combat men for the first time, the British gave them a cordial welcome, which Halverson quickly translated into a whopping requisition on military stores. Each man drew a pair of suède desert boots, drill shorts, bush jacket, cork topee, green cashmere knee stockings and an ivory cigaret holder. Duked out in these costumes, the airmen swarmed into a Khartoum night club that boasted three Viennese hostesses. The ladies were enemy nationals, but this sort of technicality did not faze the red-blooded American boy. The hostesses would accept only officers as dance partners, so the sergeants formed their own conga line, snaking around to the band leader's calls of "One, two, three—kick!" and breaking formation only to pull up their socks.

It was a little comic gleam in a tragic period for the Allies. The Liberators were deep inland at Khartoum because German planes were raiding Egyptian air bases almost as they pleased. Everywhere the Axis was winning the war. Bataan was falling and Corregidor would soon go. General Joseph Stilwell was retreating from Burma. In Russia the Germans had taken Kerch, were besieging Sevastopol, and the road seemed open to a great prize —the Russian oil fields at Baku. General Erwin Rommel's Afrika

Korps was threatening Egypt. U-boats were killing ships off the U. S. Atlantic seaboard. There was only one Allied gain. The battered U. S. Navy had turned back the Japanese in the Battle of the Coral Sea.

Halpro's Chinese expedition was held at Khartoum, awaiting orders. Halverson ran practice missions to keep the crews on the ball. That took more life out of the planes. The best maintenance man in the air force, Captain Ulysses S. ("Sam") Nero, fought the scouring desert dust, without replacement parts and with too few mechanics. In 1921, as a sergeant, Sam Nero had flown with Colonel William Mitchell to sink the 27,000-ton war-prize battleship *Ostfriesland* in the historic assertion of the airplane's supremacy over warships. Now Nero declared one plane after another unserviceable until Halpro was down to half its original strength.

In June Halpro's destiny changed overnight. The Japanese captured Chekiang, from which Halpro was supposed to bomb Japan. On 5 June the U. S. Congress declared war on Bulgaria, Hungary and Romania. Oddly enough, Hitler's puppet dictator of Romania, Ion Antonescu, had declared war on the United States nine months before, but not until now had he been honored with a counter-declaration. Washington's belated response was to legalize an invasion of Romania by Halverson. Hap Arnold ordered Hurry-Up to strike Europe's greatest oil refinery, the Astro Romana plant, located at Ploesti, with an annual productive capacity of two million metric tons.

The airmen asked each other, "Where is this Ploesti? How come?" Their top commanders knew the name well; capturing or destroying Ploesti had long been a classic problem in the world's war colleges. The name was being used frequently in the secure rooms in Washington, London, Berlin, Moscow and Cairo. Ploesti's refineries produced one-third of Adolf Hitler's high-octane aviation gasoline, panzer fuel, benzine and lubricants. From Ploesti came half of the oil that kept Rommel's armor running on the sand seas of Mediterranean Africa. At that bitter moment, destroying Astro Romana seemed the only move that could stop Rommel in deltaic Egypt and the smashing German drive to take

Baku. If Hitler seized the Baku oil, it would quench the thirst of the Nazi machine for a long time to come, and it was far beyond bombing range of any Allied base in prospect or any bomber in production. In the airman's thinking, Ploesti was the key to many doors.

President Roosevelt's bright friend Harry Hopkins had been urging a blow at Ploesti. Royal Air Force Chief Marshal Sir Arthur Tedder offered petrol and bombs from his meager African stores to hit Ploesti. The U. S. military attaché in Cairo, Colonel Bonner F. Fellers, declared that the Ploesti refineries were "by far the most decisive objective," in fact, "the strategic target of the war," and they were "within striking distance of American heavies." In ordering it to be bombed, the Joint Chiefs of Staff overruled the misgivings of some airmen who said that Ploesti was too far for planes to carry an effective bomb load. They would have to trade bombs for extra gas to bring them back. A Liberator could not carry much more than a ton of bombs that distance and Halpro was down to thirteen planes.

But the time was now or never, in view of Rommel's rapid progress toward the Nile. Sam Nero painted fake insignia on the B-24's and moved them to the take-off base, the R.A.F. training school at Fayid on the Great Bitter Lake. It had been raided four times by the Luftwaffe in the past fortnight. Halverson was jeopardizing his force merely to reach the forward base. Halpro landed at Fayid the day the gallant Free French garrison was forced out at Bir Hacheim and the Afrika Korps was laagering up for the victory march to Egypt. There was a rumor in Cairo that Hitler had reserved two floors in Shepheard's Hotel to accept the surrender of Africa.

Washington asked Moscow to permit Halpro to land behind the Russian lines, to shorten the flight over Ploesti. The Kremlin was silent. The American privateers faced the longest bombing flight in history. None of them had ever been in combat, dropped a live bomb, or seen an enemy pursuit plane. They were going to fly over unknown blacked-out lands at night, without proper charts, flouting the U. S. daylight bombing doctrine for which they had been trained and the Liberator designed.

The airplane had never been tested in combat by Americans. The first production run of the B-24 had gone to Britain, where it had been dubbed the Liberator. It was a fat, slab-sided machine with a radically thin, high-set wing that looked incapable of bearing the ship's weight. It had twin oval rudders and a low-slung tricycle undercarriage. Yet the "pregnant cow," as airmen called her, could fly faster and farther at 20,000-25,000 feet than the vaunted B-17 Flying Fortress, and with a greater bomb load.

Before take-off Kalberer ran into an Australian mechanic who was familiar with the LB-30, the Royal Air Force designation for the Liberator. "Would you have a look at my right wheel?" asked the pilot. "It won't retract." The Aussie got under the machine and said, "No wonder, sir. The strut you have on 'er was not made for the Liberator. I'll have a look in stores." He came back and installed a proper Liberator strut.

An R.A.F. officer briefed Halverson's men for the mission. He warned them about a fake Ploesti the Germans had erected ten

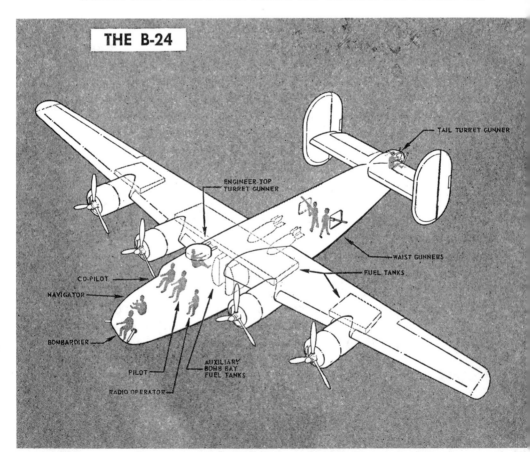

THE B-24

TAIL TURRET GUNNER

ENGINEER-TOP
TURRET GUNNER

WAIST GUNNERS

FUEL TANKS

CO-PILOT

NAVIGATOR

BOMBARDIER

AUXILIARY
BOMB BAY
FUEL TANKS

PILOT

RADIO OPERATOR

miles east of the target, and announced the course: they were to cross the Mediterranean to a lighthouse on the Turkish coast. "However, gentlemen, you are not—and I repeat *not*—to enter neutral Turkish territory," he said. The fliers glanced at each other; the direct line to the target was over Turkey. The briefing officer continued, "You will swing out to the west and skirt Turkey in this fashion, then turn back northeast across northern Greece [which was German-held] to the Romanian port of Constanta on the Black Sea. Follow the pipeline west to the Danube. You will follow the river inland until you come to a fork and a diamond-shaped island. From that point take your northern heading direct to the Astro Romana refinery." The fliers groaned. An American Intelligence officer concluded the briefing. "This will be a momentous mission," he said, "and can have a tremendous effect. You will bomb from thirty thousand feet and land at Ramadi in Iraq."

Captain John Payne, one of the pilots, said, "To us the briefing was straight out of *The Wonderful Wizard of Oz*. Many of our ships could never make thirty thousand feet with an extra bomb bay tank and six five-hundred-pound bombs. And range! We calculated the round trip was twenty-six hundred miles. Even if we stripped the bombs and put two gas tanks in the bomb bay, we'd never make it back on the briefed route."

The mission navigator, Lieutenant Bernard Rang, a civil air transport alumnus, called a navigators' meeting in his room without telling Halverson. Rang pinned up a National Geographic Society map of the Middle East and pointed out, "It can't be done. If we have to veer all around Turkey, nobody will make Iraq. But, for God's sake, don't anybody land in Turkey, or you'll be interned for the rest of the war. If your pilot insists on it because you're about out of gas, try your damndest to talk him into Aleppo, Syria. Or try to hit the Euphrates River and follow it to Ramadi." Although the Kremlin was still silent on the request to land in the U.S.S.R., Rang said, "Maybe you can land in Tiflis. They got red-headed women there."

The rump briefing was interrupted by the dramatic entrance of Hurry-Up Halverson. The navigators leaped to attention. The colonel drew his finger down a well-worn crease in the map—the

line of 30 degrees east longitude running from Egypt through
Turkey to the Black Sea. He said, "Can we help it if the National
Geographic put this line through Turkey? Furthermore, I suggest
that we bomb at fourteen thousand feet." Without another word
he stalked out. The navigators roared with relief.

The first U. S. mission to Ploesti—indeed the first U. S. Air Force
mission to *any* target in Europe—took off at 2230 hours, 11 June
1942. Each plane was on its own. The pilots could not keep formation at night, although prowling fighters could spot the un-
dampered engine exhausts at a short distance. *Babe the Big Blue
Ox* was the last ship airborne at 2300 hours. One-Eyed Shea felt
hopeful of his navigation; the sky was transparent, a diamond
mine of stars. Shea hit the Turkish lighthouse "right on the money"
and the pilots pulled the giant bomber into the substratosphere
over sleeping Turkey. Another machine, *Little Eva,* co-piloted by
Wilber C. West of Pine Bluff, Arkansas, climbed into the freezing
heights. Her navigator, Charles T. Davis, the Pittsburgh newspaperman, said, "The penetrating, almost unbearable forty-below
zero cold sapped our strength. It froze the oxygen mask on one
of the gunners and West stumbled back through the windy, frigid
bomb bays in time to bring him a spare and save his life. It thickened the machine oil on our bombsight until it would hardly
operate." The bombardiers were using a sight manufactured by
a cash register company, of which they said, "Maybe it's good for
ringing up sales, because you sure can't bomb with it." A few
hours after take-off the Kremlin granted permission for them to
land in Russia, but the airmen were keeping complete radio silence
and could not be advised of it.

Kalberer, conning the lead ship, reached Constanta in the first
glimmer of dawn and sighted no other Liberator in the sky. But
to the east there was something that looked like the aurora bore-
alis. It was caused by the glowing trajectories of 36-inch German
mortar shells falling into Sevastopol in the ghastly battle of the
Crimea. Kalberer turned west and looked down at the Danube.
The river outlines were completely unlike the largest-scale map
he had seen in Egypt. Then he realized that the Danube was in
heavy flood, the shorelines blotted out by muddy water. There

would be no neat fork and island to use as an Initial Point from which to turn for Ploesti.

Behind him, over the Black Sea, One-Eyed Shea squinted for his second landfall, a Romanian lighthouse near Constanta. After a period of suspense he said, "I got her, fellows. But she seems to move." Wilkinson asked for the bearing and took a look. He said, "Shea, you've got a damned good fix on the planet Venus." The navigator said imperturbably, "Check. Give 'er a ninety-degree turn, Lieutenant." *Babe* was over Constanta harbor. Wilkinson said, "Kindly give me the bearing for Astro Romana." Shea scribbled something and took his fur-lined jacket off the bombsight; he had shivered the whole way across Turkey to keep it from freezing up. In the Halpro force navigators also served as bombardiers to save weight.

The crew, now over German territory, was solemn and silent, thinking of fighters. Shea heard a shout on the intercom and thought, "Oh, boy, here they come!" He looked out and saw Lieutenant Mark Mooty's Liberator, the first plane they had seen since take-off. Shea waved to his colleague, Lieutenant Theodore E. Bennett, in Mooty's greenhouse. Bennett shrugged eloquently. He was lost too.

Below, they saw explosions flashing on the dusky earth. They didn't know whether they were bombs bursting or muzzle flashes of flak guns, having seen neither phenomenon before. The scattered mission, unable to pick up landmarks, now came into thick cloud. *Little Eva*, with her frozen fuel transfer system, lost three engines. The crew struggled to regain them as the plane turned back. *Little Eva* dumped her bombs on shipping at Constanta.

"Well, navigator?" said the pilot of *Babe the Big Blue Ox*. Shea figured he *had* to be over the Astro Romana refinery and toggled the first live bombs he had ever dropped. *Babe* leaped with relief and Wilkinson wheeled her about and streaked for the Black Sea. He landed at Aleppo, Syria, and was surrounded by tommy gunners. A French officer said to his men, "Put down the guns. They're the same types as those who have just landed." Another Halpro plane was at Aleppo.

Lieutenant Mooty landed safely on an Iraqi waste near the

Euphrates. The Liberator was encircled by a band of desert brigands. The American gunners prepared to defend themselves in the fashion of a wagon train beleaguered by the Sioux, and were saved in the nick of time by the cavalry, in the form of a French armored car.

Short of gas, *Little Eva* landed on the civil airport at Ankara, Turkey. The airport manager rushed over and gave Charles Davis a box of candy. A Turkish officer looked at the plane and said, "*Little Eva?* If this is little Eva, what must *big Eva* be like?" As the crew breakfasted in the airport café on syrupy coffee and goat cheese, two more B-24's landed, followed by a Messerschmitt 109, which had chased them all the way from Romania. All three were out of gas.

Another B-24 "christened" a nearly completed Turkish fighter base at Istanbul. Aboard were the first U. S. Air Force men to be wounded over Europe, pilot Virgil Anderson and gunner Enoch G. Kusilavage. They had been hit, not too seriously, in a brush with a German fighter. The remaining ships reached Iraq.

Halverson's Balkan incursion dealt little or no damage to the refineries. Nonetheless, it was an outstanding feat of World War II airmanship, especially in view of the extraordinary staging flights to Egypt. Twelve of thirteen planes reached the Ploesti area. None were lost to the Germans and not a man was killed. Halverson's mission had fared better than Doolittle's Tokyo raid, the other product of Washington's revenge impulse. Doolittle lost his sixteen aircraft; five men were killed and four taken captive. Doolittle's "thirty seconds over Tokyo" received great publicity for the benefit of home-front morale. Halverson got none.

The day after Halpro went to Ploesti not a word about it appeared in the press. Washington did not issue a communiqué. The big air news from Cairo that day was the stopover there of some Doolittle repatriates on their way home from parachuting into China. The second day, newspapers carried a squib from Ankara saying that unidentified bombers had landed in Turkey. Washington's silence dealt German Propaganda Minister Joseph Goebbels all the wild cards. He put out a communiqué saying that the bombers had force-landed while dropping propaganda leaflets on

Turkey. Vichy Radio said they were American lend-lease planes trying to reach Sevastopol. Goebbels thought of a better one and broadcast that the bombers were Chinese. On the third day the New York *Times* rounded up Turkish dispatches under a six-column front-page headline: U. S. BOMBERS STRIKE BLACK SEA AREA: BASE IS MYSTERY. Washington remained mute. No books, songs or war bond tours by Ploesti heroes were laid on.

Few Romanians were aware that anything had happened; the best-informed people in Bucharest adopted Vichy's line that U. S. planes had passed over on a lend-lease flight to Russia. However, there was one man in Romania who marked the event. Luftwaffe Colonel Alfred Gerstenberg, military attaché to the German Embassy at Bucharest, called a meeting of his Nazi "military assistance" staff and announced, "About fifteen American heavy bombers of the newest long-range type penetrated Sectors Sixty-five, Seventy-five, Eighty-five of Defense Zone Twenty-four East [Ploesti-Constanta]. This is the beginning."

As the Halpro crews filtered back from Syria and Iraq, the defense of the Mediterranean world was at its critical stage. Every man, ship, tank and plane was committed to battle. German and British land forces were fighting it out at Mersa Matrûh. The British garrison at Tobruk was *in extremis*. An immense air-sea battle was forming around two British convoys from Gibraltar and Alexandria which were taking relief to Malta. The Royal Air Force and Navy in the Mediterranean were totally engaged with the Luftwaffe. Even the temporizing Benito Mussolini, prodded by the Germans, sent out the Regia Aeronautica and the Italian fleet, which was the strongest in the sea.

Hurry-Up Halverson had not yet returned to base from Iraq. The R.A.F. told Alfred Kalberer that the Italian fleet was out, and he asked Sam Nero for bombers. It was precisely the situation for which the Consolidated Liberator had been designed. In the spell cast by Mitchell and Nero's battleship-sinking in the twenties, U. S. air strategy had dwelt on bombers to defend the country from battleships. No one was more interested in the practical test than Sam Nero, who furnished Kalberer with seven B-24's plus a volunteer R.A.F. LB-30 Liberator.

Kalberer borrowed a young British Navy officer for each plane to distinguish naval friend from foe. The bomber men were warned not to attack submarines; a Royal Navy pigboat was stalking the Italian fleet. And the fliers were to be careful about those whom Kalberer called "the bravest men in the battle"— R.A.F. pilots in old Beauforts, who were flying out of a patch of ground in encircled Tobruk with torpedoes slung beneath their craft. These lads were jabbing at the Italian battleships through swarms of Junkers 88's that provided fleet air cover.

Kalberer took his small force over Mersa Matrûh. Below, there was a dun blanket of tank wakes and shell bursts from which came occasional signal flares and flames. British and Germans were dying by the hundreds beneath this pall of dust. The Liberators tightened up into two flights and went hunting over the blue sea, the Royal Navy boys in the greenhouses intent with their binoculars. Kalberer's spotter called, "Smoke smudge to the north, sir. Believe it is Admiral Vian's convoy, but we should go closer to be sure it's ours." The spotter was right, but Admiral Sir Philip L. Vian's naval escort was no longer with the convoy. He had had to turn back the night before with just enough oil left to reach his only bunkering port in Alexandria. The merchantmen were alone with the Italian fleet rushing toward them at thirty knots. As Kalberer went closer to have a look, "everything that convoy had started busting around us." The merchant gun crews were taking no chances. They had no idea that the four-engined bombers might be trying to help them. Some of the freighters were American.

Kalberer's formation scattered from the fire. He broke radio silence to reassemble the planes out of gun range. The R.A.F. Liberator radiophoned, "Flight Leader. We've been shot up. Must turn back, sorry." As the LB-30 turned back, Kalberer's tunnel gunner handed him a six-inch piece of spent flak that had arrived through the skin of the plane and said bitterly, "I'll bet it's from a lend-lease shell." This set them all laughing and they settled back to combat intent. The saucy convoy fell behind and Kalberer began bridging the distance from it to the Italian fleet. Only unfriendly fire was expected ahead.

He was flying at 14,000 feet. He planned to hold there until the Italian naval gunners had fused their shell bursts for that altitude. Then he would lead his B-24's into a rapid banking dive of a thousand feet to throw off the enemy aim and fuse settings, and cross the ships at beams' ends to bomb. Soon he saw a magnificent sight—the oncoming warships steaming close together at flank speed with bones in their teeth, led by what seemed a capital ship, speeding along, flanked by two cruisers and the darting white wakes of nervous protecting vessels. About 1,500 feet above the Italian fleet the Junkers shuttled.

As the B-24's roared on into the climax, no fire came up, yet everyone below seemed alert and busy. The German planes buzzed back and forth, but showed no climbing profile to the Liberators. Bernard Rang, Kalberer's navigator-bombardier called, "I've got the battleship. What are we waiting for?" Kalberer nearly overshot the dreamy target. He dived his four Liberators, and the second flight went for a cruiser. Even on the bomb run there was no opposition. Kalberer said, "The Ju-88's were looking for low-flying Beauforts and we were flying into a headwind that carried off our engine noise."

Bernard Rang toggled five 500-pound bombs and his colleagues dropped fifteen more almost in unison. Most of them crashed on the main deck of the big ship,* setting fires. The second flight dropped a higher percentage on the cruiser *Conte di Cavour*. The Liberators were out of range before the flak started. "It was the rare perfect bombing operation," said Kalberer. "We attained complete surprise and wasted very few bombs. The two ships stopped dead in the water, and the Ju-88's climbed after us. We dived to within ten feet of the waves and made it home untouched, except for the "friendly" damage.

Germans aboard the stricken vessels tried to force the Italian commanders to continue toward the convoy. While the intra-Axis issue was being debated, the British submarine sank the cruiser. The two remaining Italian capital ships limped back to Taranto and never went to war again. The Allied freighters reached Malta

---

* In 1945 an Italian admiral from this ship told Kalberer it was the *Littorio*.

carrying the supplies that guaranteed the island's fortitude would win out.

Back in Fayid, Sam Nero greeted Kalberer with laurels, the first can of Spam in Africa. "It tasted great," said the victor. His crew walked three miles across the desert to the operations shack and found nobody around except a ground officer, staring into his fourth pink gin. "Ruddy show is finished," said the reception committee. "Rommel's broken through. Army's pulling out of Egypt." In came the R.A.F. officer who had briefed them on the Italian fleet. He heard Kalberer's story with eyes shining. "Bloody well done!" he said, running to Signals to spread the news.

Rang was interviewed by an American reporter. To convey the impression of hitting a battleship, the bombardier said, "It was like shooting fish in a barrel!" The British communiqué on the Mediterranean battle properly acknowledged the contribution of "four-engined American Liberators." This cracked Washington's silence on Halpro. The Air Force announced that the Halverson Detachment was responsible and had earlier attacked "the Balkans." It was Washington's combined birth and death notice for Halpro.

Harry Halverson, whose remarkable feats were thus meagerly acknowledged, was down to a fraction of his task force; moreover, he was overloaded with personal problems. He fell into a heated argument on bombing tactics with a very senior and stuffy R.A.F. officer and was sent home and retired.

Mickey McGuire and Al Kalberer took over what was left and ran 63 short-range raids against Rommel. They were reinforced by a dozen battle-weary Flying Fortresses from the other side of the world, the remnant of the U. S. Far East Air Force, under a chipper little general named Lewis H. Brereton. Brereton was a 1911 graduate of the U. S. Naval Academy who had switched to a second lieutenancy in the Army Coast Artillery, then to the Flying Corps. He was smarting with defeats; the Japanese had chased his planes out of Indonesia and then out of Burma, and now it looked as though those left were joining another losing cause against Erwin Rommel. Brereton was immediately obliged to remove his B-17's and the Halpro Liberators from Egypt to Lydda, Palestine, to save them from destruction on the ground.

Thirty-seven Ploesti men were still interned in Turkey in a modern hotel on Attaturk Boulevard, the main street of Ankara. They were paroled from morning to midnight, dined in the best restaurants, drew full pay from the U. S. military attaché, and enjoyed romantic flutters. A gunner lost his head over an exquisite German refugee girl and mooned to his pilot, "I'd marry her grandmother just to get in the family." The fliers became acquainted with thirty interned Soviet pilots who taught them to play chess. Navigator Harold ("Red") Wicklund was a superb swimmer and worked out daily in a pool, beating Turkish natatorial champions with such sprints as fifty meters in 25 seconds.

On the Fourth of July the internees dined with American Ambassador Laurence Steinhardt at the embassy. Over cigars they heard a news broadcast: "Today United States Air Force crews penetrated Europe for the first time. In a joint raid with the R.A.F. to Holland . . ." * The Ploesti men looked at each other in amazement and the ambassador sent an aide to find out what the broadcast was all about. A dozen R.A.F. Bostons, six carrying uniformed U.S.A.A.F. crews, had flown a propaganda sortie from England on the American national holiday. The Halpro men, who had bombed Europe three weeks before, were hurt and puzzled. Five weeks later they were upset by a broadcast announcing that "for the first time U. S. Air Force heavy bombers have attacked targets in Europe." This was a mission of twelve British-based Flying Fortresses to Rouen, France. The Halpro men had beaten them by two months, and had gone far deeper into Europe with one more plane.

The Turkish internees did not slump into the comfortable life. They wanted back in the fight. Charles Davis met a Turk who

* An error taken up in later official histories. See the Army Air Forces, *Target: Germany* (Simon and Schuster, 1943), p. 28, on the 4 July 1942 raid: "for the first time in World War II American airmen . . . fly American built bombers against the Germans."

offered to further this ambition. On certain nights, after the day's parole was over, Davis let pairs of airmen out of his hotel window on a knotted rope, into a courtyard, from which the Turkish friend put them on the Taurus Express for Allied Syria. In order not to embarrass Turkish border controls, the escapees detrained short of the boundary and were escorted across it on foot by another anonymous friend. Three who escaped in this fashion —Red Wicklund, Lieutenant William Zimmerman and Sergeant John E. O'Conner—were destined to fly to Ploesti again on a terrible raid.

Pilot Eugene L. Ziesel often took his crew to Ankara airport to see that the new owners of his Liberator were treating her well. Turkish airmen gathered around Ziesel for lectures on the prodigious contrivance. Ziesel said, "I'm worried about the engines. They'll deteriorate unless they get regular warm-ups. And it helps to keep a little gas in the tanks or they get raunchy." The Turks rationed out gas for Ziesel's frequent warm-ups. The day after Christmas Ziesel's flight engineer said, "I think we got enough." Ziesel took off and landed on Cyprus with one engine. The Turkish Government protested the theft, and the United States solemnly returned the airplane *sans* crew. Ziesel and two fellow escapees were killed over Naples a week later.

The Turks asked some of the internees to teach Turkish pilots to handle the Liberator. It was inevitable that, during one of the early lessons, a monster flying machine buzzed Ankara from end to end, panicking people in the streets.

During the winter Charles Davis continued to mete out prisoners on the knotted rope until the Turkish Government tired of the charade and offered Britain, Germany, the U.S.S.R. and the United States a clearance sale of second-hand fliers. By April they were all back with their commands, except the Russians, whose government would not treat for them. They continued to play chess in their hotel on Attaturk Boulevard.

The Halpro men came back to Egypt and found the power of the Liberators growing. Big plans for the adolescent force were shaping in Washington, where the Joint Statistical Survey, a group of elderly sages who reported to the Joint Chiefs of Staff, was talking of Ploesti as "the most decisive objective of the war." The Statistical Survey had studied enemy economics and all known industrial targets whose destruction would hurt Hitler most. Ploesti was number one.

Denying oil to Hitler satisfied the Second Law of Strategy: to deprive the foe of, or seize from him, the means of making war. It also conformed to Frederick the Great's maxim, the Strategy of Accessories: When a belligerent is unable to engage the main armies of his adversary, he sends expeditions to destroy his communications and storehouses. It was secondary, alternative thinking, but that was all that seemed possible to the beleaguered free world at this period of the war. Another mission to the deepest target, even more daring than Halpro, was in the making.

It is an approved maxim of war never to do what the enemy
wishes you to do. NAPOLEON

2

PLOESTI: THE TAPROOT OF GERMAN MIGHT

Ploesti was an oil boom city at the foot of the Transylvanian Alps,
35 miles north of Bucharest. Frequent showers account for its
name, which means "rainy town." Its 100,000 inhabitants lived
far better than the average lot of Romanians—in acacia-shaded
white villas with Roman atriums, along colonnaded streets redo-
lent with lilacs and roses. The Arcadian city was incongruously
fenced by the source of its prosperity—the smoking stacks, cracking towers, pumping stations, tank farms and noisy rail yards of
eleven huge modern refineries, Romania's main economic asset,
providing 40 percent of her exports.

Ploesti (plô-yĕsht′) was the first place in the world to refine
commercially the black blood of contemporary industrialism. That
was in 1857, two years before the petroleum strike at Titusville,
Pennsylvania. Within a half century the automobile arrived with
its croaking petrophilia, and British, French, Italian and Dutch
capital and technology came to Ploesti. By 1914 Ploesti was
coveted as an essential of machine warfare. In 1916 the Germans
invaded Romania, and British engineers dynamited the refineries.

It was a trifling setback to the city; the postwar motor car, Diesel ship and airplane drank vastly greater draughts of oil, and Western companies were ready to build bigger production capacity.

The country was ruled by one who knew how to cope with oilmen, Queen Marie, née the Princess of Edinburgh, granddaughter of Queen Victoria, out of the Russian ruling house of Romanoff on her father's side. She was a tall, provocative, blue-eyed blonde with long mascaraed eyelashes, who swayed about in a wardrobe of *violette-cardinale*. In 1920 she was forty-five years old, but she had a sexual magnetism that lasted until she was an old woman. Marie was all dealer and tough as a Tartar. While English and American vulgar journals doted on her regal progresses abroad and her romantic indiscretions, Queen Marie was striking hard bargains for Ploesti.

At the Versailles peace conference and during the amputation of Romanoff territory in the Russian civil war she got Bessarabia and part of Bukovina from Russia, Transylvania from Hungary, and Dobruja from Bulgaria, doubling the size of her country. She called this polyglot jailhouse of nationalities Greater Romania.

Marie died in 1938, leaving orders that black was not to be used in mourning her. Bucharest was draped in a non-oily shade of mauve. As the cortege passed, Adolf Hitler was peering over the mountains at Ploesti, which Marie had left to her errant, cork-popping son, Carol II. The refineries produced ten million tons of oil annually, including 90-octane aviation fuel, the highest quality in Europe. Hitler's problem was novel for him. The refineries could not be taken by the usual Nazi smash-and-grab method. They were vulnerable to aerial attack and to sabotage by resident British, French and American engineers. He needed undisturbed production.

Instead of dive bombers, Hitler used a fifth column, the Legion of the Archangel Michael for the Christian and Racial Renovation of Romania—or the Iron Guard—a fascist outfit covered with the blood of civilized politicians and teachers. Romania's 5 percent Jewish population, which after centuries had won civil equality, was subjected to window-smashings, pillage and assault. The German ambassador to Romania, Baron Manfred von Buch-Killinger, purchased the Iron Guard and its leader, General Ion Antonescu, a small, pinch-nosed Transylvanian graduate of French military schools who first came to notice in 1919 as the captain of a band that looted shops, homes and hospitals in Bucharest.

Britain and France met Hitler's gambit with a staggering sum paid into King Carol's privy purse for a mutual-assistance treaty guaranteeing military aid for Romania and containing a secret clause providing that, if Hitler tried to seize the refineries, Allied technicians might destroy them.

In June 1940 Hitler drew a lucky down card in the Ploesti game. During the fall of Paris a German column stopped one of the last trains leaving for Bordeaux and captured archives of the Deuxième Bureau, the French counterintelligence agency. They contained the technicians' plans for sabotaging the Romanian refineries. The next night Antonescu's gunmen moved down the leafy streets of Ploesti taking Allied oilmen from their villas to Iron Guard torture rooms. An American named Freeman was among the 35 men kidnapped. Shortly afterward Antonescu became prime minister of Romania. He appealed to Hitler for military aid. Der Führer's conditions were the expulsion of "foreign" oil interests and German occupation of strategic military positions in Romania. Antonescu accepted.

The German military assistance group arrived in Bucharest to take over control. Its chief was a short, little-known forty-eight-year-old colonel with red hair and an equable and scholarly air. Alfred Gerstenberg was born on the Polish border and was imbued from childhood with German xenophobia. Originally a cavalryman, Gerstenberg became an aviator and flew with Hermann Goering in the First World War. When Germany was forever denied an air force in the Treaty of Versailles, the Soviets afforded her clandestine air training at Lipetsk, 230 miles southeast of Moscow. Gerstenberg was among a secret group of German officer-instructors who formally resigned their Reichswehr commissions in 1926 and went to the U.S.S.R. as members of the Red Army. Gerstenberg reported to Marshal Klimenti Voroshilov and remained in the Soviet until Hitler took power and Stalin broke off the arrangement. Back in Germany, Gerstenberg resumed his military commission but remained aloof from the Hitlerites. He was not a member of the National Socialist Party and refused to wear the swastika on his uniform.

In Romania, Gerstenberg was nominally air attaché to the embassy in Bucharest, a modest pose which disguised his actual role as the executor of German military designs in the Balkans. He was diplomatic, far-sighted, realistic, and, as much as he stood apart from the actual party machinery, was willing to accept responsibility for *Südostraum*, the Nazi concept of a Balkan empire. Gerstenberg was a bachelor, a connoisseur of books and paintings, and a host whose dinner invitations were soon coveted by Bucharest society. General Otto Dessloch, who served with him, said, "He was a dedicated man. To better fulfill his duties he learned to speak Polish, Russian and Romanian. He worked sixteen hours a day with one goal in mind—to make Ploesti too costly for the enemy to attack." Thus, a full year before the United States entered the war an exceptionally able and resolute Protector was placed in charge of the Romanian refineries. Indeed, in the person of the genial and adroit air attaché there had come the actual wartime ruler of Romania.

Romanian nonbelligerence was Hitler's strongest shield for undisturbed oil production. The Germans consolidated control by forming the Kontinentale Oil Company, "nationalizing" the Allied-owned refineries and staffing them with German technicians, setting up new boards of directors consisting of pliant Romanian politicians and lawyers. This done, Gerstenberg turned to a more serious endeavor, that of squeezing men, guns and planes out of Goering to defend Ploesti. He bent his powers of persuasion and scare propaganda on Berlin rather than Bucharest, which he dominated with unobtrusive art. Gerstenberg thought little of the Antonescu mob. Romanian fratricide served only to strengthen German rule. One night the Iron Guard murdered 64 politicians of the Liberal party—leaving fewer patriots to annoy him. A few months later, however, Antonescu's crazed domestic fascists gave Gerstenberg a start by rising against their own leader for "selling out to the German!" Antonescu, however, controlled the Romanian Army and squelched the berserkers with 6,000 deaths. It gave

Gerstenberg a period of domestic tranquillity in which to carry on his preparations.

For Romania the result of Antonescu's embrace of Hitler's protection was immediate national humiliation. Other willing Nazi satellites waited until 1945 for territorial disgorgement, but Romania was partitioned immediately. Soviet Russia, accepting Antonescu's word that he was too weak to protect the country, and not herself at war with Germany, served an ultimatum for the return of Bessarabia and Bukovina and got them back next day. Whereupon Antonescu's Axis neighbors, Bulgaria and Hungary, twisted his arm and regained southern Dobruja and most of Transylvania, respectively. Queen Marie's Greater Romania vanished overnight. Soon King Carol II was in flight to Switzerland with Iron Guard assassins at his heels, and his seventeen-year-old son, Michael, was placed on a powerless throne.

In February 1941 Britain broke off diplomatic relations with Romania. Two months later Hitler blitzed Yugoslavia and Greece. Outnumbered Royal Air Force squadrons resisted with hopeless valor. In the fortnight left to her in Greece, Britain proposed to hurl her remaining two-engine bombers at Ploesti. The Greek cabinet forbade it because Greece was not at war with Romania. The last chance to hit Ploesti from Europe was lost. Germany had won the prize intact by a combined diplomatic and military offensive that forced Britain a thousand miles from Ploesti, far beyond bombing range.

Among the R.A.F. escapees from Greece was a long-haired, histrionic Anglo-Irish peer, Wing Commander Arthur Patrick Hastings Viscount Forbes, formerly air attaché in the British Embassy at Bucharest. Lord Forbes arrived in Cairo crying for vengeance upon Ploesti, but there was no way now to bomb it.

Gerstenberg made use of the lull to obtain more men and arms from Berlin. Hitler, preparing his onslaught on the U.S.S.R., was disinclined to strengthen a region where enemy incursion was impossible. But Gerstenberg's old comrade, Goering, helped him, and the Protector came into good luck a few days after Hitler's attack on Russia in June. During the first week, Red Air Force bombers came three times to Ploesti in small numbers. The last raid, a twilight affair, left some damage and a few parachuted airmen. Gerstenberg used it to get a substantial reinforcement from Berlin. There was no follow-up by the Red Air Force. Stalin, a leading proponent of massive long-range retaliatory bombing, quickly dropped the whole idea. Many of his heavy bombers were destroyed on the ground by the first Luftwaffe attacks; the Wehrmacht rolled over his forward air bases, and Stalin lent every resource of Soviet aircraft production to ground-support craft for the Red Army, and fighters to defend his cities. Gerstenberg gained another epoch of calm for his preparations. He was promoted to *Generalmajor* (brigadier) and was moving along briskly toward the unique result of his mission, an autonomous theater command, not subject to *Oberkommando* politics or Hitler intuition.

Antonescu drove a half-million unwilling, ill-trained and poorly equipped peasants into the U.S.S.R. under the name of the Third Romanian Army. Hitler sacrificed 50,000 of them to win Odessa. (During the war Germany consumed about one-third of the ablebodied farmers of Romania, a nation with an 80 percent agricultural population.) As a consequence, Gerstenberg's new troops came to a land of lonely women. From hardship, deprivation, blackout and bombing in Germany, they came to peace and plenty. Werner Nass, who arrived with the 622nd Antiaircraft Battalion from the Ruhr, said, "As an NCO I got fourteen thousand lei a month; that bought ten pounds of bacon. You could buy anything—things no longer known in the Ruhr—eggs, sausages, ham, fruit and as much wine as you wanted. From our first home leaves we brought old clothes to sell to the Romanians. Our pockets were full of money. We were everything but soldiers. It was like Feldmarschall von Mackensen said when he went to Romania in 1916: 'I came with an army of soldiers and returned with an army of salesmen.'" The only flaw in the good life was the exacting Gerstenberg who fought obesity, alcoholism, venereal disease and laziness with incessant drills. Every day the gunners in their pale blue, short-sleeved shirts and mustard-colored shorts—an Afrika Korps fashion—ran through firing exercises. Russian POW's in Red Army uniforms with insignia removed served up the shells, and on some guns a "reindoctrinated" Red even pulled the firing cord.

Life became even sweeter when 1,200 Luftwaffe airwomen and hundreds of German civilian girls came as secretaries and technicians. Romanian women also were kind to the rich soldiers. However, a German having relations with Romanians or Russians outside the line of duty had to report each contact to an Intelligence officer. There were a few Romanian antifascists who would risk espionage work, but most of the information leaving the country was carried by diplomats or commercial travelers going to neutral Turkey. The United States and British embassies there received generalized impressions and Bucharest café chatter but very little about Gerstenberg's strength or dispositions. He allowed no one but German troops near the flak batteries, airdromes and warning installations. He divested Ploesti of occupants not holding essential refinery or commercial jobs. On the ruling level, Gerstenberg had a singular strength; he spoke Romanian, which his Ambassador Buch-Killinger did not, so that the General controlled intimate communications between him and Antonescu. Gerstenberg disdained both of them. He permitted them to think they were running Romania while having his own way on matters of importance. Colonel Bernhard Woldenga, Gerstenberg's fighter controller, said, "He was absolutely the key man. He knew everyone and all combinations in court circles, the Romanian staff, businessmen, estate owners and people who knew what the peasants were thinking." Only his immediate staff knew what Gerstenberg was thinking. His plans for holding Ploesti were quite un-Nazi. Berlin had no notion what to do about defeat or insurrection until they occurred. The Protector, however, was cooly anticipating an Allied bombing offensive, a Romanian rising and a Soviet rollback of the Wehrmacht three years before they in fact occurred.

To handle bombers Gerstenberg required the world's heaviest concentration of flak guns and warning systems. He was defending a curious city; it had a soft civilian center five miles in diameter and, close around it, an almost solid belt of oil plants and transportation systems. The Protector wanted an outer ring of powerful, highly mobile guns which he could shift and concentrate quickly in the most likely tangents of aerial assault. He demanded 250 first-line interceptor planes standing by and 75,000 Luftwaffe troops, mostly technicians, to serve the planes, guns, radar and communications systems.

On the second possibility—the national rising—Gerstenberg's thinking was subtly realistic. Although the Iron Guard's anti-German outbreak had been smothered in bullets, he was aware of a more tactful, pro-Allied, or opportunistic, core in the Romanian general staff and among the aristocracy and big landowners. He was surrounded by Romanian toadies whose fortunes had improved under the German rule, but he did not delude himself that they were any more than an ineffectual and expendable minority when the patriotic war came.

The Protector held Saturday afternoon staff meetings in which he elucidated his analyses and plans. He reminded his officers that the Antonescu crowd would be broken quickly in a rising and it would be entirely left to the Germans to save themselves and the refineries. Ploesti was the key. It lay astride the main road and rail routes from Germany to the southeastern front. If the Romanians rebelled, Gerstenberg would pull his outer flak rings in tight against the oil city and use the guns as artillery against the insurrectionists. He called this concept *Festung Ploesti*, an unconquerable redoubt. At the same time, he insured that a corridor would remain open to the Reich by fortifying both sides of the Predeal Pass north of the city. As the peasants threw themselves at his 88's, he would continue to receive supplies from Germany and send oil to her through the armed corridor.

Gerstenberg considered Bucharest of no strategic importance and was confident that a gun battery and a few squads could quell a revolution in the capital.

Festung Ploesti also was the answer to the Red Army if it came through the Danubian Plain. The fortress would bar the Soviets from crossing the Transylvanian Alps into Central Europe and the city defenses could be quickly and steadily enlarged through the bristling Predeal life line.

In the spring of 1942 the premature Halpro mission helped

Gerstenberg's *Festung Ploesti* project. He flaunted the daring attack before the *Reichsmarschall des Grossdeutschen Reiches,* which was Goering's shy title, and Goering began to eke him air troops amounting to 50,000 people by the end of the year. Gerstenberg had in addition about 70,000 Slav prisoners and civilian slaves who had been driven out of the conquered eastlands.

During the winter the British Eighth Army rolled back Rommel's threat to Egypt and Brereton's bombers came back to Egyptian bases. Halverson's successor, Mickey McGuire, received a dribble of Liberators. McGuire jeeped to each arrival as though Washington was going to snatch it back before he could put his unit symbol on the rudder. From the second replacement ship came a small pilot, Norman Appold, a chemical engineer recently graduated from the University of Michigan. He looked nothing like the prognathous aviators in the comic strips. Instead of the standard bulging jaw, Appold's could be held slightly recessive. In place of eagle brows, his formed two quizzical circumflexes, and the eyes were round instead of squinty. He wore a large grin and was full of gab and gags instead of the Olympian silences of the classic birdmen. McGuire thought for a moment that America was running out of manpower. What stood before him, saluting casually, was the first of the college boys, children of the Great Depression, who were about to take over air combat from the prewar set.

Appold's vivacity was deceptive. He was deadly serious. He resented the war for interrupting his engineering career and he was resolved to get the damn thing over with as soon as possible. To him that meant absolute application to the bomber business, preserving his life by laying it on the line at every opportunity. He held iconoclastic views on air tactics. Even in training, Appold had tossed the book out the window by practicing low-level attacks with the cumbersome Liberator.

The bombers blasted ahead of Montgomery's army, reducing Tobruk and Benghazi and gaining them as bases. When Appold arrived in Benghazi—a "weather-beaten wasp's nest fallen to pieces," as the war correspondent Ivan Dmitri put it—he found the Ninth Bomber Command moving into one of the few surviving structures, a hotel compound south of the city. Since 1940 it had housed, in order, war staffs of Italy, Britain, Germany, Britain, Germany, and now the U.S.A. In barren battlegrounds, opposing generals sometimes leave each other suitable headquarters in their wills. Appold leafed through the guest book, noting such previous registrants as Marshal Graziani, Vittorio Mussolini, Erwin Rommel, Sir Arthur Tedder, Sir Archibald Wavell, and a recent hasty German scrawl: "Keep this book in order. We'll be back." Appold signed in and drove off to inspect the city and its important deep-water port. The ruins of Benghazi were clinically interesting; he had helped considerably to put them in this condition by breaching the flak defenses when the Germans last held them.

The R.A.F. had opened up the final offensive on Benghazi with night pathfinders, dropping flares for following bombers. The Germans dispersed them with jungles of flak and lured them to bomb phony target flares ten miles away on a barren beach. Next time the pathfinders dropped flares in the flak sites to guide oncoming B-24 trains with Norden bombsights. The glare was too intense for the U. S. bombardiers, who once again hit the false Benghazi. During a subsequent night raid Appold decided to pull a counter-ambush on the flak men. He went over at 20,000 feet. Shells ranged toward him and the Germans lighted the mock target. But Appold dropped no flares. He crossed Benghazi, turned and deliberately flew back over it, bringing more ground guns into action. On the third pass every muzzle on the grounds was belching brightly, revealing the complete geography of the antiaircraft positions, nicely picked out in the dark. Appold flipped into a steep dive to 12,000 feet, throwing off the fuse settings of the German shells, and distributed three tons of high explosive and antipersonnel bombs on the exposed flak guns. After that the Germans could not break the bomber array. The Allies took the upper hand and systematically reduced the defenses.

From Bucharest, General Gerstenberg watched the enemy bomber bases marching west in Africa. At Benghazi the Liberators were nearly 200 miles closer to Ploesti than they had been in Egypt. The Protector also noted Italian reports of higher, faster B-24's, whose markings revealed a new bomb group operating from Benghazi. This was the 98th, the Pyramiders, led by a sulphurous Texan, John Riley Kane, whose name began appearing in Luftwaffe intelligence summaries as "Killer" Kane. He had come to fight, loud on the intercom and hard on the power settings. "Every bomb on the Axis!" Kane preached to his troops. Once he took the Pyramiders over an Afrika Korps objective with his tail and top turret guns jammed. He missed the bomb heading during spirited Messerschmitt attacks, and went back over the target, calling on the open radio for his planes to follow. The German pilots got on his frequency and drowned Kane's commands with taunts. Kane yelled, "Get the goddamn hell off the air, you bastards!" The Messerschmitt boys shut up, Kane bombed, and dodged through them to get home safely.

Then Gerstenberg noted still another new group of Liberators entering Mediterranean combat. Unlike Mickey McGuire's and Killer Kane's tawny desert-camouflaged ships, these planes wore green and loam colors, and they flew tight formation with well-disciplined gunners. This was the 93rd Bomb Group out of England on temporary loan to the desert forces. It was called Ted's Traveling Circus, after its commander, Colonel Edward J. Timberlake, a West Pointer with a nose bent playing football on the Plain. Timberlake was a ruggedly built, easygoing blond, a style setter and an elegant manager of men. He spoke his own argot; if he called a man "a good Joe," that man was *in*. "A joker" was *out*.

At this augmentation of enemy air power, Gerstenberg sent to Goering for more men, guns and planes to defend Ploesti. He got a first-class reinforcement, including an outstanding airman, Colonel Bernhard Woldenga of Hamburg, who became Romanian fighter controller. Trim, blue-eyed Woldenga was a former master mariner of the Hamburg-Amerika Steamship Line. In the 1920's Hamburg-Amerika planned its own airline and trained a half dozen of its ship captains, including Woldenga, as air pilots. He joined the Luftwaffe in the mid-thirties, and after Hitler marched in 1939, flew both bombers and fighters in Poland, Britain, Greece and Russia. Gerstenberg especially welcomed Colonel Woldenga, who came straight from eight months in North Africa managing fighters against the B-24's of McGuire, Kane and Timberlake.

The quality of the enlisted technicians in Gerstenberg's new draft was evidenced by Willi Nowicki, *Waffenwart*, or armament warden, in the 614th Antiaircraft Artillery Battalion, which was pulled out of Germany Christmas week and drawn nonstop to Ploesti in a double-locomotive train. In civilian life Nowicki was a Brandenburg locksmith. He won a master mechanic's certificate at the age of twenty-two, had worked before the war constructing British air bases in the Suez, and, after the war began, was a sub-contractor in the German aircraft industry. Willi could knock down and reassemble flak guns in astonishing time. His battery sat on the southwest quadrant of Ploesti, through which Gerstenberg estimated the American bombers would come, when they came. Battery Seven staked out and dug in with six officers, 180 men and a hundred Russian prisoners to do the heavy work. The battery implanted six 88-mm. rifles, the versatile high-velocity artillery piece which served as an antiaircraft, antitank, naval and general purpose gun. Waffenwart Nowicki's 88's were named *Adolf, Bertha, Caesar, Dora, Emile* and *Friederich*. *Bertha* had four white rings painted on her muzzle, one for each bomber she had shot down in Germany. On the periphery of the battery there were four 37-mm. and four 20-mm. guns.

Before long there were forty such batteries embracing the Anglo-American salients of *Festung Ploesti*. Outside of them were lighter batteries manned by Austrians and Romanians, and hundreds of machine-gun pits and towers. More guns were mounted on factories, bridge approaches, water towers, church steeples, and concealed in haystacks and groves. To exercise the gunners, Colonel Woldenga sent old Heinkel 111 and Junkers 52 bombers on unannounced mock attacks. In case the Americans should actually be able to bomb through this awesome protection, Gerstenberg secured from Germany a crack 500-man unit of fire police, despite their urgent need at home in the mounting Anglo-American bombing offensive. Corporal Werner Buchheim of Ulm, one of the fire fighters, operated a mobile radio car with the call letters ICEBEAR, to link up the active air defenses and the passive fire fighters and reconstruction engineers. Gerstenberg was building the first air fortress in the world—around an exposed industrial installation that could not go underground or be dispersed. Ploesti was a colossal land battleship, armored and gunned to withstand the heaviest aerial attack.

In addition to the massing of arms, Gerstenberg conceived a system to restore production quickly if some of the bombers got through to the refineries. He erected a trunk pipeline around Ploesti linking all the refinery units. Refinery managers protested that they were competing with each other and that a common circulation of oil would be uncapitalistic. Gerstenberg paid no attention to them. His brilliant scheme provided that if parts of several refineries were destroyed the pipeline would marry their surviving units to begin processing oil immediately after a raid. The emergency pipeline stood exposed above the ground so that bomb damage to it could be repaired quickly. Allied Intelligence knew nothing about Gerstenberg's rapid recovery system.

In contrast to Gerstenberg's situation, his coming opponent's was most uncomfortable. On the Libyan desert, crawling with scorpions, in dust blowing shoulder-high, the Americans lay in a vast, unprepossessing encampment, scattered forty miles north and south on the beach behind the ruins of the Bronze Age city of Benghazi. Their threadbare tents were patched with scraps of aluminum from neighboring junk yards of Axis air wrecks. Around the tents bloomed "desert lilies," conical urinals made from gas tins; oil drum privies; and cordons of fluttering rags marking off old German mine fields and shell dumps, cunningly booby-trapped for souvenir hunters.

In the morning the inhabitants of this unholy bivouac shuffled out, fisting dust from their eyes, to a breakfast of pressed ham and dried cabbage boiled in alkali water. Each man was rationed to one pint of water a day. They were lean and dirty and some had beards and shoulder-length hair. They wore tatters of U. S. uniforms, save for a lucky few with British battle dress or German and Italian garments pulled out of dunes shifted in the wind. Their shoes were held together with wires. They seemed the final camp of a broken and demoralized army at the end of a hopeless retreat. Actually they were among the early elite of the mightiest air force the world has ever seen. This was Lewis Brereton's Ninth Air

Force Bomber Command in January 1943. It was incapable of bombing Ploesti. However, at that moment, on the other side of Africa, at Casablanca, a secret meeting was assigning just that mission to it.

At the Casablanca Conference, Franklin D. Roosevelt and Winston Churchill met to settle on European land strategy once the Germans were expelled from Africa. Both were under pressure from Stalin and agitation in their own ranks for a second front— mass landings in Atlantic Europe to grapple Hitler from behind while Stalin hammered him from the east. Churchill opposed a second front in 1943, as he had in 1942, on the grounds that the Allies did not have the strength for it.

When the Casablanca elders chose Sicily as the next land objective, the Prime Minister noted that the Americans were probably thinking, "At any rate we have stopped Churchill from entangling us in the Balkans." Churchill yielded gracefully on another friction point—American high-level daylight bombing out of England, which he had come to Casablanca to oppose. General Ira Eaker, chief of the U. S. Eighth Air Force, who was trying to prove the concept with inadequate forces in a season of foul weather, met Churchill privately and read off a list of ten arguments for high daytime strikes. The master propagandist rolled one of them aloud on his tongue—"round-the-clock bombing" by the R.A.F. and U.S.A.A.F.—and withdrew his opposition until Eaker had had a chance to demonstrate whether the tactic would work.

The British delegation came to Casablanca with a cautious brief for an Allied invasion of the Balkans. It became apparent in the preliminary *pourparlers* that the United States would be very difficult to persuade to this course. Foreign Minister Anthony Eden made the Balkan proposal while Mr. Churchill remained quiet. The Americans strongly opposed the strategy, and Britain swiftly withdrew without involving the Prime Minister. Later Churchill wrote about the incident somewhat elliptically: "The American chiefs do not like to be outdone in generosity. No people respond more spontaneously to fair play. If you treat Americans well, they always want to treat you better." Perhaps it was this trait that brought out the Ploesti folder and resulted in unanimous and enthusiastic approval of the blow at Romanian oil production. Generals George Marshall and Henry Arnold and the political side of the U. S. delegation were strongly for the assault as a strategic imperative and as a project that would please both Stalin and Churchill. Ploesti was a minor matter compared with the momentous "unconditional surrender" declaration and "Husky," the planned invasion of Sicily. Destroying Romanian refining capacity would relieve pressure on Stalin and the Allies in Sicily. It was estimated that the bombers could destroy one-third of Hitler's fuel production and shorten the war in Europe by six months.

There was a large content of hope in the plan. An uninfluential group at Casablanca regarded Ploesti as another "panacea target," the sort Sir Arthur Harris, R.A.F. bomber command chief, railed against. Analysts were always telling Bomber Harris that huge single raids on pet German industries would shorten the war by six months. The skeptics had no weight at Casablanca. The conference directed the Ninth Air Force to bomb Ploesti sometime between the end of the African campaign and the invasion of Sicily in order that bomber support would not be withheld from these operations. The plan was called Tidal Wave. It was one of the few instances in World War II in which the High Command handed down a major task to a theater commander without asking him if it was feasible. At this stage—early in 1943—the only Ninth Air Force airmen who knew of the intent were Brereton and his immediate staff.

The Ploesti mandate passed to General Arnold's inner circle, Generals Heywood Hansell and Lawrence Kuter and Colonel Jacob Smart. The generals assigned Smart to work up the bombing plan. He was a tall, sandy-haired Southerner and a crack pilot whom Arnold often entrusted with viceregal missions to overseas commands. Colonel Smart flew to Britain and enlisted British Intelligence and R.A.F. tactical specialists, the most important of whom was Lieutenant Colonel W. Lesley Forster, an old Balkan hand who had managed the Astro Romana refinery at Ploesti for eight years. Lord Forbes, the anxious avenger, was also brought in.

Forster briefed Smart on the peculiar industrial geography of Ploesti. The refineries did not constitute a single large unit like most of the familiar German targets. There were a dozen of them ringed around the city, due to the unplanned growth of the oil industry. The first oil wells in Romania were located in the Transylvanian foothills to the north and were drained off in gravity pipelines to the convenient refining city. As more refineries were built, they came to form a ring six miles in diameter with their rails and delivery pipelines, pumping stations, marshaling yards and trucking depots.

Smart did not have enough bombers to hit all the plants. He and Forster selected the five major refineries, one on the north side of the city and the others strung for five miles along the southern outskirts. The target selection confronted Smart with the challenge of his career. To drop anything in the city itself would be a waste of bombs and cause useless civilian casualties. He had to find a way to hit only the outer ring. It was like trying to bomb an atoll without dropping anything into the lagoon. In addition, there were two other highly productive refineries that should be struck if the raid was to be a telling blow at Hitler. One was eighteen miles north of Ploesti and the other five miles south.

Furthermore, Forster pointed out that simply bombing a refinery would not suffice. A single plant, like Creditul Minier, for instance, was dispersed over an area of a mile to keep volatile processing units apart in case of fire. The entire bomber strength Smart could hope for—perhaps 200 planes—could place all its bombs in the grounds of such a refinery and fail to destroy it. What had to be hit were the relatively small critical installations within the complex—the powerhouse, boiler house, stills, cracking towers and pumping stations. And Forster and Smart had reason to believe these pinpoints would be surrounded by blast walls.

The Allied chiefs had given Jacob Smart a strategic mandate with no known tactical solution.

He had also to consider that such a raid far into enemy territory would be very costly in men and planes, far more expensive than other missions. Such losses had to be offset by very heavy destruction to the enemy's fuel production capacity. While balancing these questions, Smart did not hesitate to ponder another, which is often the arbiter of battles—how to obtain surprise. To reach the target city the B-24's would have to fly a round trip of at least 2,300 miles, most of it over enemy territory. It would be the longest mission of the war, save for Halpro. The odds against surprise seemed insurmountable. The enemy certainly had radar, visual spotters and scouting planes to report the inbound attacking force.

Smart's cerebrations on what was known, what was foreseeable, and what could be imagined had a special intensity. He was going to fly the mission himself. He looked for the best way to fly to Ploesti, smash most of the production capacity, and get back with the most men, including himself. Ploughing through the morass of implausibility, he found a solution, "like bright metal on a sullen ground." It gleamed so brightly that each difficulty seemed an omen of victory.

He conceived that the bombers would attack the refineries at very low altitude.

The idea seemed to have everything. It was a cunning psychological trick. Everyone, including the Germans, knew the American monomania for high-level attack by heavy bombers. An unprecedented low-level strike would permit the utmost precision bombing of the vital pinpoints in the refineries and score with the most explosives. It would spare civilians and raise American esteem among the subject peoples of fascism. It would reduce losses of men and planes by affording the flak gunners only low, fleeting targets. By hugging the ground the B-24's would cheat German pursuit planes of half their sphere of attack. Moreover, the stratum nearest the ground was the blind angle for radar detection. And Liberators that were mortally hit in battle would have a better chance to skid-land than those that were crippled high in the sky.

Before he told anyone of the wild idea, Smart turned devil's advocate and tried to upset his own reasoning. "Of all aircraft there is probably none less suited to low-level work than the B-24," he said to himself. "To the man on the ground it appears as though he could knock it down with a rock." He took off his horns and answered, "The quality of our B-24 pilots is pretty high. With special training they could fly formation on the deck and make it work. Moreover, for the first time in heavy bombing experience the machine gunners in the Liberators will be able to fight the flak men, not just the fighter craft. Previously, flak crews have been subjected only to an occasional nearby bomb burst or strafing by fighters. How would they behave in the face of hundreds of fifty-calibers firing from the low-flying Liberators?" Each question produced a satisfactory answer. The revolutionary low road was the right road to Ploesti. The most radical tactic was the most practical. The *coup de main* would be delivered at zero altitude.

Smart placed his low-level proposal in the Ploesti folder that lay before the Allied chiefs at the Trident Conference in Washington in May. The meeting was obsessed with the invasion of Sicily, scheduled to begin in two months' time, and the conferees could pay little attention to Ploesti or whether it was to be tackled high or low. Sir Charles Portal, Britain's chief of the air staff, voiced misgivings about a Ploesti assault by either technique. He noted that the entire Liberator force in Britain, the redoubtable Traveling Circus and the Eight Balls (44th Heavy Bombardment Group), were to be removed to Africa, along with the newly arrived Sky Scorpions, to make up the mission force with two Ninth Air Force groups. All would be taken off operations for low-level training at a time when they would be sorely needed in the Sicilian invasion and the round-the-clock offensive on Germany. Sir Charles also wondered aloud whether, if the mission failed to destroy enemy oil production in one blow, the Germans would not build up heavier defenses at Ploesti to cope with the succeeding attacks which would have to be made.

The U. S. chief of staff, General Marshall, replied that even "a fairly successful" attack on the refineries would stagger the enemy. He held that Tidal Wave was the most important action that could be taken to aid the Soviet and the coming invasion of the Continent. The overtasked Trident Conference countersealed the Tidal Wave order to the Ninth Air Force.

The conferees, minus President Roosevelt, repaired to Africa to make their writ known to Dwight D. Eisenhower, the theater commander. He agreed to the mission and its time of execution, but did not give an opinion on whether it should be executed high or low. Jacob Smart was accorded a private audience with Mr. Churchill to describe the low-level scheme. The imaginative Churchill, a lifelong lover of surprise raids, responded enthusiastically. He offered four crack Royal Air Force Lancaster crews to lead the Americans to the target.

Smart replied that the Lancaster bomber and the Liberator had differing characteristics of range, load, altitude and speed, and that it would be impossible for the two types to maintain close formation on the long journey to Romania. Mr. Churchill yielded. Smart did not have to bring up the additional consideration that American airmen would resent the implication that they could not find the target themselves.

The whole art of war consists of getting at what is on the other side of the hill.   THE DUKE OF WELLINGTON

3

ZERO RAIDERS

While the inner circle of the U. S. Army Air Forces was buzzing with Smart's daring low-level proposition, the R.A.F. furnished ostensible proof that low strikes by heavy bombers were too costly. Twelve Lancasters assailed U-boat engine works at Augsburg, Germany, and five returned. Wing Commander Guy Gibson took nineteen hand-picked Lancaster crews to destroy the Mohne and Eder hydroelectric dams and flood the industrial Ruhr. Three planes aborted after take-off. Sixteen bombed from an altitude of sixty feet, and eight returned. The gallant Gibson was awarded the Victoria Cross, Britain's Medal of Honor. Bomber Harris remarked, "Any operation that deserves the V.C. is in the nature of things unfit to be repeated at frequent intervals." It was a matter of plain arithmetic. If you lost half your sixteen planes on a mission, four raids afterward you would have one plane. The U. S. Air Force in Europe demanded 25 missions of a combat flier by day, and Bomber Harris insisted on 35 by night.

Jacob Smart flew to Britain to confer with the airman he wanted to assume operational planning for Tidal Wave, Colonel Edward J. Timberlake, dean of the Liberator combat school, who had just brought his Traveling Circus back to England from the winter campaign in Africa. Timberlake had promoted squadron leaders to commanding rank, including Group Colonel K. K. Compton, who was to lead the force on Tidal Wave. As Jacob Smart braced him, Timberlake was relinquishing command of the Circus to Addison Baker, one of his squadron leaders, and moving up to command of the 201st (Provisional) Combat Wing, a cadre charged with converting the onflow of new B-24's and crews to a battle might. Timberlake accepted Smart's challenge to take over the thousand and one details of Tidal Wave, and began picking out the experts he needed.

As his operations officer, Timberlake selected one of his Circus squadron leaders, a slight, sharp-witted youth from Racine, Wisconsin, named John Jerstad, who suffered the nickname "Jerk." Major Jerstad had flown so many more missions than his quota that he had stopped counting them. He had come far since his first raid, after which he reported to interrogations, "I never saw so much flak!" Jerstad kept a notebook of lessons learned in combat; he had brought his men through many a dire sky engagement, including a 105-minute running battle with the "Yellownoses," Goering's smartest fighter group. Jersted wrote his parents, "I'm the youngest kid on the staff and it's quite an honor to work with Colonels and Generals."

The navigation officer of Timberlake's planning wing was a New York State school teacher, Captain Leander F. Schmid, retired from combat but prepared to fly to Ploesti as the target finder. Two outstanding Britons joined the wing, Group Captain D. G. Lewis, R.A.F., an expert on enemy fighters, and another ex-refinery manager from Ploesti, Wing Commander D. C. Smythe, an advocate of low-level bombing.

As the tactical motif for the assault formed among the planners, they became attracted to the idea of attacking Ploesti from the northwest, the direction of the Reich itself. Coming down from the Carpathian foothills and sweeping the targets simultaneously seemed to promise maximum surprise. Moreover, from this direction there was a shining arrow pointing straight at the target city —the railway from Floresti to Ploesti. The attack groups could guide on the railway and run infallibly upon the targets from Floresti, thirteen miles—or three minutes—away from the bomb-line. Thus Floresti, an obscure hamlet carried on only the largest-scale survey maps, was selected as the final Initial Point, the turning place for the bomb drive.

Looking down at Ploesti from the Initial Point, the planners found the refineries neatly spaced across a five-mile-wide bomb-line. Men rushing across a strange country could not be expected to learn place names, much less the names of factories, so the refineries were assigned numbers from left to right.

The lead group, Colonel K. K. Compton's Liberandos, accordingly drew Target White One on the far left, the Romana Americana plant. The second group, Addison Baker's Traveling Circus, would simultaneously strike White Two, the Concordia Vega refinery. Section B of the Circus, led by Ramsay Potts, would hit White Three, the parallel Standard Petrol Block and Unirea Sperantza units. Killer Kane's heavy Pyramider force, coming in on the center, would take out the number-one priority target of the raid, Astro Romana, or Target White Four, the two-million-ton producer that had eluded Halpro. On Kane's right, flying almost on top of the railway, would come Leon Johnson's Eight Balls, aiming for White Five, the Colombia Aquila refinery.

Johnson's deputy, James Posey, would veer off a few points further right to carry his force to Blue Target, the important Creditul Minier plant, five miles south of the White targets at a town called Brazi. The last and seventh strike force in the bomber stream, Jack Wood's Sky Scorpions, would climb the foothills and hit another isolated objective, the Steaua Romana refinery at Câmpina, 18 miles north of Ploesti. It was named Red Target.

The approach was shrewdly selected, considering the extra flying range the B-24's would be given that day, the surprise angle, the lucky railroad, and the fact that the last sixty miles to the Initial Point would be flown over wooded foothills and ravines that Allied Intelligence was almost sure had no antiaircraft defenses. Intelligence firmly estimated that the flak and detection systems were arraigned in Ploesti's eastern approaches, toward the Soviet, and denied the possibility of effective defenses in the northern, western and southern salients of Ploesti. What enemy commander could be expecting an incursion over the vast distance from Africa, and especially one that went on an extra hundred miles or so to attack through the back door? Unfortunately for this supposition, Gerstenberg was definitely expecting an attack from Africa and was right now building up his guns on the north, west and south.

Having picked Floresti as the turning point for the bomb run, the planners redoubled assurances that the navigators could find the little town. They projected a line west of Floresti and slightly south and found that two much larger towns lay along this approach, Targoviste and Pitesti. So Pitesti became the First Initial Point to find and Targoviste the Second Initial Point. Crossing them correctly would bring one unerringly to the Third I.P. In addition, there was a prominent landmark at Targoviste that could be seen for many miles, a large ancient monastery on a hill. Everything that could be done for the navigators was done. The three principal plotters of the I.P.'s, Ted Timberlake, Leander Schmid and John Jerstad, were going to fly the mission.

In England, Timberlake started low-level rehearsals among the two Eighth Air Force Liberator groups selected to go to Africa for Tidal Wave—his former command, the Traveling Circus, and the Eight Balls, led by Colonel Leon Johnson. Johnson introduced his flying officers to a specialist who would teach them how to use a low-level bombsight. Pilot Robert Lehnhausen said, "This was right after a very mean and costly mission we'd made against the submarine pens at Kiel where we lost seven out of eighteen ships. And a few days before, a squadron of speedy B-26 medium bombers had tried a low-level raid on Holland and none came back. There was much murmuring and grumbling. Colonel Johnson told us in a calm, positive voice that if it was the desire of the Air Force to fly low-level missions we would fly those missions and he would lead us. There was complete silence in the room. If he was leading, we were going to follow."

The English-based groups, together with the newly arrived Sky Scorpions (389th Bomb Group), began beating up and down the foggy East Anglian countryside in treetop practice flights. None of the crewmen knew why, but they reveled in the sudden legalization of buzzing, heretofore a highly illicit pleasure. English farmers were not as happy about it. They complained of horses in shock, cows gone dry, and bees on strike against May flowers. To satisfy speculations about the low-level target, Timberlake's Intelligence chief, Michael G. Phipps, a former ten-goal polo player, planted a rumor that it was the German battleship *Tirpitz*, hiding in a Norwegian fjord beyond the range of R.A.F. bombers. Phipps borrowed Norwegian Navy officers to walk around the B-24 bases and go in and out of operations rooms. The Norwegians had no idea why, but they enjoyed their post exchange privileges.

The planners dreaded one aspect of the low-level scheme— mid-air collisions caused by propeller turbulence or slight errors in judgment. During the rehearsals two Liberators collided, killing eighteen men. The survivors, pilot Harold L. James and Sergeant Earl Zimmerman, returned to duty. They were to go to Ploesti.

Timberlake befriended an unemployed Intelligence officer whom he found wandering around Eighth Air Force H.Q., vainly trying to sell an idea. He was a slender, ingenious Connecticut architect named Gerald K. Geerlings, a World War I infantryman, and his idea was: "Flat aerial maps do not coördinate with ground features until the navigator is directly over them. Why not use oblique drawings to show how places look as you approach them?" Timberlake admitted Geerlings to the Tidal Wave secret and gave him instructions to prepare perspective views of Ploesti and the overland route to the target.

The Allies had no such aerial pictures of the Balkans or the refinery city and were prohibited from photo-reconnaissance lest the defenses be alerted. The only way to fulfill the orders was for Geerlings to comb a large random picture bank without alerting the custodians to his regional interest. He went to the Bodleian Library at Cambridge, where there was a large picture deposit of foreign scenery, gathered by appeals to the public for snapshots and postal cards from prewar travels. Geerlings asked for files on ten widely separated parts of the world and photographed the mountain to get the mouse he was after—a slender folder on the Balkans.

Geerlings designed a novel route chart—an accordion folder with eleven oblique views of landmarks en route to the target. There were no place names on the folder. They could not be disclosed even to his printer, the secure R.A.F. Intelligence center at Medmenham. At that establishment model makers worked on another hush-hush project, scale models of a nameless valley and an unknown industrial city. The miniature of Ploesti was so accurate that Group Captain Lewis recognized his former villa. They finished the models in record time, and an odd pair came with strange devices, including a child's tricycle, and locked themselves in the model room. They were the Ploesti avenger, Lord Forbes, and a Texas-drawling New York newspaperman named John Reagan ("Tex") McCrary, chief of the Photo & Newsreel Section of the Eighth U.S.A.A.F. They produced a professional 45-minute sound film to brief the Ploesti fliers; this was the first use of movies to prepare men for a single battle. They also turned out 8-mm. silent films showing how each refinery would look from the air on a low-level approach and crossing. The camera dolly for these trucking shots was the child's tricycle. Thus, more than a month before the mission, the entire briefing panoply was designed for a low attack, even though General Brereton in Cairo was still supposed to have the final option between the low road and the high road.

Brereton was not closely involved with the operational preparations; they were left to his bomber chief, Brigadier Uzal G. Ent, who had to find the men and airplanes to do the job. Ent was a small, amiable Pennsylvania Dutchman with a searching mind and remarkably varied attainments. A graduate of Susquehanna University and the U. S. Military Academy, he was a qualified specialist in chemical warfare, engineering, meteorology, and aerial navigation and piloting. As a navigator in the National Balloon Race in 1938, Ent won the Distinguished Flying Cross for landing the bag after his pilot had been killed by lightning. He had served in diplomatic posts and was an ordained Lutheran minister. He was married to an ex-Ziegfeld Follies girl.

Ent was not enthusiastic about a low-level attack; he believed the losses would be unbearable. He intended to fly to Ploesti himself. Then a surprising and encouraging omen came, when an adventitious low-level bombing experiment succeeded beyond all expectation. It began in the restless, inventive mind of Norman Appold, who had become impatient with the often ineffective high-level attempts on Rommel's Italian supply ports. Appold asked his Liberando group commander, K. K. Compton, to let him try the low road to a particularly resistant target at Messina, Sicily. The flak there was almost interdictory. The veteran Halpro lead navigator, Bernard Rang, had recently gone over Messina in a plane rocking with flak hits, and had parachuted to his death among the bursts.

When he braced K. K. Compton, Appold had no inkling of the big low-level mission being planned. Compton was secretly pleased to have a man volunteer for a vitally needed experiment without knowing why it was important, and he endorsed Appold's plan to Uzal Ent, who immediately approved.

Appold's Sicilian objective was a row of ferroconcrete train ferry sheds protecting Rommel's supply trains from bombing after they were ferried across the Messina Strait from Italy. Repeated high-level strikes had not penetrated the roofs. Secretly, after dark on 29 March, Appold led three Liberando ships to the Luqa fighter strip on Malta, the most forward base for the novel target route he planned. As the planes were refueled, he briefed the crews: "We are going around the top of Sicily, keeping under radar all the way. The Initial Point, where we turn into our bomb run, may be hard to find. It's just an unmarked spot of water between the Lipari Islands and Messina. So let's all stick together. The alternate target is Crotone." This was another familiar and defiant high-level target, an important chemical and ammunition works on the boot sole of Italy which had resisted nine high-formation bombings.

At midnight, Appold's research flight took off from Malta on a night without moon or stars and settled into a wave-top swing around the west and north coasts of Sicily, to attack Messina not only at an unexpected altitude but from the opposite direction of previous missions. Appold's navigator, Donald O'Dell, called off estimated height above the waves. Bombardier John B. Hogan crouched on the central spar of the open bomb bay, looking down at the sea, reporting white chop, which indicated an altitude of twenty feet—as low as Appold cared to go. Hogan was soaked with spray during the all-night sweep over the Tyrrhenian Sea. A gunner said, "It was just like water skiing."

The voyage was too much for the other two B-24's, which became separated from Appold and returned to Africa. At dawn, O'Dell found the Initial Point and Appold turned south into his bomb run. The pilot saw thick morning mist in the Strait and announced, "Well, we'll never be able to see the sheds this morning. What say we go to Crotone?" Appold always polled his crew on major decisions and they always agreed with his suggestions. By now the little pilot had an awesome reputation for attempting the weird and improbable and getting away with it. Appold banked into a climbing turn for the Italian mainland.

Ahead, the Calabrian Mountains were covered with low rain-drenched clouds. O'Dell had no accurate elevation charts. Nonetheless, Appold undertook to fly the contours of these unknown mountains to keep under radar and thus give fighters and flak the least opportunity to pot him. Over hogbacks and peaks at 200 miles an hour, shaving ridges and planing low in ravines, the solitary Liberator flew. The tail gunner saw pigs running, chickens being plucked in the prop-wake, and sleepy farmers coming out of stone huts to look and wave. The B-24 leaped the last foggy mountain and slid into the plain leading to Crotone. "There's a fighter base between us and the target," O'Dell warned. Appold stormed across it at wind-sock level, noting unattended Messerschmitts and Macchis lying about. O'Dell used the enemy base as a final course correction, ten miles from Crotone. He and Appold called out terrain features for Hogan, hunched over his bombsight: "Three chimneys coming up. . . . Freight train moving across in front of target." Hogan interposed, "Hey, boss, let me try one on the train." Appold said, "Okay." Hogan dropped a yellow 500-pound bomb. Although it would not explode for 45 seconds, the effect of the dead weight was startling. The bomb cracked the train in two, tossed up cars, burrowed on, curling up rails, and disappeared in a lumberyard. The tail gunner cried, "Timber going up like toothpicks and she didn't go off yet!"

"I want a better line-up, Norm," said the bombardier. "Drop her lower." Appold jacked the boisterous bomber a few feet deeper. Hogan crashed the five remaining bombs into the factory. Not one of the fierce flak guns at Crotone was awake. With the loss of bomb weight Appold went full throttle, leaped the first smokestacks, and banked away from a higher 150-foot chimney. The bombs burst in a tremendous exhalation. The plant went up, crumbling and swelling with dust, cordite fumes and vaporized chemicals. Flames spurted out of the hanging debris.

Appold said, "Gunners! You want to paste it?" "Yeah, man!" they chorused. Appold crossed back over an undamaged section and the sergeants shot it up. Before the antiaircraft guns could go into action the Liberator was speeding to Benghazi, unscratched. Interrogation officers regarded Appold's report as a "snow job." K. K. Compton sent a photo-reconnaissance plane to Crotone. Its pictures fully bore out Appold's report. Intelligence estimated, "It will not be necessary to return to Crotone for some time." One plane at minimum altitude had accomplished what nine forces at high level had failed to do.

On the following day K. K. Compton was approached by another masterful Liberando pilot, a tall, ruddy-complexioned, dark-haired youth named Brian Woolley Flavelle, from Caldwell, New Jersey. Flavelle didn't open his mouth much, except when men gathered to harmonize—then his fine baritone sounded deep into the desert night. He had interrupted forestry studies at the University of Oregon to join the Air Force because he hated fascism. Flavelle proposed to lead three ships on a twilight raid on Messina to avoid the morning mists that had foiled Appold. Compton and Ent approved.

Flavelle took his wave-skimming B-24's into the ferroconcrete train sheds and "rammed the bombs right down their throats." The planes leaped overtop into a formation of forty unarmed Junkers 52 transports flying toward them at tree level. Jerome DuFour, Flavelle's wingman, said, "We decided to fly straight ahead and the hell with them. With all our guns opened up, we ploughed right into them. They all scattered, except one who came at us head-on. We broke him up in the air, and he crashed." Now General Ent had another successful low-level strike to consider.

In this brightening atmosphere the Circus, Eight Balls and Sky Scorpions arrived from England, completing the five heavy bomb groups assigned to Tidal Wave. Never before had there been gathered a more experienced group of American airmen. The force commanders were, with one exception, hardened survivors of the air war. The commander of the mission-leading Liberandos, K. K. Compton, was a product of the early campaign in the west under Timberlake, who placed him with Rickenbacker and Lindbergh as "a great instinctive pilot." The second bomb force was to be led by Addison Baker, Timberlake's heir at the helm of the Traveling Circus. Baker's two deputies were Colonel George Brown, who had led many high battle boxes over western Europe, and an equally experienced ex-economics professor named Ramsay Potts, set to lead a small echelon of his own. Next to Potts in the battle front would be the largest force, the Pyramiders, the old established desert firm, led by the salty Killer Kane. Beside Kane on the simultaneous sweep there would be an efficient group of green ships, the Eight Balls, led by a man of destiny, Leon Johnson, also an alumnus of the East Anglian Liberator school. His deputy and leader of another separate striking force was a cool, tight formation keeper, James Posey. The remaining force, the inexperienced Sky Scorpions, were led by Jack Wood, who maintained high technique and discipline among his crews.

When Colonel Wood arrived in Benghazi, he came up against the reality of the desert war. He and his officers had to pitch their own tents. Major Philip Ardery looked enviously at the dwellings of the pioneers. A tent near him had a marble floor two feet deep and high sandbag revetments above the ground, which made it cooler and kept out German strafing.

Jacob Smart flew to Benghazi carrying the invisible seals of the Joint Chiefs of Staff. He discovered that the low-level concept was by no means sold to those who so far knew about it—the top brass and group leaders. Smart jeeped around the forty miles of dust, visiting the colonels and arguing for his conception. He let them know that he himself was going to fly the mission. He had secretly picked the co-pilot's seat with an old reliable squadron leader of the Circus, Major Kenneth O. ("Kayo") Dessert, who was to lead the second wave over Target White Two.

One of the Circus pilots who had come to the desert was Walter Stewart, a big, ebullient blond from Utah. If you did not know this fact you could read it in very large type on the side of his machine: *Utah Man*. Before the war Stewart had been a Mormon missionary in England. When he returned there in uniform he resumed his rapport with English crowds by speaking at war bond rallies. One day, after selling a fortune in British bonds at King's Lynn, Norfolk, he was introduced to two members of the audience who had asked to meet him. Stewart shook hands with Queen Mary and her fifteen-year-old granddaughter, Princess Elizabeth. He put the girl at ease with a chat on literature. "I've just finished *The Robe*," he said. "I'll bet you'd like it." The future queen averred she would. "I'll lend you my copy," said Stewart. "Where are you putting up?" Elizabeth said, "Sandringham."

The next day Stewart borrowed Colonel Timberlake's cub, *Fearless Fosdick*, flew low over the palace lawn, and dropped the book. When he got back, Timberlake was waiting with a teletype from the Air Ministry. "H. M. Government takes a dim view of aircraft dropping objects on Sandringham Palace," said the CO. "A servant took your number." Stewart received a series of reprimands, although the admonitory officers had a hard time keeping straight faces.

Surrounding the American bases in Libya and filtering ubiquitously through them, peddling melons and eggs and salvaging bits of loose gear, was the indigenous population, mostly nomadic herdsmen belonging to the Senussi Brotherhood of Islam, which believed that the next Prophet would be born to a man. Senussi males wore tight trousers with incongruously baggy seats in readiness for this event. The American security people were not much concerned over them. Before departing their Libyan colony, Italian forces had delivered Senussi allegiance to the Allies, free of charge. The fascists punished petty thievery by cutting off Arab noses. To teach respect for Mussolini, they seized the Great Mukhtar, the spiritual head of the Brotherhood, trussed him up, and dropped him from an airplane two miles over the Senussi village of Solluch.

During the fluid land fighting, Senussi rangers, unbidden by the Allies, stalked Axis movements and reported them to the British. When the Americans came, they too fell under the protection of the stealthy Brotherhood. One night Italian saboteurs landed from a submarine, killed two American guards, and blew up four airplanes. The Senussi fell on the gumshoe men and cut them up sorely before the Italians could find British antiaircraft men to take their surrender.

Life was elemental in the bomber encampment. "About dusk the desert comes to life with all manner of animal and insect life," said Captain Jack Preble. "The greatest pests are jerboa mice and desert rats. Herodotus described the jumping rodents of the Libyan deserts as being 'two-legged.'" The airmen tried to protect food by hanging it in bags on lines between tent poles. The rats leaped six feet, clutched the bags, and gnawed through to the delicacies. Captain Ernie Parker sat up one night with a .45 gun to ambush rats. He spied one forcing its way into his roommate's locker and killed the animal with one shot. The bullet went on through his friend's dress uniform.

Captain Benjamin Klose, a Circus bombardier, was trudging through the rain when he saw a sight that made him philosophical. "Out in the open," he said, "there sat a lieutenant general on an oil drum privy. This desert is the right place to fight a war. They ought to ship the generals and politicians from both sides down here and let them slug it out." A muddy clerk put it another way: "This war in Africa is being fought to see who *doesn't* have to keep the place and the Eyetalians have us licked."

Mail from the States was months late, but the men had plenty of time to write home. A mechanic, lacking anything better in the way of news, wrote his girl, "Last night we licked the officers at softball." When she opened the letter there was a postscript: "Like hell they did. Capt. Harry Schilling, Squadron Censor."

The airmen had nothing to drink except boiled water and coffee, although an enterprising sergeant found the only bottle of cola in Egypt, scrounged a tot of Nelson's Blood, and advertised on his tent: CUBA LIBRE, 250 EGYPTIAN POUNDS. However, a miracle was passed one day in the officers' mess. Captain James A. Gunn, who was to be lost at Ploesti, greeted a weatherbeaten visitor in South African naval uniform, who introduced himself, "Peter Keeble. Working in the harbor." Gunn said, "Sorry, Commander, I can't offer any refreshment." Keeble said, "Matter of fact, I've got a flask in my car. Would you have your guards pass it through the gate?"

A British lorry entered and discharged a hundred cases of Scotch. "Gift of the Royal Navy," said Keeble. "Where the hell did you get it?" Gunn asked. "Bottom of the harbor," Keeble replied. While clearing shipwrecks, his divers had entered the S.S. *Hannah Möller*, sixty feet down, to dynamite her, and had found an intact cargo of 1,000 cases of whiskey and 200,000 quarts of Canadian beer.

Companionship was one of the few of life's pleasures available to them. They were lucky in their chaplains and special service officers. Captain Brutus K. Hamilton, the famous Olympic track coach, was a much-loved morale officer for the Circus, as was its Protestant chaplain, James Burris. Captain Gerald O. Beck of Cincinnati, Ohio, was the picturesque white-haired Roman Catholic chaplain of the Sky Scorpions. A Protestant, Philip Ardery, said of him: "If there was no rabbi on hand, Father Beck would preach a Jewish funeral service with perfect form and dignity. When no Protestant chaplain was available, he would give all aid and comfort to Protestant boys, without pushing his religion on them. He slept in various tents with the enlisted men, carrying his cot and bedding from one group to the next, each anxiously awaiting the visit. The crews superstitiously believed they would not be shot down as long as he was sleeping in their quarters. Father Beck also had a worldly side. He loved to gamble on cards and dice, was nearly always a heavy winner, and gave the money to charity. I saw him make six straight passes with the dice one night and break up the game. No one dared fade him on the seventh roll. One time before we went on a rough mission, I lay in my cot and heard him talking to the Catholics outside the tent: 'I want to urge you now to prepare yourself for this dangerous task. Go to confession before take-off. And, if you find a *good* priest, let me know and I'll go with you.'"

Souls were one thing and serviceable airplanes were another. In the bomber domain the omnipresent, indispensable man was a short, big-chested, swarthy individual with graying hair who drove a jeep day in, day out, coming in a pillar of dust or a fountain of mud to the far-flung aircraft. He was the legendary Ulysses S. Nero, Billy Mitchell's sergeant, now a colonel charged with providing an impossible number of airplanes for the missions. At breakfast General Ent might say, "I want a hundred planes tomorrow," and Sam Nero would say, "There are only eighty-seven fit to fly." The general would say, "I want a hundred." The next dawn would find dogged mechanics putting the last touches to No. 100 as the mission warmed up. Nero slept adequately only when the three-day khamseen blew, and he never took a leave.

The men wore any sort of uniform they could find. One day in the chow line, a G.I. noticed an elderly, unshaven individual in a U. S. leather flight jacket without insignia. He looked again and ran for Colonel Timberlake. The colonel arrived on the double and said, "Sir, we had no idea you were here or . . ." It was General Sir Harold Alexander, the British commander in chief for Africa. He grinned at Timberlake's costume—British Army battle dress.

The greatest pleasure was bathing naked in the warm blue Mediterranean, generals and privates stripped to the same rank. A thousand miles away their coming adversaries went swimming too. Colonel Woldenga, on an unannounced inspection of the Mizil fighter base near Ploesti, found a large swimming pool that had not been there two weeks before. His fighter pilots were vying in fancy dives before a throng of Romanian and German girls. They had scrounged the cement from Gerstenberg's blast-wall construction.

As Tidal Wave came nearer, the Liberator men were ordered on missions to Italy to soften Rommel's rear for the Sicilian invasion. Over Naples, bombardier Alfred Pezzella made a quip that immortalized him in the force. He was glued to his bombsight when a hunk of flak entered between his feet and ripped out a hole over his head. Without taking his eyes from the crosswire, Pezzella flung up an arm and called, "Ball one!" He was to die at Ploesti.

The desert air war got little attention from war correspondents. They were in England, helping put over daylight, high-level, precision bombing. Few noticed the absence of all of Eaker's Liberator groups, which had gone to Africa for Tidal Wave. The occasional visitor from the States who ventured into the inhospitable desert came with the impression that the Ninth Air Force had an easier war than the embattled Eighth. Alfred Kalberer, the Halpro holdover, said: "A War Department wheel and two big air force doctors happened to be visiting Benghazi when a plane came in firing flares for wounded aboard. We took the V.I.P.'s with the ambulance to meet the ship. The inside looked like somebody had been sloshing buckets of red paint around. It was frozen to the metal during the high altitude flight. The top turret gunner's head had been blown off, and he became a fountain of blood before his fingers, half frozen to the grips, came loose and let the body fall to the deck. One of the doctors fainted. An old crew chief dismissed the retching men, lifted the body out, and cleaned the airplane."

A few weeks before Tidal Wave a disturbing personality came to Benghazi. He was a short, fair-haired Royal Air Force squadron leader named George C. Barwell, the world's leading air-gunnery theoretician. Barwell, a masterful mathematician, was the son of a Cockney officer of the London Machine Gun Regiment who had died in the Great War. Barwell had been washed out of R.A.F. pilot training because of his annoying habit of questioning the instructors' dogmas. Training Command had to grind out pilots by the book and would not slow down classes to deal with Barwell's challenges. He was shunted into bombers as a gunner. After several night missions Barwell announced to one and all that gunnery training was unrealistic. "The gunner's limited practice firing at towed targets has no relation to the ultimate problem of defending his aircraft against fighters traveling at great speed in three dimensions," he said. "In combat, the ill-trained men blaze away at multiple simultaneous attacks and self-inflicted damage is a terrifying by-product of their training."

Barwell proved his own theories in fifty night battles over Germany, during which he shot down several opponents. Once, when his pilot turned back from flak over the target, Barwell berated him on the intercom: "Your job is to put it straight through the letter box." Back in England the pilot so couched his flight report that he received a decoration, so Barwell denounced him again in the officers' mess. Soon thereafter "flak-happy" Barwell found himself assigned to Berka Two, the R.A.F. base at Benghazi, as a gunnery instructor. The field was surrounded by five Liberator bases building up for Ploesti. Barwell was drawn to the bristling guns of the B-24's like a politician to so many baby carriages.

He met General Uzal Ent, "a charming man, who liked to talk gunnery." The American knew there was plenty wrong with U. S. aerial marksmanship and borrowed the incisive Britisher from the R.A.F. as a gunnery lecturer to help his airmen through the coming Ploesti ordeal. Next day they were enticed from their tents by an earnest Englishman who drew pictures in the sand and angled his hands, talking big air battles. "Now, you chaps are doing it all wrong," said Barwell. "Here's Jerry coming at you from ten o'clock high at three hundred fifty miles an hour. And you make the mistake of leading him." They treated him with scoffing tolerance. For Barwell's first formal lecture Uzal Ent had to drive them into the briefing hut. The Briton began, "The gunner's problem of calculating relative air speeds, altitude, temperature and a dozen other variables, is beyond the ability of most mathematicians, let alone a hurriedly trained air gunner." That brought an American groan comparable to the parliamentary cry of "Oh, sir!" The gunners reassured themselves by looking down at the silver wings on their chests that proclaimed them qualified marksmen.

The pest continued, "Fighters are shot down largely by accident, at tremendous cost to your own planes." The crowd growled. "You have wonderful computing gunsights," Barwell ploughed on, "but they are so complicated that it is impossible to use them properly in combat. For example, take your gyro gunsight . . ." Laughs broke out from men who had decided Barwell was a Limey double-talk comedian masquerading as a flier. He continued, "The system of gunnery that has proven itself in combat is called position firing." It was his own theory, at variance with British and U. S. doctrine. "Position firing is based on the fact that the attacking fighter's problem is equal and opposite to that of the gunner in the bomber. This applies, of course, only during the curve of the pursuit fighter attack." Snores were heard, and laughter in growing volume, despite the British Distinguished Flying Cross on the lecturer's tunic. But there was also a puzzled element, whose minds turned over during this upsetting talk. After the lecture they surrounded Barwell. "Look, if you know so much about it, how about coming up with us and showing how it works?"

Barwell was a grounded instructor, and besides, foreigners needed special permission to fly U. S. missions. He said nothing about this. Some Americans muttered, "The Limey is yellow." Barwell turned up uninvited at the first briefing of the freshmen Sky Scorpions. Their leader, Colonel Jack Wood, said Bomber Command had offered a choice among four relatively shallow targets for their initiation. Sentiment veered toward the nearest one, a German air base at Maleme, Crete. Barwell said, "That one won't be easy. It hasn't been hit for a fortnight and Jerry will be quite eager." The Americans voted defiantly for Maleme. Barwell said, "Very well, I volunteer for top turret in Tailend Charlie." The last plane in the formation was the most vulnerable to fighters.

He did not put his name down as a member of Philip Ardery's crew in Tailend Charlie as they flew off to the target he had warned them against. Worse was in store at Maleme than Barwell had anticipated. The night before, British forces had staged a fake commando and paratroop invasion of Crete in which they dropped thousands of plastic doll parachutists with toy guns that sparked on the way down. The Germans were kept up all night wasting shoe leather, ammunition and tempers and were eager to sock back at somebody for the stunt. Wood's greenhorns flew right into it. On the bomb run, three dozen hot Messerschmitts of the latest mark climbed savagely into the B-24's.

The Liberator gunners freighted the sky with bullets, firing continuously in all directions. Friendly shells crashed past a waist gunner's ear. Furiously rattled, he was going to fire back at "the bastard," when his buddy knocked his aim away from the other Liberator. During the bedlam Barwell's twin fifties remained silent. He stood in the top turret with a chronometer and note pad, recording incidents that would prove instructive later.

A Liberator exploded and fell. The young men stared in disbelief at the injustice. The age-old shock to the maiden warrior's soul—"They are trying to kill *me!* What did *I* ever do to them?"— was felt in all hearts save one. Barwell saw a fighter coming with blazing guns. He said, "Tail gunner, don't lead him. Fire right into him." As the fighter passed undamaged, Barwell gave him an economical squirt and the Messerschmitt broke up. "Navigator, credit one certain to the tail gunner," said Barwell. On the next fighter pass, the Briton's borrowed guns jammed, and he returned to note-taking.

Carried away by his educational opportunity, Barwell flew mission after mission, sometimes two a day, never putting himself on the sortie roster. "It was rather nerve-racking," he said. "The Americans swung from ridicule to extravagant praise. Since they were always given to extreme claims of enemy aircraft destroyed, they went around saying I personally shot down everything. If I'd destroyed all those Jerries, there'd have been no German air force left. Actually, I may have gotten seven or eight while flying with the American chaps. The boys wrote home to their mums, talking big about me, and I got touching letters and homemade biscuits from the States. They called me Lucky Barwell. I was trying to be scientific, but don't forget, one did need luck."

Leon Johnson's Eight Balls also entered the air war in the Mediterranean theater. On their first raid, Pilot Robert Lehnhausen was shot down into the sea. He was picked up from a life raft by a British mine sweeper carrying General Montgomery's staff to Malta for the Sicilian invasion. In a Maltese hospital an

American infantry colonel asked him, "Did you people come out here to bomb Ploesti?" Lehnhausen had never heard of the place. He said, "I wouldn't know, sir."

At the time, from Brereton's Cairo H.Q., General Richard Royce was writing General Arnold, "Security around this headquarters is practically nonexistent. All the typists and file clerks are hired locally and I suspect every one of them. The city is full of people gathering and selling information." Strangers approached U. S. airmen on leave in Cairo and asked, "When are you going to bomb Ploesti?" In Bucharest, Gerstenberg was pondering the same question.

Sir Richard Grenville persuaded the company, or as many as he could induce, to yield themselves unto God, and to the mercy of none else: but, as they had like valiant resolute men repulsed so many enemies, they should not now shorten the honor of their nation by prolonging their own lives for a few hours or a few days. SIR WALTER RALEIGH,

"The Last Fight of H.M.S. *Revenge*," 1591

4

COMING BACK
IS SECONDARY TODAY

Ten thousand feet above the Bay of Biscay, the happy hunting grounds of Nazi fighters based in "neutral" Spain, five Liberators from England drummed south for Africa on the ninth of July 1943. In this area, a month before, German fighters had shot down an unarmed passenger plane, carrying the actor Leslie Howard to his death. In Captain Hugh Roper's lead B-24, the Tidal Wave architect, Gerald Geerlings, sat on a heap of numbered anonymous parcels containing the charts, films and table models of Ploesti.

Should one item fall into enemy hands, the mission would have to be canceled. Consequently Intelligence had bet on one plane arriving safely, rather than distribute the secrets among the five.

Geerlings said, "Our plane was loaded with thermite bombs. If we were hit, the entire contents would go up in a single splendid flash, leaving no trace of the secrets. Only Hugh Roper and I knew about the incendiaries, to save the crew unnecessary worry."

As Roper steered through broken cumulus off Saint-Nazaire, France, his bombardier called, "Junkers 88's below!" Roper said, "I sure hope they have some other business." The bombardier rejoined, "Looks like they do. They're chasing a big fat Sunderland in and out of the clouds." Geerlings said, "It wasn't exactly Christian, but it was some minutes before we hoped the British flying boat got away." Roper's explosion-prone Liberator drummed on, its people thinking of the long travel ahead through German fighters. But the Mediterranean skies were empty. The Luftwaffe was occupied over Sicily, where the Allied invasion had begun that morning.

At Benghazi the briefing paraphernalia was carried to a green hut in the H.Q. compound, and Geerlings and a corporal took turns sleeping against the door with loaded .45's. Only command and group leaders were admitted to the shack. Alfred Kalberer, leader of the original Halpro mission to Ploesti, by this time the grounded operations officer of the Liberandos, said, "This thing can't work. I'll have nothing to do with it. I figure we'll lose thirty-two planes." He was relieved and sent home.

As more officers were admitted to its secrets, the stuffy, smoke-reeking green hut became a theater of ill-concealed emotions. The initiate felt awe and pride in taking part in one of the great efforts of the war, and then he felt fear. This one was going to be rugged.

The group leaders groused to General Ent about the low-level plan. Leon Johnson of the Eight Balls said, "I asked the planners about barrage balloons, and they replied, 'We think your wings'll break the cables.' Think! I'd rather know we'll be able to break them." Uzal Ent embodied the complaints in a note to Brereton: "We estimate that seventy-five aircraft will be lost at low level.

Fifty percent destruction is the best we can hope for. You have guessed our recommendation—to attack at high level until the target is destroyed or effectively neutralized."

Brereton was unable to take the advice. He had already submitted the low-level plan to Eisenhower and had received the theater chief's approval. The remaining problems of Tidal Wave were left to those who would fly it.

Eisenhower kept demanding planes. Italy was cracking ahead of plan. The high command ordered a dashing propaganda raid. Ent was called on for 150 Liberators to strike precise military objectives in Rome on 19 July. Intelligence officers agreed to exempt three categories of airmen from the Rome-bound fleet: unwilling Roman Catholics (none objected); Catholic-haters who might not care too much if they hit religious buildings (three were grounded by Protestant chaplains); and men who knew the Ploesti secret. Watching them fly away, Timberlake groaned, "Damn it. I let Ramsay Potts go." John Jerstad said, "Squadron leaders like Ramsay haven't been briefed yet on Tidal Wave." Timberlake said, "You know Potts. He's probably figured out where we're going." Timberlake and Jerstad sweated out Potts's return in *Duchess*. She came in from Rome undamaged. Timberlake asked Potts, "Where do you think we're going?" The pilot had deduced that with squadron leader Joseph Tate in England two months before. Potts went to the map and silently laid his finger on Ploesti.

The day after Rome, Uzal Ent took Ninth Bomber Command off operations, quarantined the sprawl of airfields, and began intensive low-level rehearsals. South on the desert plateau British Army engineers laid out a plat of the complex refineries, the front of each vital pinpoint target marked with a furrow of lime mixed with engineers' urine. No water was available. The Americans had to find these bomb-lines in a hurry near the ground. Their flaunted high-altitude Norden computing bombsight could not be used on Tidal Wave. The bombardiers were being equipped with "ten-cent" converted gunsights to toggle and plough their explosives home.

Colonel Timberlake and target architect Geerlings examined

the dummy layout from an altitude of six miles to determine whether it could be seen by German scout planes from Crete that often passed over that high. The target was invisible. But it was also invisible to the first test flights at zero altitude. The pilots said, "You come over the white lines so fast, you can't see them. We have to get something upright. After all, the refineries are tall." The engineers planted poles topped with fluttering rags on the corners of the aiming points. Timberlake flew over them at German reconnaissance altitude and could not see them. Then pilots aimed for the poles at ground level and also failed to see them. Arabs had stolen the rag pennants overnight. When the engineers topped the poles with shredded petrol tins, the Senussi left them alone and the ground-hugging test pilots found their aiming points.

One by one the five B-24 groups roared into the mock Ploesti, dropping wooden practice bombs and having a wonderful time. Afterward, the men held mock interrogations. "Sergeant, how many camels did you get today?" "Well, sir, one certain and one probable." "Like hell you did. That certain camel was mine." Two Liberators came back from the lowest buzzes on record with paint scraped from their bellies.

The commander of the ambitious junior Sky Scorpion group, Colonel Jack Wood, who remarkably resembled the playwright Eugene O'Neill, thought beyond target marksmanship to navigational problems of the long flight to Ploesti, in which bombing cohesion could be denied by errors in navigation and formation-keeping. He instructed his deputy, Major John A. Brooks III, to take the Scorpions six hundred miles into Africa, deliberately try to trick the navigators into error and see if they could come back and hit the dummy target. Brooks made some calculations and announced, "Colonel, we'll be on target at 1603 hours."

After the planes flew off, Wood loaded his ground officers and dozens of smoke pots in a truck and drove to the dummy to surprise Brooks with smoke screens, which were expected to be a serious obstacle at Ploesti. Gasping in the baking sun, the officers planted the pots around the effigy of Red Target. One of them called, "Colonel, it's 1600, close to ETA." Wood said, "Don't worry, they'll never make it on time." Exactly on the predicted minute, Brooks brought the ear-shattering bomber front over the target at a height of twenty feet. Below, the fliers saw a Mack Sennett episode—their superiors dodging the skipping bombs, piling into a jeep that would not start, and taking to their heels again. At dinner, Brooks said as evenly as possible, "Well, Colonel, you knew our ETA."

Despite the fun of buzzing, the prolonged practice missions and the unfolding of still more special briefing material increased speculation and foreboding about the real thing. The airmen thought that a target all this important was bound to present machine-gun fire. Geerlings said, "Probably the most discussed question among all ranks was what losses would be due to small-arms fire." The architect joined volunteers who lay in desert fox-holes with broomstick machine guns which they tried to train on dust-swirling bombers coming from unknown directions at unannounced times. "It's something beyond belief," said Geerlings, "when from nowhere there is a sound of power and fury, coming and going before one's reflexes can do anything but duck. I swallowed a lot of sand and never got a satisfactory shot." Meanwhile, other men with real machine guns were crouching in pits around Ploesti tracking Woldenga's surprise practice bombings of the refineries.

During the desert rehearsals a ground crew chief grew suspicious of an officer in a clean uniform who was snooping around the base. The G.I. challenged the stranger, who identified himself as a member of the Psychological Warfare Division. The mechanic said, "Jeez, we can sure use you to examine some of the screwballs driving these airplanes."

In the last week of July all the flying officers had passed through the green hut, and then the secret was exposed to the sergeants. Not since Bernard Montgomery revealed his plan for El Alamein to all ranks before the battle had such a total briefing occurred. Walter Stewart, who was holding nightly Bible readings with his Mormon comrades, said: "As the days went by and the enlisted crews learned where we were going, men of various religions decided to meet with us—not a tough decision when the alternative was cleaning your guns again at night. The meetings became an anxiously looked-for pleasure. We knew the low-level mission was to be no breeze. To add to our little fears, one day some men came to the base and installed tanks in the outer section of each wing and even took out the right front bomb-bay shackles and installed a tank there. Now it was the *long* low-level mission. They also fitted armor plate on the flight deck for extra protection. Our little meetings became more precious to us."

The airmen, who had had virtually no reading matter, were suddenly inundated with British paperback books bearing such odd titles as *Cage Birds* and *The Tunnelers of Holzminden*. All were about British escapes from German prison camps in World War I.

Killer Kane announced to the Pyramiders, "All available crews will go on the mission regardless of completion of their combat tours." Scores of his men had logged thirty missions and were due to be repatriated. Worried about the morale of the group, Jacob Smart went to an armament shop where Kane was fixing extra machine guns into the nose perspexes of his lead ships. Kane let the Washington man wait a while before inquiring coldly, "What can I do for you, Colonel?" Smart said, "Do you think your men will follow you on the big one?" Kane exploded. "Look," he said, "if you have any doubt about it, you have the authority to remove me here and now!" Smart left. General Ent came to the shop and said to Kane, "If nobody comes back, the results will be worth the cost." Both he and Kane were scheduled to go to Ploesti.

Geerlings said, "Jake Smart was the unfailing spark plug who kept the operation from bogging down." A week before the mission a wave of amoebic dysentery hit the bases and Smart was among those ordered to bed. Geerlings dropped in to see Smart, "not daring to tell him how badly he was needed at headquarters. There was a growing pessimism at all levels." Fliers near Smart in the infirmary tent "rather hoped they would not be restored to active duty for the raid," Geerlings noted. After several days Smart staggered to his feet and drove around among the groups, rebuilding confidence.

Trucks carted the relief models of the target around the bases for the air crews to study. The smallest-scale relief—the general target area—portrayed the Alpine valleys above Ploesti with a vertical exaggeration of five times. The fliers lingered gloomily over the model, wondering what would happen to a tight, low formation tossing in the tricky drafts of these deep defiles. "No amount of explanation that the actual ravines were relatively shallow would satisfy them," said Geerlings. The men examined the miniature of the entire refinery complex and models of each refinery, which were in true scale, and glanced back at the steep canyons. All would have to fly contours over them and the Sky Scorpions were to go farthest into them and attack down one of the draws to hit Red Target at Câmpina. However, few combat men anticipated what could endanger them atop the targets. Intelligence said nothing about fire hazards to the Liberators from bombs and bullets ripping into storage tanks of volatile fuels. One pilot predicted, "It'll be like looking for a gas leak with a lighted match."

Four days before Tidal Wave the U.S.A.A.F. captured a Romanian pilot, Lieutenant Nicolai Feodor, who said Ploesti "was the most heavily defended target in Europe." There was no way to check this alarming assertion. The mimeograph machines were rolling out Intelligence estimates that "The heavy guns would be unable to direct accurate fire at low-flying formations because of their inability to follow fast-moving targets. The results would be nil. The target has been unmolested for years and is not expected to be alert."

Squadron operations officers searched files and faces to find men to fill out the combat crews. Walter T. Holmes, who had completed his own ordained missions, was the operations man in an Eight Ball squadron. Hating to do it, he called in pilot Robert Lehnhausen, who was not yet recovered from his crash in the sea. Lehnhausen said, "I have no desire to fly a mission, but will if I am ordered to go." Holmes, a shy man, mumbled something which the pilot construed as a direct order: "Okay, Bob," said Holmes, "check yourself into the green hut." Holmes had already been in the hut and felt sorry for the men he had to send there. He did not know that on the eve of the raid he would look over his crew lists, find nobody to pilot a first wave ship on Blue Target, and would write in his own name.

Lehnhausen joined the crowd in the green hut and looked at the exhibits. "Ploesti?" he asked himself. "Where have I heard of that before?" The occasion came back to him in a seizure of trepidation: in the hospital at Malta three weeks before, an American colonel coming to his bed and saying, "Did you people come out here to bomb Ploesti?" Lehnhausen wondered how many other outsiders knew the objective. "Does the enemy know it too?" The pilot left the hut, keeping "the feeling of horror" to himself, not wishing to alarm the others.

On this day in the enemy camp General Gerstenberg also received bad news. A terrible thing had happened in Germany. He went to the railway station to bid good-bye to one of his two precious 500-man regiments of fire police. They had been ordered to Hamburg to fight the fire typhoon which took 60,000 lives in three nights. The cataclysm began with one secret weapon and ended with another. On 25 July the R.A.F. reached Hamburg, almost unopposed, by dropping a blizzard of metallized paper strips to craze the German radar. The bombers dropped the new RDX-2 blast bomb, whose monstrous explosion raised a tornadic updraft that sucked in ground air in a fiery tempest that seethed through whole blocks of buildings. It carried flaming trees torn out of the ground by the roots. The survivors said it was "beyond all human imagination." Gerstenberg's people wondered whether the new weapon was coming to Ploesti. Quite the contrary was true: the Americans had only general-purpose bombs, and recent tests on a U. S. proving ground had determined the dismaying fact that 50 percent of the 1,000-pound bombs failed to detonate and a quarter of the 500-pounders did not go off.

Tidal Wave labored under another severe handicap. Normally the Liberator's Pratt & Whitney engines had a life of 300 hours. However, in the desert grit they were good for only 60 hours. Sam Nero had hundreds of "Pratt & Wog" engines on his hands— tired mechanisms that had been repaired all too often in the desert. The minimum 2,300-mile trip to Ploesti required new-engine performance. Nero called for 300 engines from the States, an order beyond the lift capacity of Air Transport Command. Washington borrowed the fast liner *Mauretania* from Britain and she brought the engines to Benghazi two days before the mission. The mechanics began a sleepless 48-hour job to install them in time.

Killer Kane's khamseen-weary ships were already in shocking condition when his engineering inspector came down with dysentery. He borrowed an inspector from the Eight Balls—Master Sergeant Francis I. Fox, Regular Army—who pronounced 32 of Kane's Liberators unfit to fly. Fox cracked the whip on the numb ground crews, teaching, hectoring, cozening, and gave Kane 40 Pyramider planes for take-off.

On Friday, 30 July, General Brereton flew from his Cairo headquarters to Benghazi, bringing along Lord Forbes and Frank Gervasi, a war correspondent of *Collier's* magazine. En route, the general sat cross-legged on the flight deck, playing gin rummy with his aide, Colonel Louis Hobbs. "As far as I could tell from Brereton's poker face," said Gervasi, "he was somewhere between worry and outright anxiety." Brereton pushed the cards away and said to Gervasi, "Well, Frank, this is it. This is where the Ninth Air Force makes history or wishes it had never been born. Hap Arnold has handed us a tough one." The correspondent did not know what this was all about until he was signed into the compound, forbidden to leave, and admitted to the green hut.

To cover one of the war's greatest stories there was only one other correspondent present—Ivan Dmitri, who was stopping over at Benghazi by chance while on a globe-girdling assignment for the *Saturday Evening Post*. Four other civilian visitors happened to be on the base—the Yacht Club Boys, a variety troupe on a camp show tour. Caught in the Tidal Wave quarantine but not admitted to the secret, the Yacht Club Boys feared that they were being held as cultural hostages by the entertainment-starved desert rats.

On Saturday morning, the day before the mission, the five bomb groups went on a full-dress rehearsal on the desert mock-up, using live hundred-pound bombs. It was a spectacular success, the widest, tightest and lowest heavy-bomber front ever flown.

Five miles wide, wing tip to wing tip, the Liberators crossed the facsimile target and obliterated it in two minutes. The wildly elated men finished with an unauthorized buzz of the bases, clipping the tops from palms and tearing up tents by the stakes with their prop-wash. The days of gloom and doubt were done. Tomorrow there would go against fascism the poised strength of the finest aerial task force the world had ever seen.

In the afternoon the airmen convened on bomb-fin containers to hear Brereton's final campaign address. Their small, bespectacled general, in full medals, beat his riding crop against his pants to punctuate his stirring remarks. As Walter Stewart remembers it, Brereton said: "Gentlemen, I am the only person I know of who has held a commission in both the Army and the Navy. I have seen the fleet steam up the Hudson and I have seen the corps of cadets pass in full-dress parade. These sights are soul-stirring. But today, as I saw your hundred seventy-five four-engined bombers come roaring across the African desert at fifty feet altitude, bringing dust from the ground with your mighty roar, I enjoyed the great thrill of my entire life. Tomorrow, when you advance across that captured country, you will tear the hearts out of them. You are going in low level to hit the oil refineries, not the houses, and leave your powerful impression on a great nation. The roar of your engines in the heart of the enemy's conquest will sound in the ears of the Romanians—and, yes, the whole world!—long after the blasts of your bombs and fires have died away."

The general concluded with special injunctions for the bombardiers. He wanted precision, precision, precision, on the targets. "When you get on the bomb run, bombardiers," he cried, "I want you to go in like—" Before he could point his simile, a dust devil blew him off the platform into the crowd. The general picked himself up and shouted, "I want you to go in like that!"

Sir Arthur Tedder addressed them. "I am proud to be here with you just before this job," said the R.A.F. desert chief. "I want to wish you the best of luck with it. It's a hard, dangerous mission. It will take all your famous American courage and resourcefulness."

A gunner visited an operations clerk who had chased him over a lot of airdromes to get him to recognition and gunnery classes. He gave the clerk his watch, ring and billfold with £200 in it. "I've had it," said the airman. "There's my mother's address. Go see her after the war." In the evening the chaplains received hundreds of men. They brought their worldly goods—family photos, high school rings, camel whips, medals, and money for the chaplains to hold "just in case." One chaplain kept $3,300 for his men. John Jerstad, who was to fly co-pilot with Addison Baker in *Hell's Wench*, the lead ship of the Circus, gave Chaplain Burris money to pay up a lapsed Sunday school pledge in a Wisconsin church. Jerstad was among the hundreds who gave the chaplains last letters to mail if they should not return. Jerstad told his parents, "I'm to be one of the boys to try out the planning, so if you don't hear from me for a couple of days, don't be too concerned, because it will take time to work out some details and I probably won't be near a post office."

A young Mississippian named Jesse D. ("Red") Franks wrote the pastor of the First Baptist Church at Columbus: "Dearest Dad: I want to write you a little note before our big raid tomorrow. It will be the biggest and toughest we've had yet. Our target is the refineries that supply Germany with three-fourths of her oil. We will get the target at any cost. We are going in at fifty feet so there will be no second trip to complete the job. We will destroy the refineries in one blow. Dad, if anything happens, don't feel bitter at all. Please stay the same. Take care of yourself, little Sis, and don't let this get you down, because I would never want it that way. Hope you don't get this letter, but one never knows what tomorrow may bring. My favorite chapter is the 91st Psalm. Your devoted son."

In Ploesti it was market day; the rich 1943 harvest was evident in heaps of corn, beans, tomatoes, apples, chickens, cheeses and salamis in the white-tiled market place. The stalls were tended by women in embroidered skirts and old men in white tunics and hard black hats; the young farmers were dying for the Germans in Russia. Plump corn-fed pigs could be bought without ration cards

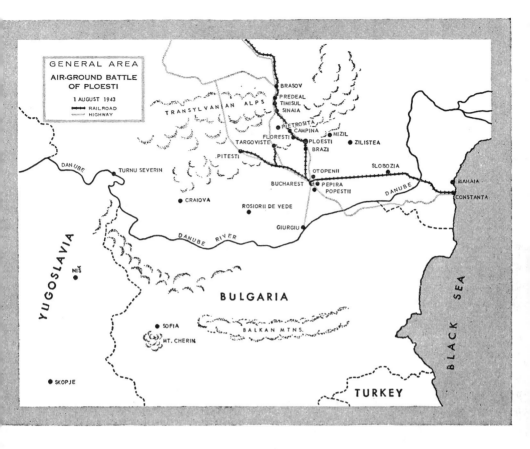

GENERAL AREA
AIR-GROUND BATTLE
OF PLOESTI
1 AUGUST 1943
RAILROAD
HIGHWAY

in the only wartime country in Europe where such a fantasy was real.

Around the oil city the defenses were ready. At Mizil, twenty miles east of Ploesti, lay the main German air base, where four wings of Messerschmitt 109's, totaling 52 aircraft, formed Jaegergruppe 4. Hauptmann (Captain) Manfred Spenner, leader of Yellow Wing, was one of the few pilots who left the station that Saturday. For him Romania was a blessed respite from endless battle. The winter before he had been four weeks in the chopper at Stalingrad, and he had served in the battle of Tunisia after that. Spenner had an appointment in Bucharest with a dentist who was swapping fillings for flying lessons.

A few miles east of Mizil, at Zilistea, seventeen black, clipped-wing, two-engine Messerschmitt 110 night fighters were ready under Major Lutje. In addition to the pilot, the Me-110 carried a radioman with swivel guns, which often made this machine a testier bomber opponent than the single-seat Me-109 with its fixed forward guns. Months before, Goering had promised to replace all of Gerstenberg's solo Messerschmitts with the twin-engine machines, but the half strength of Nachtjaegergruppe 6 at Zilistea represented all that had arrived so far.

More than half of Gerstenberg's total fighter strength in the target area was Romanian. One of the Me-109 wings at Mizil was commanded by Romanian Captain Toma, whom the Germans accounted "a first-class flier." He was a close student of U. S. bombers. In front of his operations building on a flagpole as high as the flanking swastika and Romanian flags, Toma had perched a huge wooden model of a Flying Fortress mounted on a universal joint so that its angle could be adjusted to various perspectives. Captain Toma studied it so closely from the air that one day, during a mock attack, his propeller chopped off a piece of the wooden enemy. However, one of the German pilots said, "Most of the Romanian pilots were wealthy boys from the play-sports set. They took poor care of aircraft. Considering the few they were flying, they wrecked many Messerschmitts, although every time they got a new one a bearded Orthodox priest came out and blessed it."

On the eastern outskirts of Bucharest, at Pepira, there was an all-Romanian base with domestically built fighters—IAR-80's and IAR-81's, heavy, low-winged machines, each armed with four light and two heavy machine guns. On this Saturday before battle only 20 of the 34 IAR's at Pepira were serviceable, due to the Romanians' frolicsome attitude toward flying. The Germans called them "Gypsies" behind their backs, and had a low opinion of the IAR, although admitting that most of the Gypsies were daring fliers.

On this particular Saturday in high summer, some of the Gypsies were out joy riding, as though the war were just a super aeroclub outing. Lieutenant Brancu Treude flew low over the bathers at Lake Znagov, a popular resort north of Bucharest. He spied a tall yacht. Buzzing sailboats was exquisite fun. You dived from the rear, pulled over close, and sent the terrified yachtsman sailing backward in your prop-wash. Dreamily, Treude dived on the boat. He clipped off the topmast, shredded the mainsail, and staggered away fouled with staylines, barely airborne. The skipper of the yacht, King Michael of Romania, took Treude's number, and the joy rider came to the officers' mess that evening to find himself confined to quarters for six weeks.

After dinner, Lieutenant Carol Anastasescu, a frustrated variety artist, improvised a comedy sketch on Treude's bad luck. The young boyars shrieked with laughter. Two older ones, the commandant, Captain Alexandru Serbanescu, and Lieutenant Florian Budu, who sat together, merely smiled. They had seen the laughter stopped in many such merry lads as these. They were veterans of the eastern front. By the Romanian system of crediting enemy aircraft destroyed, Budu had forty Russian kills.

Not far from Pepira, at Taxeroul, there was another Romanian group, with 11 Junkers 88's and 23 Junkers 87 dive bombers ready for action. One hundred fifty miles east, on the Black Sea, at a resort called Mamaia, near Constanta, there was a mixed Romano-German base under Major Gigi Iliescu. He had a mélange of about twenty IAR's, Messerschmitts and oddments, which could intervene in action around Ploesti. The modest strength of Mamaia was reinforced on weekends by many "liaison," "technical" and "inspection" visits of fighters from the inland bases. Mamaia was the one untouched seaside resort in warring Europe. There were no tetrahedrons, mines, blockhouses, wire or armed patrols on the beach, and above its golden sands stepped arcaded terraces to the Rex Hotel, which had been built to rival the Elysian establishments at Cannes and Nice. And the girls were there.

Such was Gerstenberg's inner fighter ring. The outer ring included bases on Crete and Greece, with the pursuit quality centered at Kalamaki airdrome at Mégara, where twenty Me-109's stood ready. There were also fighter groups in southern Italy which could interfere briefly with a Benghazi-Ploesti bomber stream, although these fighters were now heavily engaged in the Battle of Sicily. The largest force in the outer ring lay athwart the bomber route. It was the Sixth Royal Bulgarian Fighter Regiment, under Polkovnik (Colonel) Vasil Vulkov. His *polk* (regiment), which had never been in battle, had 124 fighters on three bases at Sofia and Karlovo. The majority of Vulkov's machines were Avia 534's, manufactured in Czechoslovakia in 1936 and captured there when Hitler raped the republic in 1939. One of the Bulgarian groups at Karlovo was being trained to fly the Me-109, but only a handful of its pilots were as yet competent to fight in the German machine.

Considering that Germany desperately needed interceptors in Atlantic Europe to meet the multiplying Anglo-American round-the-clock bomber offensive from Britain, the fact that Gerstenberg had so many fighters standing by in a quiet theater was a noteworthy achievement. Its extent was not fully appreciated by Allied Intelligence.

Saturday night Hauptmann Spenner returned from the dentist's and favored his stinging gums with a glass of brandy in the officers' casino. His fellow pilots, in contrast to the brooding air in the American camp, were at cards, drink and song. Spenner noticed two who stayed apart from the others. The first was the matchless leader of Fighter Group Four, Hauptmann Hans Hahn, who was spelling out one *fine à l'eau* to last the evening. He was a straw-haired ace, six feet five inches tall, who had been fighting in the skies of tortured Europe since 1939. His hands and face were covered with scar tissue from a flaming crash at Stalingrad the winter before. He led his airmen with the same virtues as a Timberlake or Leon Johnson—by personal example of calm boldness in battle and respect for their fears and egos on the ground. Hahn's men called him *Gockel,* or Gamecock. The Gamecock slanted his long skeleton against a bar stool and discreetly watched the other pilot in the casino who was not mixing in, a twenty-year-old named Werner Gerhartz, who sat under a model Liberator drinking his way into another sulk. Gerhartz' father was a professor at Bonn University and his mother was a physician with the German Red Cross. The youth had been schooled in England. Although the Luftwaffe spent the lives of his class by the score every day on its wide air front, Gerhartz reproached himself for having flown fighters for a year without a proper crack at the enemy. A month before, he had complained to the Gamecock, "Seven months here without action! I want to have battle too, and not always drink." Hahn, using the English nickname that the youth preferred, said, "Ben, suppose I send you on temporary duty to Jever-Wilhelmshaven? It's the hottest corner on earth. Day and night our fellows go up to meet bombers from England." Gerhartz went to Wilhelmshaven and returned even lower in spirit, to report to the Gamecock, "Seventeen days without an enemy alert! Finally we went over the North Sea to meet Flying Fortresses. I made two passes and did not hit a thing. I was determined to make a successful attack before my petrol warning. I dived again. The Americans turned tail and went back to England. Just my rotten luck." Hahn recognized the turnback as an Eighth Air Force feint to draw fighters from a raid elsewhere. He said, "Well, Ben, at least you stopped them from bombing."

This Saturday night the Gamecock watched the youngster downing plum brandy and wondered if he would survive his first battle. An orderly called Hahn to the phone. He came back and announced, "You fellows go to bed now. It is possible that tomorrow we'll have a fight." The phone call was a checkup on combat preparedness. Nobody knew what was coming, or where or when, but something was. For eleven days the Ninth Air Force had not been seen over southern Europe.

In Bucharest, General Gerstenberg was concluding his regular Saturday staff meeting, going over familiar precautions and reminders. Although he would not admit satisfaction to his staff or to Goering, he must have felt that his three-year labor to defend Ploesti was going well. He had decided to take one of his rare holidays the next day at the mountain resort of Timisul. People were leaving the sullen heat of Bucharest for the sea and the mountains. General Antonescu and several cabinet members were headed for Lake Znagov.

A thousand miles away, in the desert heat, the American airmen were watching a movie for the third or fourth time. Of all the special briefing materials they were impressed most by *Soapsuds*,* the talking picture made especially for them. It opened with a

* A discarded code name for the Ploesti mission.

shot of a nude woman. Tex McCrary's confident newsreel an-
nouncer's voice said that Ploesti was a virgin target. He assured
them that "The defenses are nothing like as strong here as they
are on the western front. The fighter defenses at Ploesti are not
strong, and the majority of the fighters will be flown by Romanian
pilots who are thoroughly bored by the war. The heavy ack-ack
should not trouble you at low altitude. All the antiaircraft guns are
manned by Romanians, so there is a pretty good chance there
might be incidents like there were in Italy at the beginning of the
war, when civilians could not get into shelters because they were
filled with antiaircraft gunners. The defenses of Ploesti may look
formidable on paper, but remember: they are manned by Romanians." The narrator depended on Allied Intelligence estimates of
a month before.

The movie audience did not know of a thunderbolt hurled into
their camp that afternoon which was already altering the fate of
the mission. From Washington, General Arnold had sent a signal
forbidding General Brereton to fly to Ploesti. The order also
grounded Jacob Smart, who knew too many high Allied secrets to
be risked to Nazi captivity. Brereton, moreover, had passed his
own version of the order to both Smart and Timberlake: "You are
not to fly and I cannot see you." Geerlings was with the two
colonels when the order reached them. "Timberlake's face became
grim," he said, "and he cursed softly but vehemently. He handed
the message to Smart. Jake's hands trembled as he read it. There
were tears in Timberlake's eyes. 'God, my men will think I'm
chicken,' he said."

The mission had lost its three top men a few hours before
take-off. An urgent reshuffling of air assignments began. Brereton's
place in the command ship was taken by General Ent, who had
been scheduled to fly with Killer Kane. Kane had to find a co-pilot.
Captain Ralph ("Red") Thompson, skipper of the command ship,
was bereft of his three familiar officers and found himself with
K. K. Compton, General Ent, a new bombardier and the group
navigator, Harold Wicklund. "The only people I knew were my
gunners," Thompson lamented. Jacob Smart's place with Major
K. O. Dessert was taken by a retired pilot named Jacob Epting.

Timberlake decided to do some ordering. He had always practiced crew integrity—keeping the interreliant men of each plane together. Now, since K. K. Compton was going to use Wicklund, Timberlake pulled his planning navigator, Leander F. Schmid, off the raid. Schmid had finished his missions and had many dependents. Timberlake tried to induce his young comrade, John Jerstad, not to go. The little major comforted him. "Don't worry, sir. Bake and I will make it all right." All night the operations officers played musical chairs as a result of the groundings, the normal strain of manning a maximum effort, and the dysentery epidemic in the camps.

Squadron Leader Barwell talked with General Ent that night and got the impression that "He was flying as a sort of protest. He had opposed the low-level plan from the beginning." Ent sent out the official mission directive, Field Order 58, which contained the final Intelligence appraisal of enemy defenses according to "information from sources believed to be reliable." Intelligence said there were less than a hundred antiaircraft guns in the refinery area, probably half of them manned by Germans. At that moment at Gerstenberg's Pepira H.Q. an adjutant was closing out the strength report for July. Around Ploesti, as of that day, the Germans had 237 flak guns, 80 percent of them with German crews, plus hundreds of machine guns.

The Intelligence annex continued: "It is estimated that the defense has been calculated against attacks developing from the EAST and NORTHEAST. The briefed course to the target has been devised to avoid all antiaircraft defenses en route. Enemy radio-detection-finding stations are believed to be located in the valley lying east of the Danube covering the EASTERN approaches to the oilfields."

Now the only thing that could cancel the mission was an adverse weather prediction for the target area. Some weeks before, Allied cryptographers had cracked the German weather code, which was changed monthly. The first of August had been selected as mission day because the last German prediction of which the cryptographers could be sure would be that of 31 July. Then they would be faced with the next month's German code which they could not guarantee to solve as quickly. They got a clear intercept on the next day's forecast, which predicted overcast in the Balkan mountains with general fair conditions in the Danubian basin and some thundershowers. The weather was not perfect, but it was not prohibitive. The mission was on.

The next day was the thirty-sixth anniversary of the United States Army Air Forces, founded by three members of the Army Signal Corps and now mustering two million men. The occasion was not announced to the fliers. They had been provided enough inspiration already.

After midnight Colonel Kane walked about his camp at Lete. "There was a quietness, quite unlike the usual buzz," said his diary entry. "Some crews were quietly giving away their belongings. I sat on my favorite perch on an old engine and stared for a long time at the stars. In my short lifetime, the stars have stayed in their places as they have for countless lifetimes before mine. They would remain unaffected whether I and the men with me lived or died. Whether we died in the near future or years later from senility mattered not in the great scheme of things. Yet the manner of our dying could have far-reaching effects. I have a young son I may never see again, yet I shall be content if I feel that his freedom is assured and he is never forced to be humbled in spirit and body before another man who proclaims himself master."

At 2:00 A.M. Philip Ardery heard "the racket of alarms going off, and jeeps tearing from tent to tent, blowing horns, and men shouting, 'Get up! Get up, you guys! Roll out of those sacks. This is the day!' " The airmen walked through the dark to the last briefings. Sergeant Patrick McAtee, rear gunner, came to the Eight Ball meeting in a Class A uniform with full decorations and polished silver wings. "The general said this was going to be a rough mission," he explained. "If the Germans get me, I want them to know they really have somebody."

At Terria, the new commander of the Circus, Colonel Addison Baker, spoke to his men. He was a tall, stern-jawed Regular Army man from Akron, Ohio. New civilian youths tended to shy away from him until old hands pointed out, "Baker is all heart. He'll do more for an enlisted man than any joker in this outfit." As a squadron leader he had led the Circus through sanguinary air battles in the west. In the briefing tent he looked at the drawn faces of seven comrades who had completed their missions with him and were flying with him today. Baker said, "We're going on one of the biggest jobs of the war. If we hit it good, we might cut six months off the war. She may be a little rough, but you can do her, fellows. Good luck." A navigator asked, "What'll happen if you and Jerk don't make the target?" Baker replied, "Nothing like that will happen. I'm going to take you to this one if my plane falls apart." A radioman asked, "What are the chances of staying off detection?" Baker grimaced. "Don't think there will be any surprise to it," he said. "When we get in the air, they'll hear us clear to Cairo. Low-altitude bombing is the only thing that will take us through."

Pilot John R. ("Packy") Roche's flight engineer, Fred Anderson, a telephone linesman from Washington, D.C., left the briefing thinking, "There comes a time in every man's life when he hits something big and feels it all over. This is the biggest thing. The target must be destroyed to win the war. The idea is to take the bombs exactly to the AP's [Aiming Points]. Coming back is secondary today."

The co-pilots distributed the escape kits. They contained a handkerchief map of the Balkans, a British gold sovereign (or a U. S. twenty-dollar gold piece), ten one-dollar bills, and six dollars worth of drachmae and lire—the latter equal to three months' wages for a Balkan peasant. There were pressed dates, water purification tablets, biscuits, sugar cubes and "desert chocolate," which Walter Stewart said "looked like modeling clay and tasted like it too." There were tiny compasses to secrete in the body and hair, and one type could be assembled from two suspender buttons. Ardery saw his men concealing so many compasses on their persons that "the only way they could walk was north." He taped a hacksaw blade to the sole of his foot. "I had spent weeks planning my escape after I was shot down," he said. "I had complete confidence in my ability to come through it." He was convinced most of the planes would go down and there would be enough wandering Americans in Romania "to call a general election, vote the Germans out, and make peace with the Allies."

The men also received mimeographed vocabularies in Romanian, Bulgarian, Serbo-Croat, Turkish and Greek—the phrases chosen to cover wounds, hunger, concealment and obtaining civilian clothes. Men who found themselves in Romanian forests were advised to avoid wolves and bears, but not peasants. "The people of Romania, especially the peasants, are honest, friendly, kindly and hospitable to strangers," said the escape notes. "Amongst the middle and upper classes, however, there are many grafters, friendly to the Germans. Generally speaking, it is safer to keep to villages and small towns."

After the briefing, thirty men attended Stewart's Mormon meeting. "We talked about death, resurrection and the life to come," the pilot said. "I told the boys that no Nazi gunners could end that which has always been—the soul and intelligence of man. I was convinced beyond question that this life was just part of a great, everlasting, progressive existence that ruled before we came here, moves on according to our diligence and obedience here and then to the next life, forever growing without limits or bounds. This testimony was much appreciated by the warriors of the 93rd. It does not remove fear, which is fixed by nature, but it gives great purpose to this life."

Charles L. Roberts, a tail gunner, thought of "the general who told us the mission would be a success even if none returned."

Faraway storms of engines sounded, and dust blew all night as the mechanics tuned them up at Lete, the Pyramider base, and on the long plains of the Eight Balls at Benina Main, the Sky Scorpions at Berka Four, the Liberandos at Berka Two, and the Traveling Circus at Terria. R.A.F. ack-ack men on the perimeter came out of their tents and brewed up tea, wondering what the bloody hell the Yanks were up to after this past strange fortnight. Sam Nero's men were producing a triumph—seventeen more planes than were called for in the field order. The 10 percent increase in aircraft would partially offset the high percentage of bombs that would not burst. Duds or not, the bomb loaders grunted under the open bays, hoisting 311 tons of them into the shackles. The Sky

Scorpions had only skeleton ground crews, and the men who would deliver the bombs helped load their own. During the night, orders came down to put two boxes of British incendiaries in each plane. The gunners could throw these thermite sticks into the highly combustible refineries as they passed over.

The people on the ground were also busy in the enemy camp that night. "Willi, something big is in the air," said Armament Warden Nowicki's CO, Major Maier. "Do the best you can." Nowicki checked out 36 flak guns and fell asleep in exhaustion at midnight. After two hours a battalion clerk awakened Nowicki. "You're wanted immediately at Battery Four. No time for breakfast." The *Waffenwart* motorcycled across fragrant harvest fields and reported to the fire controller of Battery Four, a slim, bespectacled Viennese sergeant named Aust. "The elevator panel on *Bertha* is out of order," said Aust. "First, I must report to your officer," said Nowicki. Aust waved glumly toward the officers' billet. Nowicki found Oberleutnant Arnold Hecht profoundly out of the war in a tobacco-stale bedroom littered with empty brandy bottles. He stirred the officer, reported, and went to *Bertha*, the big 88. The man in charge of the malfunctioning elevation panel, Corporal Walter Becker, in peacetime a diamond cutter from Idar-Oberstein, helped Nowicki turn off the nuts on the panel. Inside there were intricate circuits and indicator lights, manufactured by Zeiss, the camera people. "Hand me this, hand me that," said Nowicki to Becker. The gun crew and the Russian slaves came on duty, yawning and scratching, surprised to see a *Waffenwart* at work so early in the morning.

At Benghazi, about a third of the combat men were weak with dysentery. Normally, half of such cases would be medically grounded. But the flight surgeons, like the operations officers, had to produce air crews. Three army nurses and eight Red Cross girls, the only women among eight thousand men, helped the medical effort to man Tidal Wave. The doctors grounded two extreme cases of dysentery, a man with an impacted wisdom tooth, and three flight neurotics. Three able men refused flatly to fly and are remembered by those who did. The empty places were taken by some who had never been in battle and some with no air-crew training, including three privates. That all posts were manned indicated the summit of resolve the Ploesti men had reached.

In a dozen ships additional gunners volunteered, despite the high odds against coming back. Pilot Richard L. Wilkinson carried two extra people. Lieutenant Howard Dickson, a Circus ground officer who had flown twenty combat missions to learn what the men went through, got a berth on *Euroclydon* (The Storm) with Enoch Porter. The pilot asked, "What's the book for today, Dick?" It was Dickson's habit to read classics on the long hauls to and from the target. He said, "*As You Like It.* Shakespeare." Porter said, "Well, don't get too deep in the book. You're going to see some sights. We're going over in the first wave with Colonel Baker."

At Benina Main, Colonel Leon Johnson, commander of the Eight Balls, stood under his ship, a collection of patches called *Suzy-Q*, and chatted with his ground staff officers. A jeep arrived with the news that Johnson's pilot was prostrated with dysentery. A retired combat man, Major William Brandon, took his place. Johnson handed his wallet to the group chaplain, James F. Patterson. Out fell a four-leaf clover given to Johnson by his wife. Colonels and majors got on their knees, looking for it. The tower controller shot a flare. The searchers found the charm and handed it up to Johnson as *Suzy-Q* rolled away.

At Berka Four, Father Beck visited the planes before take-off. He was a jovial, sunburned, white-haired man with a happy, confident smile. He blessed the Catholics and anyone else who wanted a prayer. A co-pilot said, "You got good connections up there, Chappie?" Beck said, "I pray through channels." The men in the plane grinned down at him and held their thumbs up. "Make contact for us, Padre," a gunner shouted. The engines were turning.

Silent cannons, soon to cease your silence,

Soon unlimber'd to begin the red business.

WALT WHITMAN, "Drum Taps," 1865

5

THE GREAT MISSION AIRBORNE

During the summers in Cyrenaica the khamseen comes punctually in the afternoon, flooding dust across the coastal shelf. The Liberators used to stand in it like elephants bathing, while mechanics cleaned engines and bombardiers swaddled bombsights against the scouring disease that took a third of an airplane's life. On this Sunday morning, the first of August 1943, the dust storm came before dawn, roaring like no wind of nature. For forty miles along the Libyan bulge, 712 engines blew up earth upon which no rain had fallen for four months as 178 cruelly burdened B-24's queued up for take-off. Each plane carried at least 3,100 gallons of gasoline and an average load of 4,300 pounds of bombs, bullets and thermite sticks, exceeding the Liberator's maximum load allowance. The first, and possibly suicidal, problem of the flight to Romania was simply to get off the ground.

The first wave aircraft in the seven target forces had extra fixed nose guns; some had armored the flight deck, most had extra belts

of fifty-caliber shells. The mission force carried more than 1,250,-
000 rounds of armor-piercing, incendiary and tracer shells and
311 tons of bombs—more killing power than two Gettysburgs. In
Romania much greater fire power awaited it. The aerial army
rolling through the red dust consisted of 1,763 United States
citizens from every state of the Union and the District of Columbia. Also aboard were a Canadian, Sergeant Blase Dillman of
Kingman, Saskatchewan, flight engineer of *Daisy Mae,* and an
Englishman, Squadron Leader George C. Barwell, Royal Air
Force, London, flying top turret with Norman Appold. Barwell
was present without leave. The R.A.F. had not given him permission to fly, but for the Americans his combat art was to be one of
the luckiest things of the day.

As the Liberators gathered at the end of the runways and
waited for the dust to settle, tank trucks came around and topped
off the gas loads in the regular wing tanks and the special bomb
bay tanks. During the wait, Flight Officer Russell Longnecker of
Broken Bow, Nebraska, co-pilot of *Thundermug,* sat on top of his
ship against the top turret wondering how he could become a first
pilot. His squadron operations officer, John Stewart, came by in
a jeep, checking crews. He asked the pilot of *Thundermug,* "Well,
how do you feel now?" The pilot, who had just left a hospital bed,
still suffering with a bad case of dysentery, said, "I don't think I
can make it." Stewart yelled up to Longnecker, "The lieutenant
isn't going. You think you could take her there yourself?" Longnecker shouted, "Can I take her! This is what I've been waiting
for since flight school!" "Okay," Stewart said, "I'll find you a co-
pilot," and he jeeped away.

He returned with another sprouting flight officer, Donald K.
("Deacon") Jones. The senior officer aboard was now the bombardier, Second Lieutenant William M. Schrampf, twenty-three, a
mathematics teacher, who concealed his misgivings from the boy
pilots. Neither had ever taken a loaded airplane off the ground.
Their first try would entail lifting an overload of combustibles
and an extra man in the crew, Flight Officer Odin C. Olsen, an
observer.

At 0400 hours Greenwich mean time,* the command meteorological officer, having stirred the entrails, pronounced the weather auguries favorable in the Balkans, and with that last ground decision of six months of ground decisions, the tower controllers shot the flares. At Berka Two, the lead plane of the mission, Brian Woolley Flavelle's *Wingo-Wango*, carrying the mission route navigator, Lieutenant Robert W. Wilson, started the long and dangerous take-off run.

Flavelle was the volunteer who had attacked the Messina ferry slip and had broken down its ferroconcrete roofs. He had completed twenty-seven missions without mishap, but had been downed on the twenty-eighth just prior to Tidal Wave. That was a small epic. His plane was crippled by enemy attack and forced down in enemy-held Sicily. Flavelle sank her carefully into a small rocky pasture, with his wheels down, and braked her so skillfully that the ponderous B-24 stopped with her nose crumpled against a stone wall without injuring anyone. The crew took to heel and found an English-speaking Sicilian who had helped excavate the New York subways in his youth. He put them aboard a fishing vessel for Malta, where Flavelle's people were forwarded to Benghazi to resume military duty. Sam Nero gave Flavelle a brand new airplane called *Wingo-Wango* to fly at the brunt of Tidal Wave.

Out of seven leagues of dust the lumbering monsters heaved into the air at two-minute intervals and climbed into the five formations circling 2,000 feet up. Through thickening dust they continued taking off for an hour and finding their places in the swarms slowly turning over the airdromes. Dawn touched the pink ships and the green ships as they took up group order, with Flavelle out front pointing to Corfu, 500 miles away. Many of them saw what happened to one of the last ships to leave the ground, Robert J. Nespor's *Kickapoo*, which had been loaned by the Circus to the Pyramiders for the day. John C. Riley was the

---

* All times of day in the book are given by Greenwich mean time on the 24-hour European system. The Benghazi bases ran on Egyptian summer time—GMT plus three hours—while Romania was on eastern European time—GMT plus two.

co-pilot. One of its engines failed shortly after take-off. Nespor banked back into the dust for a blind emergency landing. His wing struck a ferroconcrete telephone pole and *Kickapoo* crashed and burned. There were two survivors, Second Lieutenant Russell Polivka and tunnel gunner Eugene Garner.

Behind K. K. Compton's 29 pink Liberando ships the battle order stood: 39 green planes of the Traveling Circus, led by Addison Baker; Killer Kane's 47 lion-colored Pyramiders; 37 green Eight Balls following Leon Johnson; and at the end, Colonel Jack Wood's 26 factory-fresh Liberators crewed by the novice Sky Scorpions.

The armada now standing for Corfu was the most intensively prepared and most experienced large force that has been dispatched in the history of aerial warfare. Except for the Sky Scorpions, each man aloft had flown an average of fifteen raids, most of them over western Europe in the hardest theater of the air war. Three hundred of them had made more than 25 missions and had long since used up their odds on staying alive or out of captivity. There might be 50 percent casualties—some even predicted 100 percent—at Ploesti. They flew to shorten the war.

Each group was formed of V's, the basic three-plane units adopted by American heavy bombers in World War II. The V permitted the fullest concentration and field of fire from thirty guns. The V's were stepped up toward the rear of each group. The air fleet, gleaming in the sunrise, streamed north, laying five miles of fleeting shadows on the quiet sea. It was a flying city. Its metal and glass terraces passed like a legend of the Mediterranean, stranger than Minos or Troy. It was a dumb, cloistered city. The men in each plane could talk to each other on the interphone, but there was no talking between planes. The command radio frequency was to be silent the whole way to avoid the enemy's radio-detection.

The precaution was useless. The Germans knew immediately that the force was up from Benghazi. Unknown to Allied Intelligence, the Luftwaffe had recently placed a crack Signal Interception Battalion near Athens. It had broken the Allied code and was reading Ninth Air Force transmissions. Although the attackers were not broadcasting their destination, they had to spread a short, essential message to Allied forces in the Mediterranean theater, simply announcing a large mission was airborne from Libya. It was necessary to alert friendly air, sea and ground forces not to jump to the wrong conclusion if a big formation was sighted. Only a few weeks before, in the invasion of Sicily, the U. S. Navy had tragically shot down dozens of American troop carriers, mistaking them for Germans.

In Greece, one of the German Signal Interception officers, Leutnant Christian Ochsenschlager, took the decoded message and relayed it to all defense commands "interested or affected." The message said that a large formation of four-engined bombers, believed to be Liberators, had been taking off since early morning in the Benghazi area.*

Conceding the greatest possible round-trip range of the B-24's, the area affected spread from central Italy to Austria, Romania and Greece. This comprised six Luftwaffe defense zones, each covering about 115,000 square miles. These huge rectangles were in turn divided into a hundred sectors each. The most important one today, as it turned out, was Zone 24 East, and the bombers would first enter it at Corfu, which was Sector 00 on the southwest corner. Zone 24 East was controlled from Luftwaffe Fighter Command at Otopenii, five miles north of Bucharest. It was housed in a windowless two-story camouflaged building sunk in the ground near a small clearing in a wood. The meadow was used to land liaison planes. In the building a two-story amphitheater faced a huge glass map of the war theater, cross-hatched with defense grids. Here 120 specialists were on duty around the clock. A long bench of *Luftnachrichtenhelferinnen* (Luftwaffe Airwomen), wearing headphones, sat facing the map. They were hooked with radio-detectors, radar and audio-visual spotters throughout Gerstenberg's command. When they received the location of a plane, friend or foe, they directed a narrow flash-

* Allied Intelligence people interviewed as late as 1961 were still unaware of the radio intercept at Athens.

light beam to its map position, and airmen on ladders crayoned it on the glass—white marks for Axis planes and red ones for the enemy.

A second-floor balcony looked into this elegant war room. Off the balcony were the bedrooms and offices of the commanders. Due to the absence of Colonel Bernhard Woldenga, a young Prussian fighter pilot from Gerstenberg's staff was the senior controller at Fighter Command that morning. This officer arose, bathed and shaved, and glanced from the balcony into the war room before he went to breakfast. He noticed an unusual stir in "the business end of the room," and went down to see what it was. Bombers were up from Benghazi.

Aboard the Liberators were hundreds of men with German names, enough to make up a Luftwaffe squadron. Indeed, the highest-ranking U. S. officer aboard, General Ent, bore a name from the German Palatinate. The name of this young Prussian officer who would give them battle today was Douglas Pitcairn of Perthshire.*

Pitcairn of Perthshire was descended from a Scottish Protestant clan which had emigrated to East Prussia in 1830 after religious quarrels with Catholic neighbors. One of his ancestors was the midshipman who first sighted Pitcairn Island, the haven of H.M.S. *Bounty's* mutineers. The German Pitcairn had grown up in Memel, joined the revived German air force in the early thirties, and was secretly trained as a fighter pilot in Gerstenberg's school at Lipetsk in the Soviet Union. He entered combat in the Spanish Civil War in 1936 with a Heinkel 51 squadron flying for Franco, and his first enemy aircraft destroyed was a U. S.-built Curtiss, piloted by a French volunteer for the Loyalists. The next year some of Pitcairn's former Lipetsk instructors turned up in Spain in four-cannon Ratas. The Russians knocked down fifteen of the twin-cannon Heinkel biplanes in the first fifty encounters. Soon after the rehearsal war in Spain, Pitcairn was flying in the Battle of Britain, fighting his own clansmen in Hurricanes and Spitfires. Pitcairn was grounded after crash injuries and sent to help create

* His legal name includes the seat.

the Fighter Command he was now to move into battle for the first time.

Pitcairn greeted the five liaison officers seated at a desk near the girls. They were linked by phone to the day fighters, the night-fighter base, the flak command, the Romanian fighter bases, and the telegraphic and radio network which terminated in a room visible behind the glass. Pitcairn checked the Würzburg Table—the central radar monitor, linked to the radar antennae ringed around Ploesti and Bucharest. He glanced at a prominent red button which set off the civilian air raid sirens in Romania.

Examining the swarm of red marks over Benghazi, Pitcairn re-marked, "It looks like another training mission. If I were running a training mission in the desert, I too would take advantage of the cool morning hours." A few minutes later the signals officer got a fresh decode from the room behind the glass. It was from Luft-waffe, Salonika, reporting that the bombers were at 2,000-3,000 feet and headed north over the Mediterranean. "It can't be a training mission," said Signals.*

On the fighter base near Constanta, Colonel Woldenga received the news from Salonika. He felt no concern over being absent from his post; it was by no means clear that the target was Ploesti, and three capable men were on duty as fighter controllers near the target. In addition to Pitcairn at Otopenii, there were two controllers in Gerstenberg's headquarters at Pepira: Major

* The authors have found no evidence on how the Germans determined the altitude and course of the mission this early in the Mediterranean cross-ing. The Liberators were far out of range of enemy radar on Crete, Sicily and Italy. It is highly doubtful that the Germans in 1943 had detection ap-paratus that could pick up planes maintaining radio silence. There are three circumstantial possibilities for the oversea course detection. When Rommel was chased out of Libya, he left three German weathermen hiding in a gulley near the Benghazi bomber bases. They radioed the Libyan weather to Crete and could have reported sighting the take-off and northerly course. These spies, living on ambushes of lone Allied vehicles, were not discovered until April 1944. A further possibility is that, following the Athens intercept, Crete sent a high-altitude reconnaissance plane to have a look at the American formation over the water. Also, one Liberator crew reported sighting "a slim gray warship" at 30° N. and 19° 50′ E., which may have been an enemy spotter.

Werner Zahn, for night-fighter operations and Major Hermann Schultz for day fighters. The news about the U. S. force was still confined to command level. There would be no need to alert squadrons and batteries until, and if, the bombers could be detected on a course for Ploesti. Their objective could still be the Messerschmitt plant at Wiener Neustadt in Austria, or Sofia, or even Athens. When the planes came over land, there were plenty of visual spotters and Würzburg units to report them again.

In the war room at Otopenii, Pitcairn raised his voice. "All right, everyone, let's have a big breakfast. We may be here quite a while." The staff went out in relays to eat. Before joining them he sent the first-stage alert out to the next lower echelons of command. This merely required them to turn everyone out on duty.

At the main day-fighter base at Mizil the German and Romanian pilots were confined to the field. They hung around the operations room, or lounged outside staring at sheep grazing on the grassy field, against the blue Carpathians. The station kept the sheep as lawn mowers for its airstrip. Some pilots gathered around fence posts upon which were mounted models of Liberators and Flying Fortresses. It was hard to avoid seeing an American bomber model at Mizil; inside they hung from the ceilings and stood on tables.

One of the most diligent students of U. S. craft was the commander of First Fighter Wing, or White Wing, Hauptmann Wilhelm Steinmann of Nuremberg. He was called "Uncle Willie" because of his advanced age—he was thirty. He understood bombers. During the Blitz he had hauled tons of high explosives to Hull, Manchester, Sheffield, London and Glasgow. One night over London, Uncle Willie was trapped in an apex of searchlights and the tracers closed in. He could not shake the cone and he knew he was moments from destruction. He turned on his running and landing lights, fired "friendly" recognition flares, and went into a steep dive. "I wanted the searchlight and flak battery people to think, 'No German could be that crazy.' " The British fire stopped and he passed safely beyond the searchlights.

Defeated in the Blitz of England, and facing frantic demands for more fighter pilots to defend the Reich, the Luftwaffe put bomber pilots like Steinmann into fighters. His combat philosophy was simple and adequate so far: "You've got to have belief. You've got to have confidence. It's either you or me." Uncle Willie even managed to radiate this confidence to his wife, Else, in Nuremberg, who never worried about him.

A pilot who thought about combat and death with the same self-confidence as Steinmann was the ex-Mormon missionary, Walter Stewart, flying *Utah Man* next to Baker, the Circus leader. As the B-24's paraded over the blue sea, Stewart, a 25-mission veteran, was thinking about the Luftwaffe. He had faith in his gunners, each at his post by his "wonderful fifties." Stewart said, "I was especially attached to those guns because my great-uncle, John M. Browning, used to sit on the porch and tell us kids how he invented the machine gun. Uncle John never got anything out of his invention, but we certainly did." Stewart was scanning the horizon for fighters when his heart missed a beat. A blast of machine-gun fire came right over his head. "Then I heard the fiendish laugh of the big logger," Stewart said. Richard Bartlett, the top turret man, a lumberjack from Montana, was test-firing his guns without warning the edgy crew. Around the sky the other gunners cleared their weapons with short bursts.

Stewart decided to return Bartlett's scare. "I moved over to another B-24, showing how close the old baby could fly formation." As he brought the prop tips right over the other ship, the logger said, "Skipper, do you have the D.F.C.?" Stewart replied, "I think so." "Do you know what it stands for?" Bartlett asked. "I guess so," Stewart answered. The turret man said, "It's not what you think. It means Don't Fly Close."

The boy pilots Longnecker and Jones had gotten *Thundermug* off the ground in their first try at taking off a loaded airplane. The newly appointed first pilot, Longnecker, now demonstrated an administrative trait of command—that of confidently placing responsibility on a junior. He said to Jones, "Deacon, you fly 'er a while and I'll go back and check on the enlisted men." He came upon Sergeants J. C. Pinson, Bernard C. Strnad, Edward A. Sand, Howard J. Teague, Leonard J. Dougal and Aloysius G. Cunningham sitting around on ammunition boxes, stark naked.

Cunningham, who wore the only adornment—a headset and a throat mike—reported to the master of *Thundermug*, "It was so damn hot before take-off, we just sort of . . ." Longnecker strode forward, the first hair pigments fading at his temples—the mark of a seasoned first pilot.

An hour out, some of the dust-scoured cylinders began to fail. Captain William Banks of Kane's Pyramiders noted, "Every once in a while I would look off and see one or two Liberators feather a prop, wheel out of formation, and start for home." Their crews gave thumbs-up signals as they turned back for Africa, jettisoning bombs and gasoline into the sea to lighten ship for emergency landings. Watching them pull out, a gunner said, "Those guys look too happy about it." Seven of the ten abortives came from the Pyramiders. There were 167 planes left.

The bombers passed into a light haze. The formation began to swell as the pilots instinctively spaced farther away from each other. In the soft, luminous air it was hard to distinguish the make-up of the group in front or behind. The leaders had been instructed to maintain 500-yard visual contact between groups at all times. Although the range of visibility was still much greater than that, the outlines of other ships became blurred.

The situation brought out one of the inherent problems of intergroup formation flying—the varying styles of the leaders. Three of them, Compton, Baker and Johnson, had been schooled in the Eighth Air Force's tight combat box formation on raids out of Britain. Wood's people had had these close formation practices drummed into them in recent training in the States. But the tactic was not strictly followed in Africa. Kane's crews had not met the prolonged, repeated and resolute Luftwaffe attacks, fought over hundreds of miles of German territory, experienced by the green ships from England. Moreover, Kane's aircraft were the worse for wear; a group leader expecting battle will set his speed to that of his slowest member to bunch his defensive strength. Two and a half hours out, the distance between the second group, the Circus, and Killer Kane's third group had widened to the extent that they could barely see each other. From the vanguard K. K. Compton could not see Kane at all. Johnson and Wood could do nothing but hang on Kane's tail as they obediently kept to their fourth and fifth places in the bomber stream.

Young Longnecker in *Thundermug* had a difficult time holding formation with his flight leader, Hugh Roper, in *Exterminator*. "I had no previous experience in the left seat," he remarked. "I admired Vic Olliffe, who was flying *Let 'Er Rip* left wing on Roper. Olliffe was a very muscular man and could fly the B-24 like it was a Piper Cub. He was holding in so close to Roper, the two planes seemed welded together."

Three hours out, the landfall was imminent—Cape Asprókavos, the southern tip of the Nazi-held island of Corfu. The anxious sea journey was over; soon they would turn on a northeasterly heading into the unknown continent, over forests and mountains to the deepest target in Europe. Norman Appold, sitting at the bottom of the ladder in his B Section of the Liberandos, looked in front at A Section and the mission-leading aircraft, Flavelle's *Wingo-Wango*, in which the mission navigator, Wilson, had brought them unerringly to Corfu. Then Appold stared incredulously at the lead plane. "*Wingo-Wango* began to stagger, dipping down and nosing up in ever-increasing movement, until its nose rose higher and higher into the air," said Appold. "The section scattered away from the wild gyrations. When virtually standing on its tail, *Wingo-Wango* slid over on her back, and slowly gaining speed, planed straight down and dove violently into the sea. I watched this episode with considerable disbelief. Flavelle was gone in thirty seconds." No one knew why Flavelle went down. Sergeant George K. ("Bud") Holroyd watched the crash. The bombardier of *Wingo-Wango*, Lieutenant Jack Lanning, was his closest friend.

Fiery waves radiated from the crash and a tower of dirty smoke rolled a thousand feet high. Flavelle's wingman, Guy Iovine, turned down, hoping to drop rafts to survivors, despite the fact that breaking formation, even for compassionate reasons, was forbidden. Iovine found no trace of men or plane. It was impossible for him to climb his overloaded craft back into the formation. He turned back for Africa. With him went the deputy route navigator. A Section reformed, with Lieutenant John Palm in

Brewery Wagon slipping into the empty lead positions. His navigator, a young lieutenant named William Wright, was now suddenly the route navigator of the Ploesti mission of 165 planes. The
first two groups turned inland, with Kane's three trailing groups
lost from sight. Kane and Compton dared not speak to each other
on the radio to reunite the mission. The radio-silence edict was
now working against them.

Another pilot now learned for certain that he would not return
to Africa. Lindley P. Hussey, piloting an old B-24 called *Lil Joe,*
discovered that he had lost 800 gallons of gas through a faulty hose
connection to the bomb bay tanks. "Unless we turned back and
aborted then and there, we would never make Benghazi," said
Hussey. "They told us before take-off that if none of us returned
the mission would be well worth it if we hit the target. On this
basis I decided to go on to Ploesti."

A spotter on Corfu had some real news for Pitcairn: "They are
turning northeast in Sector Zero Zero! Air Zone Twenty-four East.
New heading thirty degrees." Pitcairn projected a line from Corfu
on this bearing. The line ran slightly north of Sofia and north of
Bucharest. "It no longer looks like Wiener Neustadt," said Pitcairn. "They are too far east already." He ordered the second-
stage alert, which went down to squadron and flak battalion level.

Gamecock Hahn told his pilots, "We'd better have lunch early."
They ate soup, eggs and fried potatoes. As they finished, the
third-stage alert came and all Luftwaffe personnel in Zone 24 East
went to duty stations. Major Ernst Kuchenbacker in Gerstenberg's
Bucharest H.Q. thought it time to advise the commanding general. He rang up Gerstenberg at the mountain resort. "It is unclear
what is developing," he told the general, "but we think the objective must be Ploesti." Gerstenberg said, "I am returning immediately." It was a three-hour drive.

The Liberator pilots and navigators unfolded their special
Geerlings oblique drawings of the unfamiliar territory ahead. Up
the folder, through the views, ran the red line of the flight heading.
The red line ran over the northern tip of Greece and into Albania,
passing along the mountainous Greek border. The first geographi-

cal obstacle was the Pindus Range, which swings southeast from Albania to form the spine of the Greek archipelago. Its 9,000-foot summits demanded an 11,000-foot climb to clear them prudently. "It seemed just minutes later," said Appold, "before towering cumulus clouds began to show above the mountains." The clouds stood to 17,000 feet. The mission leader, K. K. Compton, faced a swift decision.

Formation flying of clumsy bombers through cloud was a dangerous matter. In zero visibility, air turbulence or slight divergences from course could bring planes into rending collisions, the doomed craft plunging in pieces, perhaps taking lower planes with them. When passing through cloud the Air Force practiced a maneuver called Frontal Penetration. Before the cloud the mission leader began circling, and when all his ships were turning on the carrousel, his three-plane wing peeled off, spread apart, and drove into it. The others turned off three by three, and followed him through in tandem. On the other side of the cloud they repeated the circle, took up battle order, and continued on course. Frontal Penetration took time and fuel during the circling and sorting out.

The mission leader did not like the idea of losing this time and gas. Keith K. Compton was a short, dimple-chinned pilot proven in battle. He had been deputy commander of the Traveling Circus in Britain, where he caught the eye of the generals. He was sent to Africa in 1942 to command the Liberandos, the 376th Group, the residue of Hurry-Up Halverson's minutemen plus new people from the States. Compton sent some of Halpro's guerrillas home, spread others in key jobs, and absorbed new crews in a competent group of his own design. He made life miserable for pilots who kept sloppy formation in the air, but indulged the men living miserably in the desert. Once Washington had sent him an officer to "whip the men into shape by push-ups and close-order drill." Compton exiled him to Cairo, where the physical culturist wore out his war service appealing from café terraces for people to keep fit.

K. K. Compton sat in the left-hand seat of the flagship beside co-pilot Ralph P. Thompson. Red Thompson was a transfer from the Pyramiders. He had served restlessly under Killer Kane until the day he saw his commanding officer fist-fighting with a lieutenant, and then he had asked for a transfer. On a stool between and behind the pilots sat Brigadier Ent, wearing a crash helmet. He and the pilots could look down at the navigator's desk, where sat Captain Harold A. Wicklund, who had flown to Ploesti before on the Halpro raid.

Facing the Albanian cloud, the mission was up against the reality of what had been theoretical problems in the long briefings. In the fortnight past, the force leaders had intently absorbed information that would help them journey to the target, bomb it truly, and bring back as many men as possible. In the last days a serious difference over tactics, verging on acrimony, arose between Killer Kane and K. K. Compton. Compton argued that the entire mission should use normal cruise settings on its engines during the first oversea leg, to keep good formation, and then use increased power for the climb over the mountains. Then, at the Danube, they would be together for the dash to target.

Kane had disagreed. "Why not save power so we can pour it on, getting away from the target?" was his plea. There was also another difference between African and European practices. The Eighth Air Force always carried oxygen breathing units for the high thin air from which it bombed. The Ninth often flew lower and did not always need oxygen. Today, many of Kane's planes had none aboard. They had not expected to fly higher than 12,000 feet.

Now, confronted with the high cumulus, K. K. Compton decided definitely what to do. He waggled his wings and climbed in straight battle formation without ringing around in front of the clouds. Compton was going to snake through the cloud tops without breaking formation. Behind him, Colonel Baker, leading the Circus, shot a flare to instruct his people to climb straight. The two lead groups leveled off at 16,000 feet and the crews donned oxygen masks. They droned through pinnacles of cumulus, spaced far enough apart so that visual contact held the formation together.

Killer Kane got the Pyramiders, Eight Balls and Scorpions

turned at Corfu and faced the clouds. He signaled for Frontal Penetration and began circling at 12,000 feet. The front and rear groups were already dangerously separated. Now the gap was widening between Kane and Compton.

Bounced in pearly mists, the airmen took lunch, Kane's crews shivering in their cotton clothing. Some of them were wearing sandals. They clawed open wax boxes of K-rations, warmed up cans of bacon and eggs on the heat vents, munched hard biscuits, and cursed the lemonade powder, one of the nutritive fiascos of the Quartermaster Corps. They drank hot coffee from big vacuum flasks. (At Luftwaffe Fighter Command, Pitcairn ordered coffee for his tense staff, watching the red marks inch toward them on the big glass map. But there was no coffee in the German stores.)

Soon Compton's Liberandos came on a far-ranging radar up ahead. Atop the 7,250-foot pinnacle of Mount Cherin, near Sofia, there was a German Würzburg unit living in wretched boredom. Eight months before, they had packed their tons of equipment a mile up the mountain on muleback and carried it the rest of the way on their backs. All these weary months they had monitored the air without a single trace of enemy aircraft. Suddenly they were talking with soft-voiced airwomen in ops rooms from Vienna to Salonika. "Many wings! Zone Twenty-four East. Sector Eleven. Bearing thirty degrees."

K. K. Compton drove across the Yugoslavian mountains, through wells of midday sun among the cloud tops. Kane was almost a mile below and sixty miles behind as Compton crossed the last mountain barrier, the Osogovska Range on the Yugoslav-Bulgarian border. Compton passed Mount Cherin, where the radar men were phoning ahead, "Big wings! Zone Twenty-four East, Sector Twenty-two."

The last possibility that the force could reunite by visual contact was now lost by a quirk of nature. At 16,000 feet Compton and Baker were kicked along by a brisk tail wind. But it was not blowing at 12,000 feet. K. K. Compton was gaining ground speed and pulling farther away from Kane. In Compton's rear, Circus pilots phoned tail gunners, "Any sight of the guys behind?" The answer was always, "No, sir. Nobody in sight."

Appold said, "Compton began a snaking descent of the mountains to allow the straggling groups to close in." The Liberators zigzagged down the slope, losing time but spending gas.

As the mission entered Bulgarian airspace, Colonel Vulkov sent up two squadrons of Avias from bases near the capital, Lieutenant Marlin Petrov leading Squadron 612 from Wraschdebna, and Lieutenant Rusi Rusev commanding Squadron 622 from Bozhurishte. Their old Czech fighters carried two to four 7.92-mm. machine guns and were stripped of oxygen and radio systems to get more speed. None of the pilots had ever been in battle or had seen an enemy bomber. The Bulgarians took up an interception course toward Berkovitsa, north of their capital, and Colonel Vulkov ordered fighters up from his main base at Karlovo, east of Sofia, where he had sixteen Avias and six Me-109's, the only fighters capable of battling on good terms with the Liberators. Vulkov was angered to learn that the Karlovo pilots were away from base on Sunday. He set off loudspeakers and phones to get them back from café and brothel.

The Bulgarians estimated that the Americans had come to bomb Sofia. Petrov and Rusev were very hard put to maintain the air speed of the bombers and arrived at the rendezvous barely in time to sight the rear echelons of the last groups, the Scorpions and Eight Balls, driving northeast, stepped up to 15,000 feet. The Bulgars could not climb to that altitude without oxygen, and, without radios, could not confer on what to do. With awed glances at the giants pulling away from them in the zenith, Petrov and Rusev arrived independently at the same decision—to return to base, refuel and try to catch the Americans on the way out.

Several Liberator crews saw the fighters and concluded they were spotters. Unaware that their mission had already been tracked most of the way, these few Americans had a sinking feeling. The mission was betrayed. The suspense was over. They wanted to tell the other ships, but could not. Up ahead, Killer Kane's Pyramiders, and still farther ahead, K. K. Compton's Liberandos and Addison Baker's Circus flew on in happy ignorance of the "spotters." The Bulgarians had been sighted from Leon

Johnson's plane and he was the only group commander who now knew that the raid could not be a surprise. But he was in fourth place in the bomber convoy, sentenced to keep off the radio.

Pitcairn's operations room did not hear of the Bulgarian sighting for some time—that spent by the mute Avias on the return flight and in translating phone calls. Before their news came, he got an alarming report from the Würzburg station on Mount Cherin: "The devils have vanished! We get no more traces of them in Zone Twenty-four East, Sector Forty-four. Last bearing, thirty degrees." The bombers were descending the eastern slopes, putting mountain tops between them and the radar on the peak. Pitcairn said, "The blackout was terrible for us. The bombers were still outside range of our radar units on the plain around Ploesti."

By now at the Ploesti flak site, Armament Warden Nowicki had discovered what was wrong with *Bertha,* the big 88. "Okay, Becker," he said, "we can start putting the panel back." Sergeant Aust ran into the gun pit yelling, "We're on alert! Willi, give me that gun!" Nowicki did not take time to look up or answer. He wasted no motion. The gun crew and the Russian loaders watched the methodical artisan. The fate of the gun, perhaps their lives, was passing through his swift, callused fingers.

K. K. Compton's leading pilots reached the foot of the mountains and adjusted their power to level off for the low onrush across the Danubian basin to the three initial points northwest of the target city. A wonderful sight spread before their dust-reddened eyes. In a light haze the ripe gold and green Wallachian plain lay before them in the splendor of harvest. The desert rats were in rich Romania. They looked at its beauty with perhaps the same emotions as the invaders of the past who had plundered this sumptuous earth since the Bronze Age—the Scythians, Goths, and Huns, Turks and Tartars, Russians and Germans. But this invasion was different: there was not a man in the American armada who did not fervently hope that he would never set foot on Romania.

As they crossed the Danube, the airman said, "Why it's not blue! It's like a muddy old river at home." For the benefit of his crew members who had not had the luck to be raised in Utah, Walter Stewart observed, "It looks just like the Colorado River at Moab."

Below them stood a Romanian spotter, phoning, "Many big bombers!" Otopenii asked, "What heading?" "Toward Bucharest!" cried the spotter.

Pitcairn paced the war room, deep in thought, wondering whether his sector was definitely committed. The bombers still might turn back on Sofia. There was no trace of the bombers on Pitcairn's nearby radar. He signaled "Stand by" to his fighter bases. He sent an officer outside the windowless room for a visual report on weather. "Hot and humid," the scout reported. "There are rain squalls in the mountains to the north. Overhead are high strato-clouds, with wind blowing holes through them." Pitcairn went to the Würzburg Table. "If they are coming here, sir," said a radarman, "they surely ought to be on our monitor by now." Compton was now well within the radius of the radar unit near the Danube, but there were no blips on the Würzburg. The B-24's were flying too low to register on radar. Pitcairn ordered the pilots on "sit-in," puzzled and alarmed over the "vanish" of the oncoming bombers.

Pitcairn told the Romanian liaison officer, "Your people may defend Bucharest as they have expressed the wish to do." Protecting the capital was distinctly secondary to saving the refineries and Pitcairn wanted the fewest possible Romanian stunt artists fooling around in the Ploesti sector. The Romanian groups climbed from Pepira and Taxeroul and went roving over Bucharest. Pilot Treude, who was beginning six weeks' confinement to quarters for buzzing the king's boat, bolted his room and was in the air with the Second Romanian Flotilla.

At Mizil, Gamecock Hahn, the day-fighter leader, tucked his long legs into the cockpit. His adjutant in Headquarters Schwarm (flight of four fighters), Leutnant Jack Rauch, got into his Messerschmitt, hoping this alert was not like the one two weeks before. Rauch had come back that day after buzzing Romanian antiaircraft guns south of Bucharest to find his whole squadron sitting in. "The civilian alarm went off," said his crew chief. "Just stay where you are. I'll fuel you up." No take-off order had come. That evening at dinner Gamecock said, "Jack, you scared those Romanians so bad they turned in an alert." The other pilots hazed Rauch, and Gamecock gave him an official reprimand.

In the third plane of H.Q. Schwarm, Lieutenant Werner Gerhartz, the unlucky warrior, closed his cockpit canopy, then opened it again and handed out his Berlin mongrel bitch, Peggi, which he often took on flights. If this was real, it was no place for a dog. (There was a dog in one of the Liberators.)

Two ground crewmen holding motor cranks stood on the right wing of each Messerschmitt. The full alert came from Fighter Command Control Center. The mechanics stuck the cranks in the motor cowling and heaved. Three-bladed props kicked and spun. The mechanics dropped off behind and scurried away in prop-wakes. Uncle Willie Steinmann watched Hahn's planes bobbing along the grass in tandem. "They always reminded me of insects," he said.

Hans Schopper took off Black Wing. Manfred Spenner, a Battle of Britain veteran with a hundred hours of front-line combat, went up leading Yellow Wing. Captain Toma got his Romanian Messerschmitts off in creditable fashion. Fifty-two fighters were airborne within five minutes. It would have been done faster if Captain Steinmann of White Wing had not had to taxi around chasing sheep off the runway. The Mizil medical officer, Hans Arthur Wagner, watched them climbing into the clouds and went into his surgery and began laying out instruments.

Sergeant Aust on the emplacement of *Bertha* yelled, "Second alert!" Nowicki closed and bolted the panel. "Sergeant, give me some test signals from the fire control box," he asked. The armament warden watched the lights flickering on and off and said, "She's working all right."

"Full alarm!" shouted the battery sergeant. Nowicki rolled up his tools and clipped them to his motorcycle. Russians bearers ran past him, cradling shells. "Hold your fire!" said Aust. "Our fighters are going up." The armament warden, having no further orders, stayed with *Bertha* of Battery Four to see what would happen. He watched the fighters ascending the sky and stretched his cramped fingers.

The battery jerked its eyes from the sky at an earthly phenomenon. Running from the H.Q. hutment toward them was a wild figure in underwear. It wore a steel helmet and carpet slippers. It was bawling orders. It was Oberleutnant Hecht, the battery commander. The event had finally penetrated his big hangover.

At Gerstenberg's H.Q., Major Kuchenbacker released the German night-fighter wing at Zilistea and the controllers ordered it into the air with its seventeen new twin-engined Messerschmitt 110's under Major Lutje.

Upstairs in the northern approaches to Ploesti, Gamecock Hahn swept his tightly packed fighters on an east-west axis 6,750 feet up, under the strato-cumulus. He was patrolling directly on the predicted bomber course, right over the final I.P. When the enemy appeared, the pilots had to remember two iron rules laid down by Gerstenberg: "Day fighters must share the same airspace as the bombers, regardless of our own flak. However, neither day nor night fighters must ever fly over the inner ring of Ploesti flak or the city itself."

K. K. Compton took the bombers low for the 150-mile run across flat ground to the First Initial Point. Roaring across the plain, the men saw the new land like tourists passing in the Orient Express. Sergeant Bartlett said, "Everything was clean and pretty. Just like in the movies." Fred Anderson declared it "the prettiest country I've seen since the States." In several planes there was a simultaneous shout: "This is where I bail out!" It was the rueful joke they made over Germany when the Messerschmitts came barrel-rolling at them with wing cannons winking yellow. There was a different reason this time. The Liberators were passing over naked girls bathing in a stream.

Harold Steiner, the radio operator of *Utah Man*, saw a woman driving a wagonload of hay along a road. "As the planes approached she got off the load and crawled under the wagon," Steiner said. "The horses ran off, leaving her face down in the dust." So close were they to the peasants below that they saw smiles on upturned faces and the brightly decorated skirts of the women. "They were very nonchalant," said gunner Robert Bochek. "They stopped working and reined up their horses hitched to carts with big painted wheels. They waved handkerchiefs at us. We thought this was going to be heaven."

The beautiful valley, the neat tree-lined roads and rivers, the friendly gestures of the Romanians, the absence still of any note of opposition, brought a holiday mood to many of the leading B-24's. The dire predictions seemed to be turning out wrong. Tidal Wave was working great. A red-haired radio operator of a Circus ship, William D. Staats, Jr., decided the occasion was appropriate for his Franklin D. Roosevelt parody. "I hate war. Eleanor hates war. Buzzy hates war, Fuzzy hates war," he chanted on the intercom. Some crews sang "Don't Sit under the Apple Tree" and "Amapola." In the middle of the thundering formation a bombardier led his crew in the doxology.

The Protector of Ploesti was speeding south from the mountain resort in a staff car, toward his headquarters. Gerstenberg's masterful plan for holding Hitler's black gold had one glaring omission. There were no civilian air raid shelters in Ploesti or Bucharest. The misled citizenry had not demanded them and the military were preoccupied preparing for battle. Civilians were too worried about the shocking loss of men on the Russian front to bother with an abstraction like an air raid. There had been no bombs on Ploesti since the scattered Red Air Force explosions in the autumn of 1941. No citizen had heard of the U. S. Halpro mission. Ploesti was bored with practice alerts, as well. During the first ones people ran for the fields and woods. Later they yawned when the test sirens blew. Ploesti's civil defense consisted of Pitcairn's red button and the sound legs and lungs of its inhabitants.

A gentle German medical orderly, Corporal Ewald Wegener of the Transport-Sicherungs Regiment, which trucked Ploesti oil to the Russian front, spent that Sunday morning in a curious way. He sang high mass in a Roman Catholic church in Ploesti. A member of the Salvatorian missionary order, he had been grabbed by

the Army while studying medicine in Vienna. After mass Wegener
walked back toward his barracks sick bay, where he looked after
fifty venereal, malarial and enteritic truckmen in the shadow of
the Colombia Aquila refinery. On the way, the priest-medic passed
citizens bound out of town with picnic baskets, and met his commanding officer, a foul-mouthed Nazi known as "The Mad Prussian."

"Hey, Wegener," said the CO. "So, I find you in town. Sleeping
with a fat Romanian woman?" Wegener meekly protested his
divine orders. "Watch yourself," said his nemesis, "or I'll pack you
off to the eastern front. If you ever get back from there you'll appreciate the need for a woman." He released the corporal, who
continued on his way.

In the target city, a German camp show musician named Paul
Baetz was in the Luftwaffe command post to arrange his next
week's concerts at military installations. Baetz was a short, dark,
animated pianist, who toured with Else Schneider, a twenty-year-
old coloratura, and Edith Rath, twenty-three, an accordionist-
comedienne. The act was popular with the soldiers, and it was just
as well that nobody wondered why Baetz, a cousin by marriage to
Richard Wagner, and a former conductor at the Weimar State
Theater, was giving troop shows in the Balkans. The little musician was staying out of sight of the Nazis, who had marked him
for a concentration camp because he continued to perform "de-
cadent Jewish music." In his exile Baetz took pleasure in comply-
ing with soldiers' requests for "Tea for Two" and "White Christmas," written by Jews, and enemies to boot.

The duty officer said *sotto voce* to the pianist, "Paul, enemy
bombers are being tracked over the Mediterranean this morning.
Life here may not always be this quiet. I believe you should take
the girls away from here." Baetz thanked him and left. Outside it
was extremely hot and humid and the streets were thronged with
promenaders. The town's picnic hampers were full of plump
roast geese and salamis, and countrybound private automobiles
honked through the streets in the only country in the wartime
world that had ineffectual gasoline rationing. The traffic policemen in their choker tunics, heavy capes and fur hats sweated

copiously. Near one of them Baetz saw a gauzily dressed Gypsy beauty, cigaret dangling from her lips, giving breast to an infant. Even Gerstenberg had been unable to keep the "unessential" Romany tribe out of *Festung Ploesti*. Baetz reflected on this strange, soft, white Mediterranean city under the Carpathians, surrounded by plants that provided Hitler's clanking panzers, roaring planes and stalking submarines with the lifeblood of war. Fingers linked behind his back, the musician strolled through the market place, where stood a soaring abstract sculpture by Brancusi, a Ploesti native who had made a name in Parisian art. In leafy parks Baetz saw soldiers fondling ripening thirteen-year-old girls in the drowsy, carnal heat. "*Rosen auf den Weg gestreut/ Und des Harms vergessen!*" (Scatter roses in your path and forget your sorrows.)

The air raid sirens screamed.

The people paid no attention, thinking it was just another test by the busy Germans. It was 1330 eastern European time, 1130 Greenwich time. The Liberator horde was twenty minutes from Ploesti. The men in the bombers saw many lovely streams flowing across their course, the waters of the Alps draining southeast to the Danube. The navigators stared hard at the streams and at their maps and kept running calculations of ground speed. The three Initial Points that would set them upon the target sweep were towns with rivers like these flowing through them.

The two lead groups were now aware that they were going across the target without the three others. Far behind them, Killer Kane was about to find that out. He came down the Balkan slope toward the Danube with the impression that the group behind was the Circus. In order to let it assume its proper place in front of him, Kane turned his ships back to the west. Then he recognized the formation as the Eight Balls and the final group as the Sky Scorpions. Kane returned to course and drove speedily to the fore. All the pilots now knew that the great mission was hopelessly split into two elements, neither knowing the other's location. Kane took up the heading to the First I.P. at higher and higher power settings.

Near Craiova, 65 miles short of the First I.P., one of Johnson's pilots, Lieutenant Charles Whitlock, lost his No. 1 engine when a fuel line clogged. Unable to keep up, Whitlock turned south for Cyprus. Although his bombs were a dangerous burden for a plane flying on three engines, the pilot did not jettison them, not wishing to harm civilians or betray what he still thought was a surprise raid. Whitlock toted them to the Danube and dropped them in the river. Over Bulgaria he lost No. 4 engine by malfunction and he was obliged to drop his incendiaries. He made it to Cyprus.

K. K. Compton passed Pitesti, the First Initial Point, which lay at the mouth of a valley with a ganglion of river, road and rails passing through it to the southeast. The leaders were now in the foothills of the Transylvanian Alps. The Liberandos and the Circus dropped lower toward the piney ridges and spread into a quasi-bombing front. The engineers and radiomen cranked up the sliding bomb doors and particles of pink African sand fell on the black soil of Europe. K. K. Compton and Uzal Ent stood on the flight deck of *Teggie Ann,* riding on the right of the thirteen-plane first element, slightly behind *Brewery Wagon,* piloted by John Palm. Although no enemy had been sighted and navigation and timing had been perfect to the first I.P., Compton and Ent were worried over the absence of Killer Kane and the three trailing groups. They also had a difficult recognition problem in the series of valleys below, all of which ran southeast, all of which contained towns, and most of which had parallel streams, rails and rivers. There were four similar-looking valleys between the First and Second Initial Points.

As they approached Targoviste, the ancient capital of Romania, located in still another valley, K. K. Compton resumed his seat beside Red Thompson and said, "Now." Thompson slid *Teggie Ann* out to the right and took up the briefed bomb-run heading of 127 degrees, parallel to the road, railway and river. K. K. Compton was taking the lead to be the first to bomb Ploesti. The others turned neatly behind, except for John Palm in *Brewery Wagon,* who shot on over Targoviste.

Teggie Ann had made a wrong turn.

Targoviste was only the Second I.P.

The lead group was turning twenty miles short of the Initial Point that led to Ploesti.

Red Thompson reflected later, "Who knows what bearing there was on it from the mysterious loss of Flavelle and Wilson, the target-finding team, and the lack of air discipline that moved Flavelle's wingman, carrying the Number Two navigator, to go down and circle his oil slick and return to base?"

Officers behind K. K. Compton were thunderstruck by the turn. Stanley Wertz, the navigator of *Utah Man*, phoned his pilot, "We're turning too soon!" Stewart said, "There's nothing we can do about it." Norman Appold broke radio silence. He switched on the command channel and cried, "Not here! Not here! This isn't it!" Ramsay Potts in *Duchess* simultaneously went on the clear air with "Mistake! Mistake!" A dozen others joined the protest on the open radio, but they had to turn. Potts's twelve planes, for instance, were surrounded by others and could not wheel back on the right course without causing air collisions.

Along the wrong route the Liberators passed through startling changes of weather, the unpredictable midsummer humors of the Danubian basin—mugginess, bright sunny patches and dark rain squalls. The main impression was of a light violet haze, limiting visibility to about six miles.

K. K. Compton drilled on, keeping the heading which they had been briefed to take after the Third I.P. This did not lead to Ploesti. It led to Bucharest. In their path lay the heaviest flak concentration in Europe, the wicked heart of Gerstenberg's surprise. His guns were packed into the fields southeast of the oil city, ahead of Compton.

In the game of supposition between the defense and attack planners, Gerstenberg calculated that bombers from Benghazi would be at the extreme limit of their flying range to reach Ploesti at all. Therefore they would have to come and depart on a straight line between the two points. So he put the brunt of his guns on this line. Now the Liberators were marching right into the ambuscade.

Near the Standard Block refinery (Target White Three) on the south side of Ploesti, men of antiaircraft Battery Four were lined up by a horse-drawn mess wagon, drawing goulash and potatoes in their mess tins. Gunners Erich Hanfland, a locksmith's apprentice from Olsberg, and his friend, Heinz Silberg, a woodcutter from the Westerwald, sat eating by the side of the lane.

When Pitcairn of Perthshire pressed the red button at Otopenii for the full alarm, Silberg exclaimed, "Always exercises! Alarms for a whole year and nobody comes!" Hanfland agreed. "And in the middle of our meal. They are crazy." Nevertheless, they abandoned their food and rushed to their gun, a four-barreled 20-mm., which they took pride in manning seventeen seconds after an alert. Hanfland, the gunlayer, put his left hand on the traverse wheel and his right on the elevation wheel and poised his foot lightly on the trigger button. Silberg stood by the electric view finder. They heard heavy flak bursts. But the battery sergeant gave no firing order. "I can't see any planes," said Silberg.

Sergeant Aust, in the center of Battery Four, received a signal from Regiment. "They're flying very low. Change your fuse settings for point-blank fire!" Aust put the Russians to work altering the 88-mm. shell fuses.

Less than halfway to Bucharest the forward line of the Liberandos walked into a massive ambuscade and the Battle of Ploesti began. The first salvo was dazzling—four enormous blue-white muzzle blasts from 88-mm. guns.

Major Appold, a mile behind K. K. Compton, was flying at 200 miles an hour, fifty feet from the ground. He and his top turret gunner, Squadron Leader Barwell, saw blue flashes and black clouds of shrapnel spreading among the leaders. Barwell observed, "Bloody eighty-eights. They're fusing point-blank to spread the stuff low." He raised his voice on the intercom: "Gunners! I'm concentrating on Jerry personnel. Recommend trying to hit men rather than guns. I say, Norm, drop the nose." Appold was folded close to his left wingman, Lieutenant Lyle T. Ryan, but managed to bank delicately to port. "The top turret began thumping away at the emplacement," said Appold. "I saw those fifty-caliber slugs churning up dust, spewing sparks off the gun barrels, and soldiers frantically running. A man went down in a puff of dust, got up and started to walk, then fell in a heap. That uncanny accuracy of Barwell's had literally saved our necks."

The outer guns were manned by Gerstenberg's second-best. One gun site now pitted against the likes of Barwell was in the hands of a unit of old men from Vienna—retired Austrian Army officers. They stood up against the storm and worked their weapons. From his turret the Englishman peered far beyond them toward another cluster of big ones, six 88's that were planting a black forest of shrapnel among the leading Liberators. "All right, old boy, let the left wing down a bit," Barwell directed. Five thousand feet from the big guns, a range that would have got another gunner Appold's reprimand for wasting bullets, Barwell began firing five-second bursts. "I would crank her down and he'd squeeze short ones," said Appold. "We coördinated successfully and the blue flashes came less and less." It was a virtuoso duet against death. Appold banked and turned the hurtling bomber, locked in low-level formation, so that Barwell could clear the emplacements passing beneath at 200 miles an hour. Appold said, "I believe George silenced three of the six guns on that spot. I am convinced that we would not have survived and a lot more planes would not have come through, save for the cool-headed gunnery of this English officer." Behind them were forty B-24's. Many took hits in the first ground fusillade, but no planes fell yet.

The opening of battle found General Gerstenberg speeding through Ploesti toward his Bucharest post. Gerstenberg said to his driver, "Turn here. I'm going to the Ploesti command post instead." The master defense architect had decided to experience the siege in *Festung Ploesti.*

"Where are the fighters?" Barwell asked Appold. "The flak was ready for us, why not the Messerschmitts?" Gamecock Hahn was exactly where he should be, had the bombers kept their projected line of invasion. But now the Messerschmitts were forty miles from the Liberators, due to the erroneous turn at the Second I.P. Battles are composed of caprice and error, and this error had some luck for the Americans. It kept the German fighters off them during the opening of the battle.

Coming down from the heights over Bucharest, George Barwell

saw low-wing fighters that were not in his mental gallery of enemy aircraft. They were Romanian IAR-80's. The Gypsies were beating Gamecock Hahn to the first encounter. Ground spotters phoned the control centers, "They're attacking Bucharest very deep!" The fighter controllers started calling Gamecock Hahn south to meet the B-24's. Amidst the nervous babble on the fighter channels he did not hear the order.

Fighter controller Schultz had an alarming thought. "If they are making a heavy attack in Bucharest it will be a catastrophe. Feelings against the war are bad enough now. This could turn the Romanians against us." Then he thought of the possibility that the bombers would attack the German airdromes. He phoned the bases, "Send up every machine that will fly! Nothing must be left on the ground." The American gunners began seeing big Heinkel 111 bombers, Junkers 52 transports, liaison Storchs, and other chore planes such as Buckers, Stieglitzes and Weihes. There was even an ancient Gloster Gladiator that Britain had sold to Romania before the war. The B-24 men could not understand why these old and often unarmed types should be up, and some jumped to the hasty conclusion that this ragtag was all the Germans had to defend Ploesti. If so, it was going to be a big day for B-24 gunners. However, these planes were in the sky not to give battle, but to avoid it.

The bombers drove on blindly toward Bucharest. Some of the IAR-80's had now gotten high behind them and were diving on the Liberator tails. Worthy A. Long, piloting *Jersey Bounce,* got a call from his rear gunner, Leycester D. Havens: "Enemy fighters at six o'clock!" There was a thump. Havens said, "Direct hit on the tail turret." A few seconds later Long heard Havens say in a weak and surprised voice, "Lieutenant Long. I've had it." He was the first American to die by the enemy's hand in the great ground-air battle.

ODYSSEUS: Curse you, Atriedês! I wish you had some other army to command, some contemptible army instead of us! Zeus it seems has given us from youth to old age a nice ball of wool to wind—nothing but wars upon wars until we shall perish every one. *The Iliad,* Book XIV

6

THE CIRCUS IN HELL

Addison Baker had led the Traveling Circus into the wrong turn at Targoviste, following the mission leader up front. As he hurtled on in the haze toward Bucharest many of his pilots passionately called the error on the radio, but Baker continued to maintain formation. Halfway down the errant road Circus crews saw a dark blur in the mist on their left—the smoke of Ploesti refineries. Russell Longnecker was anxiously watching Baker's plane, when suddenly "Colonel Baker made a decision." The young flight officer said, "There was no doubt about his decision. He maneuvered our group more eloquently than if he had radio contact with each of us. He turned left ninety degrees. We all turned with him. Ploesti was off there to the left and we were going straight into it and we were going fast."

111

Baker and co-pilot Jerstad, the mission planner, drove *Hell's Wench* hard and low for the target city at the head of the left file of the Circus. Lieutenant Colonel George S. Brown, in *Queenie*, threw the right file into the improvised turn and took up a parallel course to Baker. On the other side of Brown, Ramsay Potts, leading B Force of the Circus, swung his ships into the new heading. Addison Baker's swift decision split the Circus completely away from K. K. Compton's Liberandos, which continued toward Bucharest. Now the grand plan for a simultaneous frontal assault on the White Targets by four groups was down to two groups, parting at right angles to each other, and the whereabouts of the rest of the force was unknown to them.

Ground spotters phoned the German fighter controllers, "They're attacking Bucharest and Ploesti very deep! It's a simultaneous attack on Bucharest and Ploesti!" Controller Zahn said, "Damned cleverly done. They send planes to tie up fighters at Bucharest while the main force hits Ploesti."

The Circus ran for Ploesti across dizzy strips of alfalfa, tall green corn, and bundles of harvested wheat lying in shining stubble. Baker's 22 Liberators went lower, drawing together, until they were knit tightly fifty feet from the ground. Through fragile windows the officers faced the ground barrage and tried to find an objective. The haze dissolved and threw up a welter of stacks, storage tanks and barrage balloons, or "blocking balloons," as the Luftwaffe called them. The balloon cables were festooned with contact explosives. The weeks of target briefings and rehearsals were no use to the Circus crews now. They were going in on an entirely unfamiliar heading. Their target, White Two, was on the other side of the city. The setting factors were complete.

The Circus came to bomb. Baker was leading as he said he would. In *Tupelo Lass*, K. O. Dessert's co-pilot called off the flak batteries for his gunners. "Eight o'clock! Twelve o'clock! Three o'clock," cried Jacob Epting. "Shoot all over!" Among the shell bursts he saw "pink stuff, white stuff, red stuff, black stuff." Below, he saw "two men fall over their gun. Two others pushed them aside and took over. The planes ahead were chewing the air, but to hell with prop-wash. We went as low as we could. It was safer than

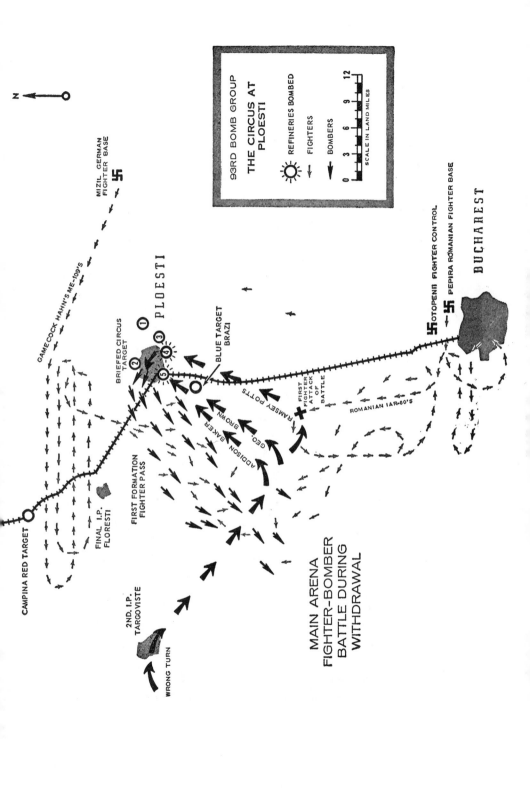

N

93RD BOMB GROUP
THE CIRCUS AT PLOESTI

☼ REFINERIES BOMBED
← FIGHTERS
← BOMBERS

SCALE IN LAND MILES
0   3   6   9   12

MIZIL GERMAN FIGHTER BASE

GAMECOCK HAHN'S ME-109'S

PLOESTI

BRIEFED CIRCUS TARGET

BLUE TARGET BRAZI

① ②③④⑤

RAMSEY POTTS

FIRST FIGHTER ATTACK OF BATTLE

GEO. BROWN

ADDISON BAKER

ROMANIAN IAR-80'S

OTOPENII FIGHTER CONTROL

PEPIRA ROMANIAN FIGHTER BASE

BUCHAREST

FINAL I.P. FLORESTI

FIRST FORMATION FIGHTER PASS

CAMPINA RED TARGET

2ND. I.P. TARGOVISTE

WRONG TURN

MAIN ARENA FIGHTER-BOMBER BATTLE DURING WITHDRAWAL

standing in the range of all those guns. We went into the target at twenty feet." Over Epting's head in *Tupelo Lass* stood one of the finest gunners in the Eighth Air Force, Ben Kuroki, turning his whining turret here and there to strafe flak towers. Kuroki had won a personal campaign against the U. S. Air Force for the privilege of performing this service. He was a Japanese-American truck farmer from Hershey, Nebraska.

Ben Kuroki had volunteered for the service on the night of Pearl Harbor and was turned away because of his ancestry. He besieged the Army and was accepted for a "nonsensitive" clerk's job in the infant Circus bomb group, whose members shunned him. His name was not on the shipping list when the group was sent to England. He pleaded with Ted Timberlake, who was at first confused, then touched and honored by the tears of Private Kuroki. Timberlake put his name on the list and Ben went to Britain on the *Queen Elizabeth,* scrubbing kitchen pots and sleeping on coiled decklines. In England, Ben slipped into air-gunnery classes and graduated with top qualifications, but no air crew would have him. Exactly one year after Pearl Harbor, Jake Epting needed a last-minute replacement gunner, and rather than ground his plane, took Kuroki on a mission. The Nisei warrior soon demolished the "yellow man" prejudice by his deeds in combat. A few months before Ploesti he was shot down in Algeria and escaped through Spain and Portugal to rejoin the Circus in England.

As Kuroki's plane ran up the twenty-mile, five-minute corridor to Ploesti, the sides of haystacks flew open, revealing spitting guns, and freight cars on railway sidings collapsed to pour out 37-mm. fire. Ahead, high barrage balloons were being reeled down and others were rising from the ground. Pits opened in the fields and sprouted machine guns. Kuroki's twin fifties joined other Circus guns in a direct fire fight with the larger German pieces, which, muzzle down, shells short-fused, interlaced the air with 20-mm., 37-cm., 88- and even 105-mm. shells. Flying gunners shot it out with ground gunners. As the flak men tried to hit the low planes from towers they killed flak gunners on other towers. The noise was beyond decibel measure as the choir of

136 fourteen-cylinder engines, with a total of more than a half-million horsepower, roared among muzzle blasts, shrapnel crumps and the ship-shaking clatter of 230 machine guns in the Liberators. Wheat shocks blew away in the bomber wakes like tumbleweeds.

In *Utah Man,* gunner John Connolly raked a man sending up a blocking balloon and saw him and the bag vanish in a puff of smoke. Connolly blew up a locomotive and did not recall it for three days afterward. He saw a flak gunner cradling a shell, looking up with open mouth, and a grinning soldier waving his cap on a bayonet.

Flight Officer Longnecker noted "an eighty-eight behind a row of trees at a crossroad. I could see the muzzle flash and the projectile as it came toward us. I forced *Thundermug* under this barrage. The shell removed the left aileron, left rudder and half of the elevator on Captain Roper's ship at my right. I went back into position with him. His plane looked like a junk yard, but he was not wavering a bit. I could see Roper in his cockpit, looking straight ahead, keeping his position. Resistance grew stronger. Our gunners were pounding away steadily. We were going in from the wrong direction at two hundred forty-five mph, sixty-five miles more than our usual speed, pulling emergency power for so long it was a question how much longer the engines could stand the abuse. All I wanted was to get beyond that inferno of tracers, exploding storage tanks and burning aircraft."

In the last ship of the Circus, a command observer, Lieutenant Colonel William A. Beightol, looked back for the Liberandos, the mission leaders last seen hanging on the rim of Bucharest. He saw their dim frontal silhouettes turning to follow the Circus into Ploesti. A minute or so later Beightol saw them turning east, breaking off the attack. He concluded that the Liberandos "had abandoned in the face of restrictive opposition."

Closing on the target city, several Circus planes were trailing smoke from smashed engines, and men were bleeding and dying on the air decks among hot bullet casings, and taking new wounds through the thin-skinned planes, their cries drowned by the deafening air-ground battle. Glittering shards of aluminum and plexiglass floated past in the slip streams. Fires bloomed from the Tokyo tanks they had brought to take them home. Longnecker said, "I saw Enoch Porter take a direct hit in the bomb bay and become a fountain of flame. Two red streams poured out the sides around the tail turret and joined in a river of fire flowing behind for two hundred feet. Porter climbed in a desperate bid for altitude, to let people parachute. The ship stalled, hanging like a cloud of fire, and out of the nosewheel door tumbled the bodies of Jack Warner and Red Franks."

Warner's shoulder blade had been shattered by flak. At his request Red Franks pushed him through the nosewheel hatch and followed him. Franks's chute did not open. Warner's silk spread just in time to save his life. He hit the ground hard and slid unconscious into a shallow stream. Enoch Porter climbed *Euroclydon* a little higher, and two gunners, Jack Reed and James Vest, bailed out safely. The first plane to go down in battle burned at the edge of a village, the pages of *As You Like It* opening and shriveling in fiery fingers.

A provident pilot named Earl C. Hurd roared toward the city in *Tarfu*. He had taught all his men how to land the plane in the event the pilots were knocked out. He struck a balloon cable, which stripped off a de-icer boot, but *Tarfu* stayed in the air. The co-pilot, Joseph Clements, opened his window and started firing a submachine gun at the German gunners. Hurd clapped his shoulder and yelled, "For God's sake, Joe, be ready to take over when they get me!"

Up front in *Hell's Wench*, Addison Baker and John Jerstad held an adamant course with Stewart's *Utah Man*. The Mormon was hit in the left aileron, but did not waver. It seemed impossible that any plane could force the city guns now belching into the Circus. "I didn't see how anyone could get through that mess alive," said Hurd.

Hell's Wench struck a balloon cable. The plane went on and the severed balloon wandered up into the air. The flagship received a direct hit in the nose from an 88. That was the station of bombardier Pezzella, of the "Ball one!" quip. Joseph Tate, leading the second wave behind Baker, saw him hit three more times—

in the wing, wing root and then a devastating burst in the cockpit. The wing tanks and Tokyo tanks took flame. The stricken command ship was still two or three minutes from the bomb-release line.

Baker and Jerstad jettisoned their bombs to keep *Hell's Wench* in the air and lead the force over the target. "You can tell from the way they drop whether it is the bombardier or the pilot who dumped them," said Tate. Colonel Brown in *Queenie*, leading the parallel column, saw "open wheat fields in front into which Baker could have mushed with ease." Instead, the flaming Liberator flew on, aiming for an opening between two tall refinery stacks. Tate saw a man coming out of the nosewheel hatch of *Hell's Wench*. "He came tumbling back," said Tate, "his chute opening. He drifted over top of us so close we could see his burned legs."

Immediately before the target, the flagship received another direct hit. "Baker had been burning for about three minutes," said Carl Barthel, *Queenie's* navigator. "The right wing began to drop. I don't see how anyone could have been alive in that cockpit, but someone kept her leading the force on between the refinery stacks. Baker was a powerful man, but one man could not have held the ship on the climb she took beyond the stacks." *Hell's Wench* staggered up to about three hundred feet and three or four men came out. She fell off on the right wing and came drifting back toward Colonel Brown. The falling flagship cleared him by six feet, and, as she "flashed by, flames hid everything in the cockpit," said Brown. *Hell's Wench* crashed on her wing tip in a field. Brown said, "Baker went down after he flew his ship to pieces to get us over the target." None of Baker's crew survived, not even the men who jumped.

The death of A Force Leader dropped into the subconscious beneath the scream of battle. *Utah Man*, sole survivor of the lead wave, pulled up to sixty feet to get on top of a refinery unit. Pilot Stewart heard "Bombs away!" and a terrific flak burst came in the left side of his ship. Stewart's bombardier, Ralph Cummings, a former Texas League baseball player, placed the first bombs of Tidal Wave between the plant and its two-foot-thick blast wall. He hit the Colombia Aquila refinery, Target White

Five, which was assigned to the Eight Balls, still coming some-where in the sky. Paul Johnston, the tail gunner of *Utah Man*, reported on the interphone, "Saw two bombs go into the target. Didn't see any more fall out. The incendiaries hit on top."

Stewart saw a 200-foot radio tower directly ahead of *Utah Man*. Its pinnacle was whipping back and forth in gusts of antiaircraft fire. "To go over it would have meant running into that flak," said the pilot. "I said to Larry [co-pilot Loren Koon, an American veteran of the R.A.F.], 'Watch out when the tower goes by.' We rolled the left wing into the street below and stood the right wing to miss the tower. Flak chewed off the high wing tip before we leveled off." *Utah Man* roared across the housetops of Ploesti, spraying gasoline from shrapnel holes.

Flight Officer Longnecker, coming in to bomb, saw up ahead "a B-24 sliding down a street, with both wings sheered off. A plane hit a barrage balloon and both disintegrated in a ball of fire. We saw bombs dropped by other planes skipping along the ground, hitting buildings, and passing on through, leaving gaping holes in the brickwork. They seemed like rats, gnawing through building after building to find a better place to rest. Suddenly a huge oil storage tank exploded directly in front of my wingman, Vic Olliffe, raising a solid column of fire and debris two hundred feet, waiting for *Let 'Er Rip*. He couldn't possibly avoid it. The next instant I glanced out and saw Olliffe crossing under Roper and myself, barely clearing us, and then going over a pair of stacks like a hurdler before putting his bombs in a cracking tower. How he missed the explosion, our ships and the stacks is a mys-tery and always will be.

"The tracers were so solid in front of us that it looked like a fishing net woven of fiery cords. I thought the flight was over for us. From the expression on Deacon Jones's face, I am sure the same thing was crossing his mind; not fear, but rather a sense of vast disappointment, like having to give up a good book before reading the last chapter. As we were about to touch this web of death and destruction, it parted and fell away. Willie Schrampf dropped his bombs and Deacon said his first words: 'Let's get the hell out of here!' "

Beneath them, near the refinery, Corporal Wegener scuttled into his infirmary as gigantic planes spread their wings over it, strafing the wooden barracks. The priest-medic and his patients huddled against the baseboards. In a moment the sick bay was riddled and smoke puffed through the bullet holes. Wegener stuck his head above a window sill; outside the world was aboil with black clouds and flickering yellow flame. "It's black as night!" he exclaimed. He turned to his men. Not one of them had been hit in the storm of fifty-caliber shells. They went outside. An officer yelled, "Don't go near the refinery! The tanks are exploding. Everything is on fire!" Wegener shepherded his patients inside. They were convinced that the bombers were Canadian.

Overhead, the second wave of the Circus streamed across White Five, led by *Ball of Fire Jr.*, which was stolen property. In England the pilot, Joseph Tate, who had lost his first *Ball of Fire* to battle damage, happened upon an unattended Liberator on a ferry base and flew off with it. As Tate bombed Ploesti he closed his mind over his comrades' deaths and a deep inner wound. A few days before, he had received a disturbing letter from his wife.

Tate came off the refinery unbelievably untouched and saw a roof-top battery addressing him directly. All at once the men and guns vanished in an explosion. Tate's tail gunner saw something he "didn't like to talk about"—a blazing B-24 climbing and two parachutes opening before the plane crashed and spread an acre of fire. The parachutes drifted into the flames. In order to deny gasoline to fascism the mission force carried a half-million gallons of it to Ploesti.

In the middle of the formation a veteran co-pilot went berserk with fright. The pilot held him and the control column until the navigator dragged the man out and sat on him.

The succeeding elements of A Force kept coming up the corridor of fire, fighting for every foot of it. It was a massive tank ambuscade upon unarmored planes racing at more than 200 mph. *Tupelo Lass* bombed, flew out intact, and K. O. Dessert banked southwest into a broad Ploesti boulevard, noting "ribbons of tracer bullets coming like an illusion of railway tracks." He lowered *Tupelo Lass* to bus-top level and drove down the street, "going through a million red lights"—the muzzle blasts of rooftop flak guns. In the top turret Ben Kuroki did not reply. They had orders not to shoot up the city.

In the meantime, to the east, George Brown's column, partially screened from flak guns by rows of lime trees along the Ploesti-Bucharest highway, approached *Bertha*, the big flak gun that Willi Nowicki had just put back in service. The roar of invisible bombers became louder, but the battery was still on hold-fire orders. Suddenly, said Nowicki, "Four Liberators swept across us at treetop level, shooting wildly." Sergeant Aust, the fire controller, could not restrain himself any longer. Breaking orders, he yelled, "Fire!"

Bertha scored a bull's-eye on the next plane to arrive. It crashed beyond the battery. All the other 88's went into action. "The concert started," said Nowicki. "It was bedlam. Our men were cheering and screaming." The Russians (the K-3's, the firing-cord pullers) worked smartly. The guns raised and lowered and turned, spouting death. The sound of bells was added to the clangor of battle. The flak guns could turn two and a half times on their bases before the electrical cables would go no farther. Then a warning bell rang and the gunners would be out of action until they traversed back to starting position.

"There was some fire power in those Liberators!" said Nowicki. "They wanted to paralyze our flak. They outsmarted us. We couldn't see our fighters anywhere." Brown's ships were felling men in the battery site, but *Bertha* and her five companions were killing his men too. The B-24 piloted by William E. Meehan fell in a sliding, burning heap, leaving a trail of burning wheat. Out of Meehan's plane ran gunner Larry Yates through a universe of fire. He was the sole survivor.

Charles Merrill flew over in *Thar She Blows* with an armored deck under his feet and got through the battery safely. The booming flak guns were soon overworked. Nowicki put on his helmet and changed an overheated 20-mm. barrel in twenty seconds. The 88 named *Friederich* had a malfunction in the automatic fuse setter and exploded, killing four antiaircraft men.

Adolf fired a shell that was fused too short. The explosion killed several other Germans.

Gunners of a Romanian battery saw a hard-hit bomber sinking on a direct line toward them. It salvoed its bombs in neat rows in a field and staggered on. The B-24 crashed in the battery and exploded, killing ten Americans and eight Romanians.

The most telling fire from the ground was coming from agile 37-mm. and 20-mm. guns. The Americans often mistook the 37's for 88's: they both threw bursting shells. Many of the big 88's were silent for long stretches of the battle. They were not maneuverable enough to hit low-flying bombers flashing by in the tree-tops on the sides. But when they got at the nose of an oncoming formation, the 88's were decisive. One such gun, manned by a corporal, was lying crouched in silence with its breech open when a B-24 flight came straight for it, fantastically low. There was no time to compute a shot. The corporal put his eye to the breech. One of the Liberators was neatly framed in the muzzle. Loading with fantastic speed, he shot it down.

Colonel Brown reached Colombia Aquila and bombed it. Now came a peril few of the Americans had anticipated. Buttoned around the refineries were the tank farms. These oil stockpiles were strategic trivia. The mission was not concerned with destroying a few days' product awaiting shipment, but neither the air gunners nor the ground gunners could avoid lacing into the storage tanks. And the airmen, as ordered, were throwing out armloads of incendiary bombs on them.

The tanks began exploding in flame. A plane skimmed one just as it went off. The bomber was tossed up like a flaming brand. Brown's following echelons flew out of the flak beds into red-hot tank tops spinning like coins, and girders blowing in the air like straws.

In the midst of his battle with the bomber column, Sergeant Aust received a phone call from the flak battalion commander: "*Wer hat den Feuerbefehl freigegeben?*" (Who gave the firing order?) Aust confessed. "I'm going to court-martial you," said the commander. The fire controller went back to work. The flak men were screaming maniacally at a sight in Colonel Brown's third bomb wave. Coming toward them was a B-24 completely enveloped in flame.

It was *José Carioca*, carrying ten young men on their first bombing mission. The pilot was Nicholas Stampolis of Kalamazoo, Michigan. His co-pilot was nineteen-year-old Lieutenant Ivan Canfield from San Antonio, Texas, whom even the sergeants called "Junior." The German gunners simply watched it fly over without trying to hit it. The plane continued on evenly in hopeless flame and disappeared in the target smoke. On the other side it came out still flying steadily. *José Carioca* went toward a refinery building from which a flak unit was firing into the onrushing bomber stream. The plane drove through the wall of the building as though it were made of confectioners' sugar. Gasoline squirted and ran in licking flamelets across the refinery grounds. From the other side of the building came *José Carioca*, in level flight, without wings. The fuselage penetrated another refinery building, where it remained, lifting a cloud of brick dust and new fires. Stampolis and Canfield had taken flame in the bomb bay tanks five miles from the target, but they reached it.

In the B-24 piloted by Roy C. Harms, the left waist gunner, Jack J. Reed, was firing at the muzzle blinks of 20-mm. guns hidden in haystacks. The flak men put a four-foot hole in Harms's left vertical stabilizer. Top turret man Arnold Holden was hit. Shells shattered the nose and tail. A fire broke out in the fuselage, sealing off the tail gunner, Michael Doka. Reed's companion at the waist guns, John Shufritz, was heavily wounded but continued to man his gun. Reed yelled to him, "Bail out if we get any altitude," and went into the bomb bay. The bombs were still in the racks and Harms was still trying to bring them to Ploesti. The plane was approaching a stall. Harms tried to climb. He reached 300 feet and Reed jumped. The plane fell with the other nine men. Reed landed with heavy injuries in the refinery grounds. "I don't know how I made it," he said. "I wish I had rode her to the ground and died with the fine men who didn't have the guts to jump."

John J. Hayes, flight engineer of *Liberty Lad*, saw "great sheets of gasoline ablaze, flowing down the roads and over the fields."

The layer of summer haze over Ploesti gave way to towering darkness, rooted in flame. As yet no Circus bombs had exploded. Their detonation times were graduated from one hour in the lead wave to forty-five seconds in the rear, and Tailend Charlie was still coming. The last plane in Brown's force was *Valiant Virgin,* piloted by Russell D. DeMont and Robert C. Murray. Laying down a bristling fifty-caliber barrage into the flak men, they got on top of the cracking plant and put their bombs into it. DeMont immediately returned to the lowest possible altitude, crossed the city and came upon Colonel Brown and one other plane in the hills north of Ploesti. DeMont tried to shape up on his leader, but one of his engines would not give full power. "Rather than waste gas to keep up," said DeMont, "I decided I would throttle back and make a lone withdrawal." *

As the two main Circus columns, Baker's and Brown's, crossed their target, out to their right were the twelve planes of B Force, led by the economics professor, Ramsay Potts, in *Duchess.* His was the smallest force of Tidal Wave and carried the highest percentage of men overdue for retirement from battle. Potts had deduced the low-level target three months before and the long anticipation had taken twenty pounds off his normally trim body. With white face, red eyes and yellow hair, his clothing hanging loosely from his worry-worn frame, B Force Leader was a ghost pilot hanging on by raw will power, as his ships ran the gauntlet of hot steel and tracers seeking their petrol reservoirs. He watched the last oval rudders of A Force plunge into the smoke, and looked for his target. Potts had been briefed to bomb the intertwined Standard Petrol Block and Unirea Sperantza refineries, small precise objectives worthy of his expert crews. They had studied the models until they could see the target in their sleep, but not from this unfamiliar angle. Ironically, their proper targets lay in the corner of Ploesti they were approaching, but Potts steered toward a nearer refinery. It was Astro Romana, the largest oil producer in Europe, the first priority objective of the mission —Killer Kane's target.

* DeMont's fuel conservation policy proved sound. He flew all the way to Benghazi alone and landed with an hour's gas in his tanks.

Potts's planes were sighted by gunlayer Erich Hanfland's battery. The young German saw, right among the Liberators, "a storage tank leap five hundred feet in the air, billowing smoke and flame." He thought, "How can anybody fly through that?" Battery Sergeant Bichler bellowed through his megaphone, "Fire! Fire freely in all directions!" Hanfland saw a dozen "furniture vans" coming, hailing bullets into the battery. Obergefreiter (Corporal) Deltester of Hamburg, who had just been married on home leave, was at his field phone when a fifty-caliber shell struck his neck and passed out under his arm on the other side, killing him instantly.

Potts and his wingmen, *Jersey Bounce* and *Lucky*, passed over as Hanfland lined up on the furniture vans and tramped the trigger of the four-barreled 20-mm. gun, loaded with armor-piercing and incendiary shells. The first fifty rounds nearly sheared the tail off a Liberator in Potts's second rank. It crashed 200 feet past the battery in a cornfield and began to burn. It was *Pudgy*, piloted by Milton W. Teltser and Wilmer H. C. Bassett. They brought the crumpled, burning ship into a crash-landing, from which they and three others—observer Willard R. Beaumont and waist gunners Robert Locky and Francis Doll—got away before it exploded. A mob of peasants closed in, thinking the men were Russians. A man in a horse cart rode into the crowd and drove the farmers away with a whip.

The seared and blistered survivors walked to a shuttered village. A middle-aged inhabitant ventured out and said, "Are you chaps Americans by any chance?" Bassett said, "That is correct." The man cried, "How nice to see you! I was with the Royal Flying Corps in England in the last war." The village poured out in gay Sunday dress, led by the burgomaster wearing a red embroidered shirt. Through the crowd came a beautiful young woman, who looked at the burned men and made way for them to a spotless infirmary. She was the village doctor. The villagers watched her strip their smoldering rags and dress the burns. She laid the shocked men on straw in the village pub, and the burgomaster admitted orderly queues of people to look at the Americans.

Alongside Potts flew *Jersey Bounce*, carrying the first man killed in action. Shortly after Sergeant Havens had died, the ship's nose was removed by shrapnel, wounding bombardier Norman C. Adams and navigator David Lipton. The bleeding Lipton continued to assail the flak pits with his machine gun. With air whistling through the open nose and tail, *Jersey Bounce* raced through hose streams of steel.

"There was a tattoo of shrapnel spraying the ship from stem to stern," said co-pilot John Lockhart. "Whumpf! A stream of black smoke. No more Number Four engine." From the ground, Hanfland, who had knocked out the engine, saw the plane lurch. "It was flying too deep for anybody to jump," said the German. Hanfland exploded a shell in *Jersey Bounce*'s control pedestal. Long and Lockhart flew on between two flak towers, which removed the rest of the greenhouse and shattered half of the instrument panel. Number One engine was struck and caught fire. With two engines gone and *Jersey Bounce* fading into a stall, the pilots saw a refinery cooling tower looming ahead. They used the last energy of the engines to pull over the tower. Long called on Adams to bomb. There was no answer on the intercom—it had been shot away.

But *Jersey Bounce* did not die. Over the cooling tower the pilots got her leveled out and walked her on treetops and telegraph poles into a fairly open field, where she went into a long slide, still without taking fire. The plane dismantled a fence, ground across a railway in a shower of sparks, and sledded to a stop. Only then did her bomb bay tanks burst and flames spring from the gas sluicing through the interior. Lockhart squirmed out through a rent in the side and ran with his head and hands aflame. Long was caught in his collapsed seat, with the catch on his safety belt pinned beneath him. He wrenched himself free and passed through "a solid mass of flames."

Adams, the wounded bombardier, plunged back into the fire and hauled Sergeant Maurice Peterson out of the waist. The two officers ripped the clothing off the badly burned gunner, and Adams went back to the wreck again to help others. The fire could no longer be approached. Four of his comrades died in the pyre of the dead tail gunner. Long watched his ship burn with "the loneliest feeling in the world." Germans marched them to a schoolhouse aid station in Ploesti, where they found their mortally hurt waist gunner, Marion J. Szaras, lying naked with heavy burns and his back and legs riddled with shrapnel. There were thirty other B-24 men there, most of them burned and others with fractures and internal injuries incurred in low parachute jumps.

Beyond the target, *Honky-Tonk Gal*, flown by Hubert K. Womble, was mortally hit by aroused flak gunners north of Ploesti, who killed an officer in the greenhouse. Womble lowered his landing gear as soon as he felt the strike. A wheat field providentially spread before him and he made a tricycle landing. A wing clipped the earth, and, as the plane ground-looped, a control cable parted and whipped off Womble's foot. His men were lifting him out as Russell Longnecker and Deacon Jones roared over in *Thundermug*, recognized *Honky-Tonk Gal*, and thanked God for the eight men waving wildly on the ground. The young pilots of *Thundermug* located their indomitable companions, Hugh Roper and Vic Olliffe, who brought their three ships together "real tight as before" to begin the thousand-mile voyage home. Longnecker said, "We had come through, but there was no sight of the three others in our wing. As I moved back into my old position on Hugh Roper, I could see the display of big holes on his right wing and side that he got on the target run."

The last Circus plane to cross the target was *Ready & Willing*, piloted by Packy Roche, a smart, lucky veteran of the high war in the west. He stayed low at Ploesti. "If we'd have climbed more than fifty feet from the ground, we'd have been shot to pieces," said his gunner William Doerner. As it was, Roche came off with five wounded. Colonel Beightol, the observer in *Ready & Willing*, watched sister ships go down and had an "intense feeling that, even though we had reached and bombed the target, the limited success scarcely compensated for the pasting we took." The Circus was paying Gerstenberg's list price. Roche's flight engineer, Fred Anderson, a "retired" volunteer, had his front teeth knocked out by shrapnel. He continued his duties, transferring fuel and looking after the ship.

As the Circus blundered across the city, Baetz, the German camp show musician, heard "loud, roaring wings" and stuck his head out of a doorway. He saw a monstrous green airplane coming toward him, its wing tips stretching nearly the width of the boulevard. He saw a gunner in a glass dome on the roof, one standing in an open window on the side, and another in a bay window in the rear, exchanging streams of bullets with a small pursuing plane, which he recognized as a Romanian IAR-81. The fighter went into a half roll and sped under the bomber, upside down, crashing bullets into its belly.

Baetz had the impression that the B-24 was out of control, "although it continued to fly at a flat angle." The IAR-81 twisted out from under the bomber and climbed. "I felt the street shake," said Baetz. "The bomber crashed into a three-story brick building." He ran toward it. The Liberator was buried inside the Ploesti Women's Prison. "Flaming petrol flowed through the cell blocks and down the stairs," said the musician. In the cells were about a hundred prisoners—shoplifters, political opponents of Antonescu, and farm girls serving short terms for watering milk. The women screamed. In the street a man yelled, "Where's the turnkey? He has the cell keys on his ring. Get the turnkey! Let's get them out." Another bystander said, "I saw the turnkey climbing the outside staircase to unlock the women, and the plane hit him."

Quick to the disaster came a unit from Gerstenberg's sole remaining regiment of fire police. Most of them came from Magdeburg in Saxony. They approached the burning prison with great valor, pried open window bars on the ground floor, and brought out forty women before the flames shut them out. The prison burned all the next night and cries were heard from it until early morning.

As the young pilots of *Thundermug* left Ploesti, Longnecker said, "We were doing two hundred forty miles an hour and planes were passing us like it was the Cleveland Air Races. It looked like we had a chance to get home, but we'd never make it on such power settings. I reduced power to save gas and conserve the engines."

Tarfu came out flying, with pilot Hurd surveying his defunct oxygen and electrical systems, a shell hole in a bomb bay tank, and severed control cables. Not the smallest loss was the shattered portable toilet. He and most of his men had dysentery.

The Mormon missionary, Stewart, swung across the chimney pots of Ploesti, still sniffing gasoline fumes, although the crew had stoppered the holes in the bomb bay tanks. His co-pilot pointed to No. 3 engine on *Utah Man*. A thick stream of gas was pouring out of the wing tank. Stewart kicked the rudder to swing the gusher away from the waist window, and told his crew to assume crash-landing positions. "Don't set 'er down now, Walt," said a small voice from the rear. "We've still got two live thousand-pounders aboard." The bombs were armed to explode in an hour. Apparently when Cummings was about to release them, a flak hit had impaired his controls and they did not fall.

Utah Man, near to mechanical failure, full of explosive fumes and streaming gas, faced sudden death from a flak or fighter strike. If that didn't finish the expedition, in about fifty minutes the big bombs would. Stewart steered toward some oil derricks, calling on Cummings to drop the live bombs to "do some good." The bombardier tripped them again, but they did not fall. "Now we've got to get them out of here, Ralph," said the pilot, "or we'll never get this thing down. Let's try this railroad bridge up ahead." Cummings tinkered with the gyro-gunsight and reported, "Bombs away!" Stewart looked at his ad lib target and cringed in horror. It was not a military objective but an ordinary country bridge with cows trudging over it, driven by a small girl, who was waving ecstatically at the oncoming Goliath.

The pilot did not feel the unburdening of bombs. The tail gunner phoned, "Hey, there's a little girl back there waving at us!" The thousand-pounders were still hanging in the slings, ruminating the acid in their nose membranes that would soon blow them to smithereens. Cummings and the engineer went into the bay to work the big ones out through the open bomb doors.

Colonel Brown, now in command of the Circus after Addison Baker's death, picked up more of his ships on the outskirts of Ploesti and led them on a southwest withdrawal heading. Brown saw that one of his wing tips was crumpled. "It doesn't look like it hit a balloon cable," he said. Top turret gunner Lloyd Treadway said, "Colonel, you hit a church steeple, remember?" Brown wondered where the Circus was. That morning 39 planes had taken off, and 34 reached the target area. Now he had fifteen in a scratch formation. Only five were relatively undamaged. Others carried dead and wounded. A feathered prop was their cockade and the marching tune was air whistling through broken glass. The Circus formed a flying hedgehog to save itself. In the shifting fortunes of battle it seemed that Brown was getting lucky. There were no fighters in sight. It looked as though the riddled Circus might slip through between the Romanians at Bucharest and Gamecock Hahn on the north.

The Luftwaffe ace was still patrolling the northern air gates of Ploesti at 6,000 feet, perplexed by the failure of the Americans to arrive punctually on their predicted time and course. His radio appeals to the controllers were lost in the yelling on the air waves.

Shouldered in with the Gamecock's H.Q. Schwarm was Black Wing, led by industrial engineer Hans Schopper in a Messerschmitt called *Hecht*, meaning a little fish that prowls and preys. Schopper had flown in the Polish campaign in '39, and later, on patrol out of Trondheim, Norway, had shot down into the freezing Atlantic a Blenheim, a Hurricane and a Sunderland. He had destroyed a Fokker in Holland in 1940 and six Soviet machines at Stalingrad in '42. Schopper was as puzzled as his commander. The mishmash of voices on his open receiver indicated that an air battle was taking place, but where was it?

The Gamecock picked a clue off the radio, an authoritative German voice calling to him, "Fly to six thousand five hundred meters." Hahn replied, "There are no furniture vans around here." Came a reply, "Then go under the clouds." Hahn spiralbanked his 52 Messerschmitts through the bottom cloud layers. Schopper hit his radio button. "Gamecock! Oh, Gamecock, I see them! Green bombers, very deep." Under the clouds the Mizil Messerschmitts saw the target drama spread before them. The south side of Ploesti was burning. The American bombs were beginning to detonate, flinging up dust through the black target smoke. The green bombers had outwitted them and were scuttling away. The Gamecock elbowed his radio-button. "Dive! Dive!" he shouted, and plunged full throttle. The brooding youngster, Werner Gerhartz, held on to his leader's wing, facing his first battle proof. He resolved that this time the Americans were not going to evade him with any North Sea tricks. The power dive of the Mizil force reached 550 miles an hour. Schopper had to throttle back quickly "to keep from pulling my wings off."

Each experienced pilot chose one of the Circus ships to attack and did not take his eyes from it during the swoop. Halfway down, the Gamecock, with reflexes trained by many battles, reached blindly to his panel and flipped on the switch that electrically armed his guns—20-mm. cannons in each wing and one under the nose, and a fifteen-caliber machine gun firing through the airscrew. He shot a glance at the red light that showed the guns were open. The light was not on. He called to the novice Gerhartz, "Ben, my guns aren't working. You take over," and slid out of the formation to climb and direct the battle by radiophone. (After it was over, none of his pilots remembered hearing a single command from him.)

Gerhartz struck at the high rear of George Brown's pinch-hit formation. The tail and top turret gunners sent up sheets of fire from their superior position in the harvest fields and broke Gerhartz' battle array on the first pass. A fighter pilot, who tried to level off and pursue, was churned up in the American prop-wake and crash-landed. Another, whose machine was full of burning B-24 bullets, ploughed the earth in flames and came staggering out of the wreckage.

The fighter formation had been dispersed by a new kind of earth-bound aerial warfare. The Mizil men went hunting in pairs and trios for lone ships, crippled ships and those that were flying too high. Gerhartz and his wingman, Hans Eder, caught on to a V-pattern of three Liberators departing at an altitude of 300 feet. They ignored one that was dragging and smoking, saving it for later. The Germans drove from behind on their selected victims. Gerhartz said, "I got high on the tail of mine and poured it into him. I don't know whether they were firing at me. It happened too fast. Eder and I came around again, perhaps two minutes later. The Liberators were scattering. One of the engines on mine was smoking, possibly the result of my first pass. As I dived I saw Eder completing his second attack. I closed in and ripped up my bomber's backbone.

"By now the two Liberators were very down, running hard for their lives, deep to the ground. As I came in I could see Eder making the third pass at his. But there was no longer an airplane in front of me. The B-24 was behind me, crushed flat. Eder's bomber was burning on the ground two miles away."

The Circus went to earth and passed out of the fighter zone. The Messerschmitts turned back to Ploesti. The controllers were yelling that new waves of bombers were coming toward the refineries.

Utah Man, the first ship to bomb, was far in the wake of the Circus hegira. The big Mormon pilot could not exceed 150 mph air speed lest his wreck fall apart. The live thousand-pounders sucked closer to their fuse settings. The engineer and the bombardier were in the bomb bay, clawing and hammering to release the ton-weight of death, their labors muffled by a screeching of wind from the torn and dangling left bomb door. Stewart's men, who had prepared for life everlasting at his prayer meeting the night before, sailed on toward that almost certain port. They counted 367 flak holes in the fuselage and wings. One hole was three feet wide. Yet the shells had missed them all, except the radioman, who fingered a crease in his hand dealt by spent flak. "Look at Steiner trying to open the cut so he can get the Purple Heart!" said a comrade.

The screeching stopped. The hanging left bay door had torn away in the wind. Now they could hear tools banging in the bay as Cummings and Bartlett worked on the bombs. There was a mighty yelp from the flight deck. Bartlett was hammering the pilot's shoulder. "Walt! They're gone!" The two thousand-pounders were tumbling into a field.

Stewart said, "Get back to crash-landing positions." Now he had a chance to save his men by skidding in. The fuselage men sat in tandem, backs to the bulkhead, nestled between each other's legs like a rowing crew, and padded themselves with their parachute packs. Stewart said, "Hey, I don't smell gas any more!" Koon said, "We're probably out of gas. Let's set down now." The pilot said, "No, let's not. Maybe the engines don't know they're out of gas. Watch them like a hawk, Larry, and we'll try to make Yugoslavia, where we have a chance of ducking the Germans." The gunners arose from the crash-landing positions and looked out. There were no other planes in the sky. The feeling came over them that no one else had come through. Shedding fragments of metal, *Utah Man* plodded on.

Il n'y a cheval si bien ferré qu'il ne glisse.   Proverb

7

TARGETS OF OPPORTUNITY

When K. K. Compton and General Ent took the Liberandos on the wrong turn at Targoviste, their mission flagship was on the right flank, a few planes behind the substitute route leader, John Palm, driving *Brewery Wagon*. The others turned southeast and knit onto the flagship, except for Palm. He kept on going straight. His tail gunner phoned, "They're all turning right!" Palm and his co-pilot, William Love, executed a tight turn and tacked onto the errant formation. Their navigator, William Wright, phoned, "If this is the correct turn, I'm lost. This heading is all wrong!" Palm thought, "Little Willie Wright always knows where he is." The navigator's protest was underscored by outcries on the command channel: "Mistake!" "Wrong turn!" "Not here!" Wright calmly said, "I'm going to try to salvage a course to the left." Palm had such confidence in his navigator that he complied. He turned off and *Brewery Wagon* headed east, all alone.

In a moment the other planes were lost from view behind trees. *Brewery Wagon* was engulfed in a blinding rain squall. For long, nervous seconds Palm ran through the murk, then shot out into dazzling sunlight, headed straight for a hill. He kicked up over it and saw spread before him a vista of glistening green and golden fields. In the distance, framed in a rainbow, were the stacks and stills of Ploesti. Palm selected the nearest refinery and drove toward it at an altitude of twenty feet. From the greenhouse Wright called off trees and power poles and Palm hurdled them.

Soon Palm was standing in the sights of the professional German gunners in the inner flak ring. John Palm was a husky, magnetic youngster who had fled his father's shoe store in El Paso, Texas, to fly big bombers. Serving with the Liberandos, he had caught the eye of K. K. Compton, who encouraged him to think of the Air Force as a career. Palm had made a good record, although he was sometimes assigned a hexed ship which was often shot up, the same *Brewery Wagon* he was now piloting. Her nominal captain was Robert H. Storz, a brewer's son from Omaha, Nebraska. That morning Storz had drawn a B-24 named *Per Diem II*, and Palm got the hoodoo plane. Before getting in to take her off, Palm threw stones at *Brewery Wagon*.

Now, nearing Ploesti, the flak men attended to luckless *Brewery Wagon*. A well-timed 88-mm. shell burst in the nose, killing Wright and bombardier Robert W. Merrell. The explosion destroyed an engine and set two others afire. The plane almost turned over. Palm and co-pilot Love fought to recover the ship. "Tramping the pedals was like fighting a bucking horse," said Palm. "Although the bombardier was dead, we were obsessed with doing good with our bombs. I was not getting much pressure on the right pedal. I reached down. My right leg below the knee was hanging from a shred of flesh." Palm jettisoned his bombs.

The rogue ship was floundering around west of Ploesti, where the Mizil Messerschmitts were diving on the Circus. As Uncle Willie Steinmann roared away from his pass at the Circus, making up his mind to go hunting singles, he espied highly eligible prey, a sandy bomber heaving along at low speed with smoke trailing from two engines. *Brewery Wagon* was nearing the end of her poor luck.

Steinmann attacked according to a theory he had worked out from studying Liberator models—obliquely from the rear at a high angle, in order to hit the right wing root and cockpit. "I

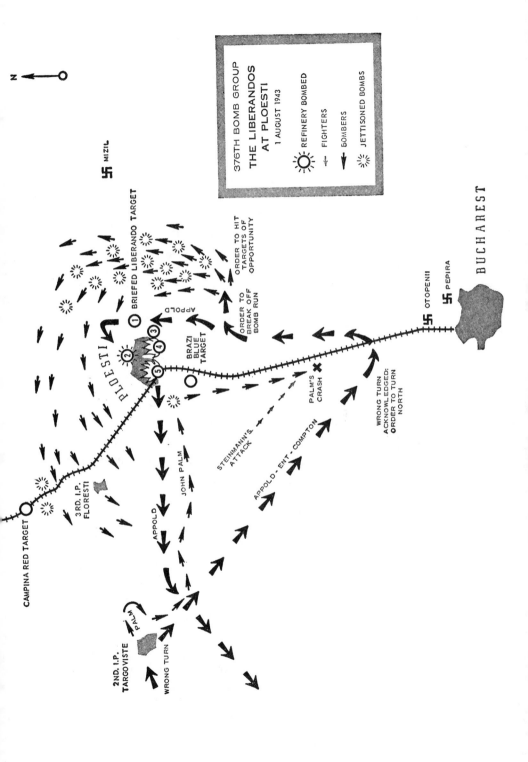

N

376TH BOMB GROUP

THE LIBERANDOS
AT PLOESTI

1 AUGUST 1943

☀ REFINERY BOMBED

← FIGHTERS

↓ BOMBERS

☀ JETTISONED BOMBS

MIZIL

BRIEFED LIBERANDO TARGET

APPOLD

ORDER TO HIT
TARGETS OF
OPPORTUNITY

ORDER TO
BREAK OFF
BOMB RUN

BRAZI
BLUE TARGET

PLOESTI

CAMPINA RED TARGET

3RD. I.P.
FLORESTI

APPOLD

JOHN PALM

STEINMANN'S
ATTACK

PALM'S
CRASH ✕

APPOLD - ENT - COMPTON

WRONG TURN
ACKNOWLEDGED:
ORDER TO TURN
NORTH

OTOPENII

PEPIRA

BUCHAREST

2ND. I.P.
TARGOVISTE

PALM

WRONG TURN

went in," said Steinmann, "and raked the tail and walked my fire across the B-24. He crashed immediately."

As *Brewery Wagon* hit the earth, Love flooded the engines with foam, preventing an immediate explosion. Palm ripped out the cockpit window with one hand, "something I couldn't do under normal circumstances with both hands in a week," he said. He dived out headfirst and hit the ground in a football shoulder roll. Love and engineer Alec Rockinson carried Palm away in a fireman's carry, and they hid in a cornfield. From the broken ship came radioman Harold Block and gunners Austin Chastain, Clay Snyder, William Thompson and Dallas Robertson. The latter had a piece of 20-mm. shell in his skull. German riflemen ran toward the dazed sergeants. Palm drew his .45 and leveled it at the Germans. Rockinson, who was at his feet, putting a tourniquet on Palm's leg stump with a web belt, said sharply, "Don't do that, sir." It was the first time he had ever called the pilot "sir." Palm put away his gun. The Germans flushed Palm's trio out of the corn and manhandled them. A big Romanian soldier menaced the Germans with his gun and they let go of Palm, who was bent over, holding his leg on with both hands. A German pulled a knife and with a swift motion cut away Palm's wrist watch. The Germans departed, leaving the Romanian with his captives.

During Palm's misadventure the main Liberando formation continued to fly toward Bucharest on the wrong course. "On the way we found that altitudes of five to ten feet, allowing for fences, cattle and buildings, were the only means of survival," said Appold. "In the haze and low altitude, I could see only the rear elements of Section A up ahead. Barwell continued to gun the flak crews with short economical bursts."

In the flagship, General Ent and K. K. Compton now realized the magnitude of the navigational error. From the haze ahead there loomed the towers of a city. They were not the stacks of Ploesti, but the Orthodox church spires of the Romanian capital.

K. K. Compton said, "At this point, General Ent went on the command channel, acknowledged the error at Targoviste, and turned the formation north toward Ploesti. We were completely disoriented on our briefed target, White One, the Romana Americana refinery. We decided it was best to attack Astro Romana, the number-one objective of the mission. It was Kane's target, but we did not know where he was. For all we knew, he had been forced to turn back. So we looked for the fractionating columns of Astro Romana as we headed north."

Norman Appold obediently winged over and took his element north with K. K. Compton. The little pilot said, "My apprehension grew as I thought of our predicament. What was General Ent going to do—circle Ploesti to the north and try to bomb on the briefed axis?" Other Liberando pilots were equally baffled over what the command intent might be. No explanation was forthcoming from the flagship, which had reverted to radio silence. The cautious Ent was not going to announce his new objective on the open radio for the Germans to hear.

Across Ent's new course north lay Lake Znagov, where a party of German officers were swimming on their day off. Oberleutnant Hermann Scheiffele, adjutant of the Fifth Flak Division, assumed that the engine noise came from Heinkels on an unannounced test of the defenses. "Suddenly twenty or thirty bombers swept over us very low," said Scheiffele. "I clearly saw up through their open bomb doors and recognized them as B-24's." He and Leutnant Egon Schantz, armament inspector of the division, jumped in a car in their bathing suits and drove pellmell for Ploesti. When he saw the colossal mushroom of smoke over the Circus targets, Scheiffele said, "Nobody can be alive in that sea of fire." But he found that only the outlying tank farms were burning and that it was possible to drive into the refinery compounds. The quick-fused bombs were done exploding. In the sepulchral gloom, Scheiffele and Schantz saw big yellow time bombs scattered around on the grounds. A stocky, bespectacled man hailed the car—their commanding general, Julius Kuderna from Vienna. "Schantz," he said, "find out how these bombs can be disarmed before they explode."

The armament inspector rallied some fire police from an underground shelter and led them and the general behind a blast wall, saying, "Everyone else stay here. I am going to have a look at that bomb over there"—pointing to a thousand-pounder about

600 feet from them. He ran to the bomb, examined it, and returned. "It has a new kind of detonator that I have never heard of," said Schantz. "The nose has two separate screw turnings, one back of the other. I think one stops the time clock and the other sets off the bomb immediately. Schütz!" His best man, fireman Schütz, moved in close to listen over the roar of flame. "I am going to the bomb and remove the first screw turning," Schantz told him. "You remain here. If it is the wrong one, you'll know how to handle the other bombs."

Peering around the blast wall, Scheiffele saw Schantz kneel and examine the nose "for a long time." He saw the armament inspector "seize the first screw with both hands and turn it slowly." The nine-inch nose came off and Schantz ran back, holding it to his ear, exclaiming, "I can't hear the clock." The detonating system inside was a silent, acid-melting type, and, if it exploded, the effect would be that of a hand grenade. "Let me try to hear," said Scheiffele. He held it to his ear, waving off others who wanted to listen. "All right, that's enough," said Schantz. "Why, is it dangerous?" Scheiffele asked. The inspector said, "If there is a clock in there, you could be minus your head." He placed the detonator on the other side of the blast wall. General Kuderna said, "All right, Schantz, get your men organized to take care of the other bombs." The firemen, encircled in flame, roofed with smoke, dispersed to disarm them.

At the time the Liberando force had alerted this bomb team at Lake Znagov, the Circus was still struggling to deliver Schantz's bombs.

Hurtling nearer to the target city, the Liberandos saw through the haze on their left front an apocalyptic event taking place— the Circus fighting the city guns. The scene sharpened through Appold's windscreen. "Flights of three or four, or single planes, were going in different directions, streaking smoke and flames, striking the ground, wings, tails and fuselages breaking up, big balls of smoke rolling out of the wrecks before they stopped skidding," Appold said. K. K. Compton was nearing this slaughter at White Five. His new target was its neighbor, White Four, where the Liberandos faced the same ferocity of guns. "A few miles from Ploesti," said Compton, "we entered so much antiaircraft fire that General Ent decided that the defenses, now thoroughly alerted, were too formidable." Red Thompson, piloting the flagship beside Compton, got a dash of rain on his windshield, distorting the red-balled horror at White Five. He glanced at the general on the flight deck. Ent looked at his watch, went to the radio desk, and opened the group frequency. "This is General Ent," he said. "We have missed our target. You are cleared to strike targets of your choice."

The Liberando pilots, released from discipline, followed a common instinct to veer off east, away from the web of flak and blocking balloons. The formation came apart, scattering over open fields where there was only light infantry fire from the ground. K. K. Compton salvoed his bombs on what looked like a power or pumping installation. Many other pilots followed suit; there were no targets ahead and the sooner they got rid of the bombs, the better were their chances of getting back.

Appold, however, radioed his section, "Hold on to your bombs. We're going to use them. Hang on to me. Keep formation." He saw A Section making another sprawling turn, to the north, and turned hard inside them, his wingmen, Robert H. Storz and Lyle T. Ryan, hugging his wing tips. Barwell phoned from the top turret, "There are four planes still with us, Norm." Appold led them north at high speed, perilously low.

Ent's wandering Liberandos passed east of a large isolated refinery and Appold skimmed across the fields west of it. It happened to be their briefed target, White One, the Romana Americana refinery. Nobody recognized it from the opposite angle of approach. Even if they had, few planes had any bombs left.

White One was third in economic importance among the seven objectives of Tidal Wave, but it was first in propaganda value. Repeatedly the planners had told the airmen, "You've got to hit White One." The plant was owned by the Standard Oil Company of New Jersey. If it were not bombed, German Propaganda Minister Goebbels would have a sharp wedge to drive between the Allies, simply by broadcasting that the Americans had hit British and French refineries while sparing their own. Among the Tidal

Wave planners there were large stockholders of Standard Oil and in the B-24's there were many smaller ones, all intent on blowing up their Romanian holdings. But all the ships, including Appold's, blindly flew past White One and the great refinery fell behind, untouched.

General Ent instructed his radio operator to send a prearranged code signal to Brereton in Benghazi. It consisted simply of the letters "M.S." standing for Mission Successful. Few Liberando men could agree with that. Red Wicklund in the flagship, pilot William Zimmerman and John E. O'Conner, a gunner in *Chum V*, were heartsick. They had been to Romania with Halpro and had now missed the target a second time after perilous flights that would total 5,000 miles before they got home.

In the Liberando rear, pilot Myron R. Conn was carrying the legendary Ploesti stowaway who has not been previously identified but has inspired several romances of the great raid. The facts are as good as the fiction. He was an elderly squadron Intelligence officer named L. J. Madden, a "retread" from World War I. K. K. Compton had refused him permission to accompany the mission, but the gaffer slipped into a berth by pulling seniority on Conn. Both were first lieutenants, but Madden's commission antedated the pilot's by a quarter of a century.*

K. K. Compton's main Liberando body passed Ploesti and climbed the foothills northeast of the city. A single Romanian fighter approached, and frustrated Liberando gunners gave him a concert. The playboy jitterbugged to escape destruction and ran away. *Teggie Ann* turned west and the ships behind winged over and began packing up again. Small-arms fire was thickening and big flaks were banging away in the west. Red Thompson saw pink bombers coming down from the north on a convergent course. "They were evidently being led by Killer Kane," said the pilot, "at what I judged was fifteen hundred to two thousand feet altitude—nice fat targets for any defense. I was pulling up to get over cows and hedgerows."

At this phase of battle all order seemed lost. Tidal Wave's

---

* Madden returned safely to Benghazi and K. K. Compton chose to overlook the matter.

planned simultaneous strikes had become a mistimed farrago of groups entering Ploesti from several sides. The leading Liberandos were west-bound, north of the city, the battered Circus was reeling off the target through Ploesti streets, and three more forces were swooping down on the briefed target run from the northwest. And Norman Appold was about to skip-bomb from the northeast.

He had found a target of opportunity while his five-plane privateering force drove up the east side of the city. Among the targets flashing by he saw the last objective he could possibly reach, a plant on the north edge of town. "Looks like dry bones over there," he said. "Tabby, we're going for that target. Are you set?" The bombardier, Clarence R. Tabb, said, "I'm okay." Appold had picked Concordia Vega, Target White Two, which had been assigned to Baker, the Circus leader. Concordia Vega's stacks and silver balloons were silhouetted against the black smoke from Baker's pyre on the far side of Ploesti. Appold radioed his followers, "Let's tuck in now. Stay with me and keep close. Course two-three-oh. Out."

The orderly turns of the mission were plotted on a three-mile radius, but there was no time for that if he was to hit the refinery swiftly sliding astern. "The turn was hard on Ryan," said the little pilot. "He had been hanging on my left all the way. I climbed a few feet over him on the sharp turn and leveled out full throttle." A mile and a half ahead were invisible balloon cables and an unknown power of guns. Appold went in ten feet from the ground.

High on the black picture through his windshield, Appold saw green insectlike shapes coming straight toward him out of the oily clouds on the far side of the city. They were Ramsay Potts's survivors, groping out of White Four without suspecting they were on a collision course with another formation. Appold was committed to his bomb run and could do nothing about the green ships. He put them out of his mind to be dealt with a few seconds later. Now a swarm of blond insects came buzzing down his windshield from the high right. Killer Kane was lowering the Pyramiders through the northern flak to carry out his orders at

White Four, which Ramsay Potts had just set in lofty fires. Appold said, "I could not think about Kane's planes and the new dangers of collision. Directly in front of us, measured in hundreds of yards, was the target we had picked. So up, gently, the elevators for a smooth ride over the towers, and a shout, 'Tabby, let's get them all in there!' "

Tabb toggled the bombs and the other planes dropped theirs in unison—three dozen 500-pounders fused to explode in 45 seconds. But there was an immediate thunderous explosion, possibly caused by an air gunner hitting something volatile. The blast levitated Barwell in the top turret. Appold's "smooth ride" over the target turned out to be a big jolt that flung him over the stacks. Almost instantaneously there came a blast to the left that displaced the hurtling airships so smartly to the side that Barwell had "the unique experience for a top gunner of seeing our bombs alongside, still falling. They crashed into a large cracking plant."

In the upheaval Appold's compass fell out of its rubber shock mount and his radio was shaken to pieces. Just past the target, roof-top gunners fired into his nose, knocking out a waist gunner, blowing the aerial camera out of its anal position, riddling the left wing, and holing an empty bomb bay tank. Appold said, "I went into a right bank, trying to gain a few feet more of altitude. I put Storz, on my right wing, in an uncomfortable position. He slid down to the right and had to practically brush his wings on buildings to keep me off." Appold's five-plane improvisation had hit Concordia Vega hard. About 40 percent of its refining capacity was destroyed.

Now Appold had to avoid crashing into Potts and the last of the Circus. The two formations were closing head-on over the roof tops at a combined speed of nearly 500 miles an hour. Potts stayed low and Appold lifted a bit. Killer Kane's higher wave was almost upon them. The center of Ploesti was roofed with three layers of interweaving Liberators. In the open street below stood General Alfred Gerstenberg, in awed admiration of the galaxy of bombers maneuvering precisely at top speed without colliding. He had no suspicion that it was all a horrible foul-up.

Appold's wingman, Storz, saw a green airplane coming toward

him, "a hundred feet off my wing, low, and laboring hard. I was quite certain we would have a mid-air collision. As our courses were about to intercept, he entered a three-story building." Storz had seen the B-24 crash into the Women's Prison.

Appold's commando crossed the city and plunged into the billows rolling off White Five. From his smoke-filled fuselage came a shout, "We're on fire!" Appold steered due west. Fresh air, entering through battle holes, ventilated the ship. Nothing was on fire. Appold went to his usual altitude, "five feet plus," and asked Barwell to count his ships. The British gunner wheeled his turret and reported, "They're all still with us. They appear to have sustained numerous hits, but none seems disabled." Appold said, "I get a smell of hydraulic fluid." The engineer replied, "The whole hydraulic system is out."

North of the city there was another unscheduled cross-hatching of bombers. As K. K. Compton's reforming Liberandos drove west across the ravines, the Sky Scorpions came down from Red Target at right angles to them. No other Liberators were supposed to be within miles of the Scorpions at this phase, yet here were desert ships crossing their course and some of them dumping bombs into outlying units of the Scorpion objective. The Scorpions looked upon the Liberandos like men seeing pink elephants. All the ships avoided collision.

Appold nestled into a semidry river course, crouching under guns and radar, and his followers streamed behind, riffling stagnant pools and whipping brush along the banks. Barwell phoned, "Directly ahead, large stone bridge. Looks like a flak tower atop it." The observation was confirmed by orange fireballs skipping toward them along the stream bed. Barwell said, "Norm, could you drop the nose a bit?" Appold thought this "an unreasonable request, but I had learned that when Barwell wanted me to lower his gunning horizon, the favor paid off." He put the nose deeper. "The top turret clattered," said the pilot, "and there, without fail, we saw the slugs disintegrate the tower, gunners and all, from a distance of at least a half mile. It was over in four or five seconds. That was the maximum time I could maintain flight with the nose pressed down, and it was all that Barwell ever needed. I felt strongly relieved. We skirted the flak tower and eased down again, to begin what was going to be a long, lonely journey to base if our gas and luck held out."

The two finest aerial marksmen in the battle of Ploesti, Gamecock Hahn and George Barwell had neither one got a shot at an enemy aircraft that day. By taking to the river bed, Appold slipped his guerrillas past the Messerschmitts and sighted no hostile planes all the way home.

As Appold fled Ploesti, the Eight Balls and Pyramiders were plunging across the city from the northwest toward their briefed targets, which were now in a convulsion of flames and explosions.

Then let each man turn straight to the front,

come death, come life—

that's how war and battle kiss and prattle.

The Iliad, Book XVII

8

THE TUNNEL OF FIRE

It was now high noon. The battle of Ploesti was fifteen minutes old. The Circus and Liberandos had left three refineries in flames, and the two biggest forces of the mission, Leon Johnson's Eight Balls and Killer Kane's Pyramiders, were still coming. They had reached and turned the correct Third Initial Point on the northwest and were coming down astraddle the Floresti-Ploesti railway. As they passed over the force-landed Circus ship *Honky-Tonk Gal*, Robert Lehnhausen saw emerging from its right waist window "a fellow without a stitch of clothing."

The two groups coming in abreast, exactly as the plan required, were divided into three target forces. On the left was Kane, bound for White Four, then Leon Johnson with 16 planes, driving for White Five, and on his right James Posey, his deputy leader, guiding 21 ships toward Blue Target.

145

In the lead ship of the Eight Balls, *Suzy-Q*, piloted by Major William Brandon, the co-pilot was Colonel Leon Johnson, the group commanding officer. Johnson was a mild, snub-nosed Kansan with a blond R.A.F.-type mustache. Following graduation from Moline High School, he had gone to work in his father's bank. After seeing a friend in a U. S. Military Academy uniform, he went to West Point and was commissioned as an infantry shavetail. In 1929 he transferred to the Air Force because "things looked more interesting from the air." While the infant Eighth Air Force in Britain was shaking out commanders, Johnson was promoted group leader of the Eight Balls. He told his men, "I never expected this appointment. Frankly, I'd be suspicious of men who do not miss their former CO, and I expect I'll be resented. But I have a feeling we'll get along all right." They did. The Eight Balls followed their quiet leader in bombing a 5,000-mile arc around Hitler's Reich, from Kiel to Bordeaux to Naples and now to Ploesti.

As he sat in front of them on the target run, Johnson squinted hard through the lilac haze for his target, White Five, the Colombia Aquila refinery complex, whose six aiming points were only 310 feet wide, strung along a bomb alley 1,000 feet deep. Johnson could see nothing but a dark shroud hanging 2,000 feet high over his target heading. He was puzzled about it, but, pending a closer look, assumed that it was smog. Soon the dark curtain sharpened into focus and Johnson saw that it was not an atmospheric effect; it was a forest of surging black smoke with mangrove roots of flame. Someone had already struck his target.

Bombs exploded in White Five. Storage tanks jumped into the air. Pilot Brandon looked at Colonel Johnson with a critical, unspoken question: "Shall we turn back?" Johnson said in a calm, steady voice, "William, you are on target." The force drove on. The bombardiers in five waves of Liberators lined up on their pinpoint objectives hidden in the geysers of smoke and flame.

As Johnson and Kane faced the chosen ordeal, a series of magic boxes opened up on the railway that they were following to their targets. On a freight train speeding south the sides of box cars

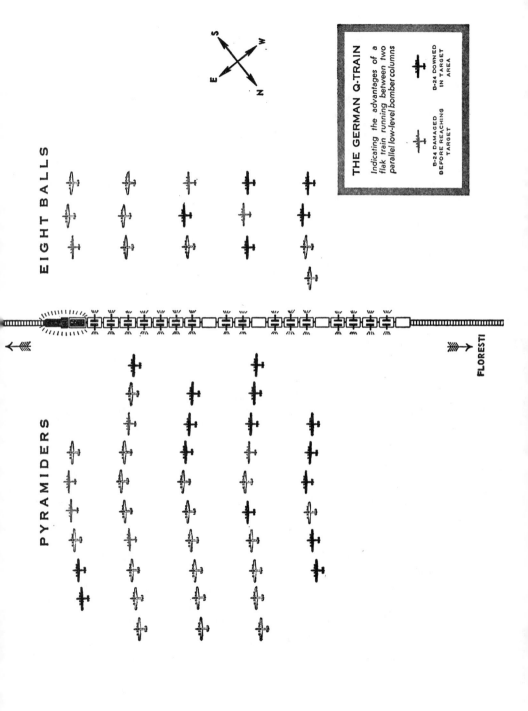

EIGHT BALLS

PYRAMIDERS

FLORESTI

THE GERMAN Q-TRAIN

Indicating the advantages of a flak train running between two parallel low-level bomber columns

B-24 DAMAGED BEFORE REACHING TARGET

B-24 DOWNED IN TARGET AREA

fell, and a line of artillery fired right and left into the flanking B-24's overtaking the train at virtually the same altitude.

The flak train was one of Gerstenberg's most effective surprises. It resembled a Q-ship of the First World War. Commanded by a captain, the Q-train was a string of prosaic-looking four-wheeled freight wagons, which contained bunk cars, a kitchen and recreation room, ammunition magazines and dozens of antiaircraft guns concealed in collapsible car bodies. This self-contained mobile destroyer could not have been placed in a better position. An hour or so before, when the predicted B-24 course spotlighted Floresti, the defenders had rolled the Q-train onto the line, and now it roared along between the two parallel bomber columns, firing into Johnson on the right and Killer Kane on the left. And the Liberators could not elude flak while holding on the bomb run. The air gunners enfiladed the train and blew up the locomotive, but not before it had hit some ships so hard they would not get far beyond the target.

Leon Johnson faced right into the seething wall of smoke. Seconds before he plunged into the holocaust there was a blast in the refinery of such magnitude that the updraft sucked the smoke high off bomb alley. The Dubbs stills and cracking towers were framed against a patch of blue sky beyond. *Suzy-Q* rode through a tunnel of clear, hot, turbulent air, arched over by crackling yellow and black clouds, and bombed her objective.

Johnson's flankers, *Bewitching Witch* and *Scrappy II,* hit their aiming points in the aerial cave and came out flying. The second wave, led by Captain Cameron in *Buzzin' Bear,* drove under the suspended fire cloud and ploughed their yellow bombs into the target. *Buzzin' Bear* came off at a height of 75 feet, with a rudder nearly shot off its hinges. Cameron's co-pilot, William C. Dabney, said, "Bill, we're too low. Pick 'er up a little." Cameron refused, and he won his point when two B-24's and a pursuing Messerschmitt crossed beneath them. The Eight Balls that had survived so far now entered the range of the guns southwest of Ploesti that had mauled the Circus. Waiting also were the roving Messerschmitts, IAR-80's, Me-110's and Ju-88's, all seeking cripples.

On Cameron's right wing, Charlie Porter Henderson was shot

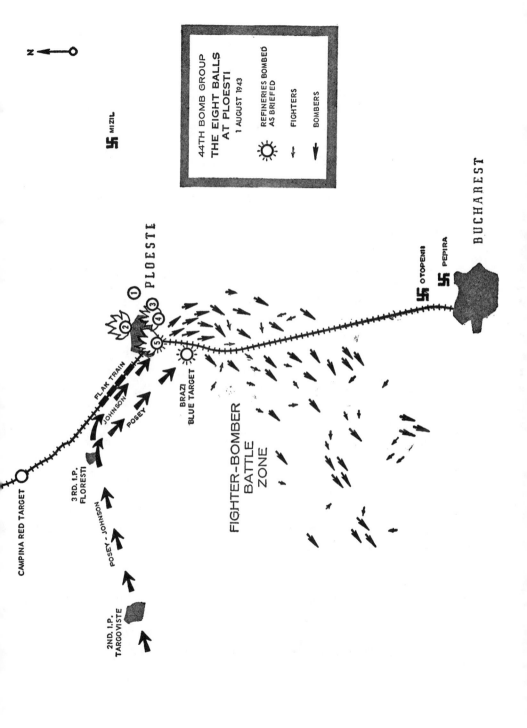

N

MIZIL

44TH BOMB GROUP
THE EIGHT BALLS
AT PLOESTI
1 AUGUST 1943

REFINERIES BOMBED
AS BRIEFED

FIGHTERS

BOMBERS

PLOESTI

BUCHAREST

OTOPENI

PEPIRA

1

3

2

4

5

FLAK TRAIN

JOHNSON

POSEY

BRAZI
BLUE TARGET

3 RD. I.P.
FLORESTI

POSEY - JOHNSON

CAMPINA RED TARGET

FIGHTER-BOMBER
BATTLE
ZONE

2ND. I.P.
TARGOVISTE

up by a JU-88, wounding navigator Robert S. Schminke and bombardier John R. Huddle. Radioman John Dayberry saved Huddle's life with a quick and efficient tourniquet while the ship was under attack by another twin-engined fighter. It drove in obliquely from the rear, cutting rudder cables and ripping up the tail. Gunner James R. Porter fell wounded. The top turret man, Harold Cooper, and tail gunner C. H. Confer hit the Ju-88, and Confer saw it strike the ground on fire. Another German crossed over them, dropping disklike objects which burst into flame but did not fall on the Liberator. Sergeant Dayberry tended the wounded and took Schminke's place as navigator to give Henderson a bearing for Malta.

The black crematory door lowered on the third Eight Ball wave, led by Worden L. Weaver piloting *Lil Abner*. He came out with three engines mangled and his controls shot away. Forty miles from the target Weaver could no longer hold in the air. He belly-landed near Visnia-Dombovitsa, and a wing tipped the ground during the skid. *Lil Abner* came to a halt with the nose rolled under the body, the bomb bay telescoped into the flight deck, and the engineer, William J. Schettler, crushed dead under the fallen top turret. The wreck burst into flame midships. Six men got out of the rear, but the pilots and the navigator were imprisoned in the cockpit. Weaver seized a crack in the windshield, forced open a hole, and wriggled out. As navigator Walter M. Sorenson followed, his parachute harness fouled in the opening, and he was stuck halfway out with co-pilot Robert R. Snyder trapped behind him. The flames spread forward.

One of the fuselage escapees, bombardier Lloyd W. Reese, Jr., went through the fire and popping ammunition and cut away Sorenson's parachute harness. Reese and radioman Jesse W. Hinley hauled both trapped men clear. The survivors split up and ran in opposite directions. A German fighter circled Weaver's party, "evidently reporting our position," the pilot thought. Weaver tried his Romanian glossary on a farm boy, who led them to a village. Women dipped feathers in a homemade balm and gently brushed their seared flesh.

K for King, commanded by Robert E. Miller, led the fourth wave into the dark and fiery target. "There was a hell of a lot of chatter on the intercom about flak batteries," said Miller, "but through it all I heard the voice of our bombardier, Robert Edwards, steady and cool even though we were enveloped with smoke and fire. One of our gunners, Daniel Rowland, got a direct hit in the thigh, which almost tore his leg off. He put on the tourniquet himself." The co-pilot, Dexter L. Hodge, said, "The way our gunners worked over the flak guys, I was convinced they were the best men ever to squeeze a trigger." *K for King* emerged with a two-foot gap in the fuselage, the top ripped open, a missing vertical stabilizer, oil gushing from the cracked hub of No. 4 engine, a shattered supercharger and the induction systems gone. In that state Miller and Hodge faced the 1,100-mile voyage back to Africa. Missing were the two wingmen who had entered White Five with them. Thomas E. Scrivner's ship came out in flames, with the pilots fighting for a crash-landing. They sledded into a wheat field, but before the slide was spent, the ship exploded in a hundred-foot sphere of flame. None of the men Scrivner tried to save came out of it.

K for King, with an engine afire, hedgehopped through twenty separate fighter attacks. Flight engineer William J. Murphy, Jr., cut off the gas on the flaming engine, pilot Miller feathered the prop, co-pilot Hodge recovered the ship, and tail gunner C. J. Ducote dueled warily with a Romanian plane that clung to him like a glider on a short tow. The Gypsy would not break off until he had learned how to deal with a bomber that refused to come off the ground and fight. The Romanian crept closer. When he came within a hundred yards, Ducote buried fifty rounds in him. The Romanian resorted to the textbook for high fighting. He peeled off, presented his armored belly to the rear gunner, and dived. "The next instant the woods for three blocks around were on fire," said Ducote.

The left wingman in the fourth wave was *Sad Sack II*, piloted by Henry A. Lasco and Joseph A. Kill, both of Chicago, flying their seventh mission. Riding the left waist gun with them was

Charles Decrevel of San Francisco, who had served in the Royal Air Force. Their story brings us close to what the red harvest of Ploesti was like for the men who went down.

DECREVEL.   Other planes were riding on black flak like trucks on a highway. We caught a hail of small-arms fire and something went through my thigh. I was strafing gun crews on a roof top and noted out of the corner of my eye that my interphone box was vanishing from the wall. I donned my parachute pack and stuck my head out the window. I noted a tree at eye level. Therefore I heroically decided to stay with the ship.

LASCO.   Our target was on fire, with very black smoke and fire high in the sky. Colonel Johnson headed into this conflagration and we followed.

KILL.   I wasn't paying any attention to where we're going except to watch a couple of rivets on the lead airplane. I glanced up ahead and thought, "How in Christ's name can we get through that?" I can't push her down, so I holler to Lasco to get on the controls with me.

The bombardier [Dale R. Scriven] is calling for corrections on the target—the boiler works and tool shed. The back end calls that the tail gunner [Thomas M. Wood] is dead. Scriv hollers, "Bombs away!" and the navigator [Harry W. Stenborn] is badly shot through the chest. Lasco shouts, "Number Two is out. She won't feather." And we hit the inferno, nothing but smoke and flame.

LASCO.   Coming out of the smoke we entered a group of six ships. Eighty-eights were firing at us at short range. The top turretman [Leonard L. Raspotnik] and radioman [Joseph Spivey] were hit. Joe Kill and I decided to head for Turkey.

DECREVEL.   A few minutes after we left the target, I began to wish I had jumped. I had grave doubts that anyone was alive on the flight deck. Wherever I looked I could see holes as big as my fist and our left wing was almost scraping the ground.

KILL.   *Sad Sack II* was vibrating badly and was extremely rough to handle. "There's a good cornfield over there," Lasco hollered.

DECREVEL. Seven to nine Me-109's were queuing up to take shots at us. They made level dead-astern attacks. The first one broke away and I caught him with a long burst in the belly at no more than thirty yards. He appeared to come apart like a dropped jigsaw puzzle. The next one was hit by Al Shaffer, my buddy at the other waist gun, who was standing on one leg, the other being almost shot off. The next Messerschmitt broke off on my side in a chandelle, and I knocked some pieces off his tail. My aim was off. The interior of our plane was full of little white puffs like firecrackers going off. Ammunition was exploding in the boxes and I felt fingers plucking at my clothing. I received shrapnel in the back, head and knee and was floored by a thirteen-millimeter in the butt. The parachute pack saved me in that area.

The fighter attacks seemed to subside somewhat. I don't know whether we had thinned them out or some had gone off looking for easier kills. There was one left hanging back about sixty yards or so with his flaps down and all his guns blinking. He really had to slow down for us. There wasn't much left in our plane but daylight. It felt like we were hanging in a total stall with one wing touching and all as good as dead.

LASCO. We were very low to the ground, probably fifty feet, when an Me-109 circled around us and came in shallow at ten o'clock on my side. I saw his wing light up and felt a tremendous sock on the jaw. I was shot through both cheeks and upper palate. I had no strength. I couldn't see anything.

KILL. Lasco called for flaps. No flaps. I reached down and started pumping them by hand. We were headed for a cornfield. I glanced up at Lasco. He was lying over the control column, all bloodied. I was coming to horizon level. We were left wing low, headed straight in. I kicked hard right rudder and picked up the wing.

DECREVEL. The pilot must have cut all his engines to crash her in, because I heard a scream. The navigator was kneeling on the catwalk and holding on to the open bomb door. He looked like he had caught an eighty-eight right in the chest. The flesh was stripped away and I could see the white ribs. I wanted to help him, but there wasn't time. We were all dead anyway. I had made up my mind to shoot it out with that sonofabitch on our tail. I leaned out the window and swiveled the gun parallel to the fuselage and fired inside the fin and below the horizontal stabilizer. We hit the ground and my last view of aerial combat was of our left rudder disappearing in a puff of smoke. I tumbled head over heels in flame and tearing metal and hit the forward bulkhead with a sweet black thud. Then immediate consciousness and a vision of green corn and blue sky from a bed of hot coals. No airplane to speak of, just a pile of burning junk. Stagger out of it, trying to run. Stop, look back. No Shaffer. Go back, drag him out. Dump him about fifty yards off. There's not enough airplane left to blow up, but ammunition is going off all over the plane.

KILL. Lasco was blindly thrashing around, pinned in his harness. All I could do was tell him I couldn't get out. Both my legs were broken and the right foot was out of the socket at the ankle. Lasco got loose and unfasted my legs from a tangle of wires and cables. He grabbed me under the arms and dragged me through a hole in the side. Then he wandered off.

LASCO. I went to look for aid as Joe's legs were bad and my mouth was in not too good shape. I saw some peasants, who ran away and threw stones at me.

KILL. Two peasants jumped me and tore off my watch and ring, emptied my pockets, and then belted me a beauty. I guess they figured I was about gone anyway, what with the legs, a cracked forehead and bad burns. Surprisingly, I didn't go out, although I prayed for unconsciousness.

DECREVEL. Drag Shaffer a bit further. Strip off my smoldering outer gear. Shaffer hollering like hell. His leg looks like hamburger. No morphine. I give him a cigaret, tell him I'll go for help. See an Me-109, having a look at me about fifty feet up. I give him a great big R.A.F. salute just for laughs.

Sit down, drag out my compass, maps and money, plan a course for Yugoslavia. Crazy! Shock wears off. I must get to a hospital quick. Burns hurt real bad in the hot sun. Have almost a full pack of cigarets. Must smoke them all up before the enemy takes them away. Get cracking! Keep walking! If you lie down you'll never get up and they won't find you until they harvest this corn.

Stumble into the edge of a village. Start hollering. Nobody appears, only eyes peeking through the window blinds. Holler some more. Crazy with pain. Stagger down main street, see sign, *Gendarmeri*. Holler real angry. Finally soldiers appear. I hold up hands and holler, *"Nix arme!"* Soldiers hang back. I drag out a dollar bill and hold it for the world to see. Ah! Immediate warm welcome and smiles. Total population turns out. Many questions. "Amerika komm? When Amerika komm?" Take me into village pub. Drinks for all. Only when they had spent all my escape money do they consent to get me aid. Out into the hot village street again. Fainted. Un-American? Too many brandies? Loss of blood? They fetch a horse cart and I ride in style. Feel like I'm dying. Don't want to die in horse cart. See nice farmyard with a big shade tree and pretty girl leaning over fence. Parade halts while I rest under tree and get a glass of milk from girl. Willing to die on the spot with pretty girl holding my head. Soldiers impatient to move on. News drifts in that more Americans are in a churchyard up the line. Parade from my village meets parade from next village. All hands into churchyard for gay festival while our top turretman dies.

KILL.   In the churchyard, Lasco was still in a stupor so I wrote out our names. For some reason I was thinking sharper than I ever had. I listed them all as officers and put an "O" in front of each name. This I had heard was wise, because it would give the enlisted men officer treatment in POW camp.*

DECREVEL.   Some hours later buses cart us to Bucharest military hospital. Sweet morphine at last!

LASCO.   The man in the next bed said, "My name is Al Shaffer. I am on Lieutenant Lasco's crew." I couldn't talk. I showed him my dog tags. "God, Lieutenant, I didn't recognize you," Shaffer said.

The last wave over White Five consisted of four planes led by Rowland M. Gentry in *Porky II*. His orders were to bomb from 400 feet at the top of the stepped-up formation that had been adopted for the five Eight Ball waves. The last wave was well

* *Sad Sack II's* sergeants spent their captivity in the officers' camp.

exposed to the German gunners. Gentry led a V-flight with a plane piloted by Charles Hughes and Sylvester S. Hunn on his left, and, on his right, George Winger, flying a B-24 that was unaccountably painted bright orange. It stood out among the others like a tangerine in a basket of limes and pears and attracted every German gunlayer who caught sight of it. Completing this vulnerable quartet was Robert Felber, flying a spare ship, *F for Freddie,* which had been added to the force the night before. Felber was alone, on the rear high left of the element, with the smallest chance of getting through.

Hunn saw waves three and four going in ahead of him. Two ships disintegrated at the same time. "Another was literally pulled to the ground by some force," said the co-pilot. "It didn't stall or drop off. It was *pulled.*" As Hunn's bombardier was set to release his bombs, Winger's orange ship was knocked aside by an explosion and crossed directly beneath him. The bomb-aimer held off until it had cleared him. In the target smoke, explosions killed two gunners and set half *Porky II's* engines on fire. E. C. Light in the top turret and the right waist gunner, Charles T. Bridges, remained in action. On the other side of the target three German fighters came up at them from the deck. Bridges, the veteran of 53 missions with the Royal Air Force, got in his last rounds of battle. The fighters left *Porky II* burning in a cornfield with the nose buried in the ground and the tail standing. Bridges staggered out of the wreck as it exploded.

The remaining three ships of the last wave came through still in the air. The orange ship was even brighter now. Its Tokyo tanks were aflame. Hunn said, "Winger climbed steeply to about five hundred feet. It must have taken him and the co-pilot enormous effort to get her high enough for people to bail out." Two men came out the waist ports and their parachutes opened as the orange ship crashed and exploded. Winger and his men had completed 27 missions and were legally "retired." The two chutists who had received the gift of life from their pilots were gunners Michael J. Cicon and Bernard Traudt. Traudt was a seventeen-year-old with a perpetual grin. He landed unhurt, concealed his parachute, crawled under some bushes and went to sleep. He had gotten no sleep the night before.

The Hughes-Hunn ship and the spare, *F for Freddie,* left Ploesti and their two crashed sister ships behind. They ran alongside some barracks from which soldiers ran out firing machine guns, rifles and pistols. The air gunners mowed them down in bloody windrows. *F for Freddie* was almost untouched, but Hunn looked back in his fuselage and was surprised how bright it was. Ground fire had turned it into a sieve.

The withdrawal plan of Tidal Wave called for all the B-24's in the simultaneous bombing front on the White Targets to continue beyond Ploesti for five miles and then wheel sharply right and take up orderly course formation to the southwest and Corfu. Leon Johnson had not the slightest opportunity to execute this order. His surviving machines were all over the air, dodging fighters and flak, or crippled and dying. By now there were about 125 enemy fighters in the immediate area of the turning point for withdrawal. Among them was young Gerhartz, who sighted a covey of Liberators "very fast, very down." As he lined up behind them, he noted that his fuel exhaustion light was on and looked at his chronometer. He had been aloft for an hour on an hour's fuel allowance. He turned and skimmed back across the fields to Mizil, not daring to climb, expecting to stall and belly-land any minute. Nearing his home sheep pasture, he lowered his wheels. As they touched earth the motor coughed out. Gerhartz rolled on momentum almost to his revetment. His dog ran to the plane.

Hans Schopper picked up a bomber flying 150 feet from the ground and assailed her from the rear high right, simultaneously pressing his cannon button on the control stick and squeezing the machine trigger. "I got him good in the right wing," said the veteran. "I gave the whole plane a good raking, and swept over top of him. His machine guns were after me, coming close, but not hitting. I full-powered a steep banking climb to the right and looked over my shoulder to see if another attack was necessary. Both of his wing tanks were blazing. He tried to gain altitude. He flew on about five hundred meters, crashed, and burned in a field. Nobody had time to jump. Apparently he had dropped his bombs. There was no explosion."

B-24 pilot Sylvester Hunn said, "We looked for a plane to tack on to. We picked one and he was shot down. We picked another and he was knocked down. A fighter got on our tail. Tracers were zooming above and around the cockpit. Hughes and I were giving it all the left rudder we could in evasive action. Our tail gunner reported the attacker suddenly hit the ground like a ton of brick. The gunner didn't claim him." Hunn, a hundred feet from the ground, saw a Liberator bisecting his course fifty feet below with a fighter in hot pursuit. "The B-24 dropped lower and the fighter went into the ground up to his neck." Hughes sailed into the sanctuary of a cloud and surveyed their situation: not enough gas to reach Libya, a large hole in the left stabilizer, a control cable hanging by a thread, and waist gunners Stanley G. Nalipa and Robert L. Albine wounded. They headed for Turkey.

Leon Johnson lost nine of his sixteen Liberators in the battle. He left behind a full measure of destruction. The combined weight of his and Addison Baker's earlier bombs on White Five totaled "the most destruction" of any Tidal Wave objective, according to later surveys. Although not totally erased, Colombia Aquila refinery was out of production for eleven months.

Vous avez mis le doigt dessus, mon Commandant.

9

THE COUP DE MAIN

The Eight Balls were assigned two separate objectives that day. As Leon Johnson struck White Five, B Force, a larger column of his 44th Bomb Group, was to hit Blue Target—the isolated Creditul Minier refinery at Brazi, five miles south of Ploesti on the highway to Bucharest. This formation of 21 ships was led by a West Pointer, Colonel James T. Posey of Henderson, Kentucky. His target was the most modern high-octane aviation fuel producer in Europe.

Posey's experienced detachment was called upon to place its bombs with utmost refinement on eleven aiming points. The target plot of a single plane, for instance, reduced its task to hitting "the near wall of Building G." No more meticulous bombing task had been given since Stalingrad, where Russian youngsters in tiny, slow biplanes were sent into the city to throw bombs into certain rooms of buildings that contained Germans, without hitting Russian soldiers in adjacent rooms.

Posey's bombing course lay three miles west of Ploesti, so that he did not have to fly into the furnaces Johnson and Kane were going through on his left. Strangely enough, twenty minutes earlier many Circus ships had flown past Posey's refinery without

159

dropping a single bomb on it. Thus the attack on Blue Target was what the planners had envisioned for all the strikes: every aircraft that had been dispatched running on a virgin target, with flak and the element of surprise the only unknowns. The flak was the same resolute stuff that had savaged the Circus, and surprise had been lost. Nonetheless, what James Posey and his men did to Blue Target was a justification of Jacob Smart's heretical low-level plan.

Posey's lead ship, *V for Victory,* was piloted by a 29-mission man, John H. Diehl. The first wave of five planes was formed like a spread "M." Following them were three more M-shaped waves of Liberators. Drumming closer to the target, Posey saw ribbons of artificial smoke dribbling across the refinery, but this was trivial compared to the inferno he could glimpse over at White Five. Alongside the speeding column a 37-mm. gun knocked off part of Posey's tail and killed a waist gunner, Truitt Williams.

In the greenhouse the target-finding bombardier, Howard R. Klekar, peered into the converted gunsight he had been given to aim the bombs and wondered if he would ever be a married man. He was engaged to a member of the Women's Royal Air Force in Britain and he and his fiancée were in the four-month cooling-off period imposed by the U. S. command to stem a wave of impulsive Anglo-American unions. Next to the preoccupied Klekar, the navigator, Robert J. Stine, was fighting the battle of his life—his twin fifties against two batteries of Bofors crouched low on a tower dead ahead and hurling destruction into B Force. The flak men had dealt with the Traveling Circus and their blood was up. Stine and the top turret man of *V for Victory* "swept those eight guns clear," according to Posey. "If the Bofors had continued, a lot more men following us would not have come through."

The ship on Posey's right, piloted by Eunice M. Shannon and Robert Lehnhausen, joined the barrage the lead planes were laying down ahead. "A heavy burst pitched some flak gunners from a platform," said Lehnhausen. He triggered two fixed guns in the nose. One shell came out and the guns jammed. "It was the only round I had the opportunity to fire at the enemy during the war," he said.

The first wave was now on target. Diehl climbed *V for Victory* to 250 feet to clear refinery stacks, and Klekar released his bombs into the aiming point. On the other side, Diehl dived back to the earth. His wingman, *Flak Alley*, piloted by David W. Alexander, dived with him, damaged by small-arms fire. "We left at a very low level," said Alexander. "People ask me what I mean by low level. I point out that on the antennas on the bottom of my airplane I brought back sunflowers and something that looked suspiciously like grass." Parallel to Posey, Captain W. T. Holmes, the grounded operations officer who had assigned himself to the mission, crossed Creditul Minier, carrying tail gunner Patrick McAtee in his Sunday uniform. The sergeant got no opportunity to impress the Germans with his costume. He went back to Benghazi without losing the crease in his trousers.

The second wave, led by Reginald Phillips and Walter Bunker, bombed its aiming points in Blue Target. Holding the center of their rank was an exceptional pilot, George R. Jansen, who had been accurately hitting low-level targets long before Jacob Smart proposed the tactic. Jansen was a former crop-dusting pilot from the Sacramento Valley in California. Jansen's pinpoint was the southwest corner of the boiler house. His bombardier was Technical Sergeant George Guilford, one of the eight noncommissioned bomb-aimers on Tidal Wave. Guilford, jarred by flak, toggled too soon. He groaned. The tail gunner phoned, "Direct hit! The bombs skipped into the boiler house." Guilford's three 1,000-pounders knocked it completely out of the war.

Another second wave ship, *D for Dog*, piloted by William D. Hughes, lined up on the U. S.-built Dubbs still, and bombardier George E. Hulpiau placed his three 1,000-pounders directly on the aiming point. "We were too low to miss," he said. "We were five feet above the target." He glanced toward Ploesti. "A flight of desert rats went straight into a cloud of fire and came out all in flames."

The third wave on Blue Target was led by W. H. Strong. He

bowled a thousand-pounder with a half-hour delayed fuse through the top of the powerhouse, and also hit a large oil storage tank. The fourth wave leader, James C. McAtee (no relation to Sergeant Patrick McAtee), had this same powerhouse as his objective. The oil storage tank Strong had hit was about to explode a few feet under McAtee's plane. Instead, McAtee noted, "the top of the tank just peeled off like a sardine can." His tail gunner, John R. Edwards saw the lidless cauldron boil over in flame after they were safely over it.

As Posey's ships left Blue Target, some airmen were screwed up to hallucinations. The radioman of *Princess*, Norman Kiefer, heard urgent shouts in the interphone. "Go back, Mac! *Mister Five-by-Five* just crash-landed back there! Go back and pick them up!" yelled the top turret man. The tail gunner joined in: "We can land and pick them up! The field is level. Go back, Mac!" McAtee hesitated and replied, "Shut up. We're not going back." (When *Princess* landed at Benghazi, her men found the entire crew of *Mister Five-by-Five* in the briefing room. McAtee shook hands with the pilots, Frank O. Slough and Raymond J. LaCombe, and confronted his two gunners with them. The sergeants vehemently denied calling on him to turn back. McAtee said, "How do you like that! You know, I almost turned around and went back.")

Posey's force did its work without losing a single plane on the target. But on the other side it entered the general misery of fighters and flak besetting Leon Johnson and Killer Kane's stricken and disoriented planes. It was a grand mêlée of airplanes trying to survive or shoot each other down or make formations or steer for favorable crash-landings. Hans Schopper, leading Black Wing of the Mizil Messerschmitts, picked out a sand-colored bomber flying southwest—"deep, very deep, not more than sixty feet from the ground"—and closed in on her. Suddenly he saw a black night fighter from Zilistea passing him, slamming bullets into the B-24's tail. He said, "The Me-110 passed under the bomber and turned up in front of him. He turned too soon. The Liberator filled him with lead and set him afire. I said, 'Okay, bomber boy, now I catch you.' I maneuvered into position behind the Liberator and improved my position before attacking. We were coming toward Rosiorii-de-Vede, about seventy-five miles from Ploesti. When he was nicely aligned, I pressed and squeezed. Nothing happened. My ammunition was gone! At that instant my red warning light came on. I was out of fuel—I must land quickly. When I got back to Mizil there wasn't enough petrol left to taxi."

Elmer H. Reinhart took the last plane away from Blue Target. With part of a wing shot off, he came out into "a crazy crisscrossing of ships," unable to catch up with any of the improvised formations. The Messerschmitts leaped on him. They shot away most of the tail turret, but George Van Son crawled out of it alive. The attackers incapacitated waist gunners Alfred A. Mash and Robert Wolf. The radioman, Russell Huntley, gave them first aid. The fighters left the bomber they had mangled but could not down. Engineer Frank D. Garrett reported: "Gas is pouring out of a hole near Number Three. The tunnel is a wreck. The tail turret is hanging by a thread. The left vertical and horizontal stabilizers are almost shot off. The left aileron is practically gone. There's a big hole behind Number One and oil is streaming out."

"I realized that we could never get back to base," said Reinhart, "so I tried to gain altitude." The crew put on their parachutes. The plane heaved and quivered from nose to tail. Reinhart managed to climb to 3,500 feet. Disintegration was at hand. Eighty miles from Ploesti, he turned on the automatic pilot and rang the bail-out gong. He stayed in his seat until the others had jumped, then went into the bomb bay and hurled himself out.

Reinhart floated down through an empty, sunny sky. The roars, the shouts, the explosions were over. The silence was emphasized by the drone of his plane, flying on, dipping its crippled wing. He saw no other chutes. He landed in a field of six-foot corn and hid his parachute. The ground trembled and a black column of smoke climbed over the corn tassels. His ship was in. He heard shouts in an unfamiliar tongue and ran several miles, thinking "how closely the corn, wheat and alfalfa resembled that of the United States." He ate some concentrated food and assembled a compass from two disguised suspender buttons.

In the disorder beyond the target, collisions were possible all over the sky, yet only one occurred among the 200-odd bombers and fighters milling around south of Ploesti. Carol Anastasescu, the debonair Romanian lieutenant, accidentally crashed into a B-24 and parachuted safely. The bomber evidently fell with a total loss of life, for none of the Americans who survived mentioned colliding with a fighter.

Rowland Houston, from the first wave over Blue Target, joined the end of an assembling formation. Willie Steinmann, who had shot down John Palm at the opening of the battle, was flying one of the Messerschmitts that pursued him. "The American machine guns were spatting all around," said Steinmann. The German ace picked out Houston's ship which was "about a hundred fifty feet from the ground. I attacked from the rear," said Steinmann. "I cut back on the throttle, slowed her with flaps, and gave the Liberator a good raking from wing tip to wing tip. I could see tracers walking across the width of the plane and flames coming out everywhere. The top gunner [Walter B. Schoer] and the tail gunner [M. L. Spears], particularly the man in the tail, were shooting me up. I closed to within seventy feet.

"My engine caught fire and there was a tremendous quivering. My speed carried me under the left side of the bomber, which was going out of control. The Liberator and the ground were coming together fast and I was in between, with no control. I had an instant to consider what would happen. The best chance seemed being thrown free in the crash. I loosened my harness and opened the latch on my canopy. I don't remember crashing. The first thing I knew I was seated on the ground with my pants torn and cuts on my legs. Near me the two planes burned. I got up from the ground and walked away."

No one escaped from Houston's ship.

Posey's perfect strike destroyed Creditul Minier. The refinery was out of business for the rest of the war. It cost only two of his twenty-one planes.

The Trojans worried Odysseus all around like a pack of grimy jackals round a wounded stag. You have seen such a thing in the mountains. A huntsman has hit the stag with an arrow: the stag gets away, and keeps good pace as long as the blood is warm and his knees are nimble: but when the arrow is too much for him, the carrion jackals tear and crunch him.

The Iliad, Book xi

10

KANE AT WHITE FOUR

The Pyramiders, the largest attacking force in Tidal Wave, reached the final Initial Point, turned it correctly, and began the run toward the biggest target—White Four, or Astro Romana, the most productive refinery in Europe. At the controls of the flagship *Hail Columbia* sat the beefy force leader, wearing a World War I doughboy helmet and an automatic, "to shoot my way out if I go down." John Riley Kane was the son of a Baptist parson at Eagle Springs, Texas. He had been reared on a farm, over which passed primitive planes flying air mail between Austin and Dallas. He had vacillated between careers in aviation and medicine. The smell of dissection rooms had finally decided him, and he entered Army aviation in 1931 at Brooks Field. Kane had a dissonant personality. His tough-hombre manner covered a sensitive, almost poetic core. He had a manner like General George Patton's. It has a place in war, which is not entirely waged by nice guys.

On the dash for Ploesti, Killer Kane took *Hail Columbia* down, and his first wave of nine planes spread into the bomb front to pick up the target lanes in White Four. He had briefed his men: "It would take an entire army a year to fight its way up here and smash this target. We are going to do it in a couple of minutes with less than two thousand men!" The Pyramider front was committed on a twelve-mile sprint at 225 miles an hour, with four waves following Kane. There were gaps in the ranks. Eight pink ships had already fallen out with mechanical failures.

Kane said, "Toward Ploesti the sky was the ominous black of a threatening thunderstorm. It would be our luck to arrive during a heavy rain, so that we could not see ahead of us. A flight of B-24's [Liberandos] passed under me. I thought I was low, but those planes were really low." Kane looked at his oblique target drawing to pick out the two tall stacks of White Four. Then "everything but the kitchen sink began to rise from the ground at us," he said. "I dived behind a row of trees and told the men in the nose to stand clear. We had to shoot our way in. I lifted over the trees and opened up with the fixed front guns. My tracer streams glanced off the ground a mile ahead. I saw natural-looking haystacks unfold like daisies, with guns spouting fire at us. On our right a flak train moved full speed down the track with guns belching black puffs at us. They were shooting eighty-eights like shotguns, with shells set to go off immediately after they left the gun barrels. A sprinkle of rain spread a film of water over the windshield." The nose guns jammed. Kane yelled at his navigator, Norman Whalen, "Clear the guns!" Whalen, who was knee-deep in shell casings, replied, "You shot up all the ammo." Kane had passed 2,400 rounds through the guns in a hundred seconds.

Now Kane came close enough to the shadow over Ploesti to see that it was not rain but smoke. His target was burning from Ram-

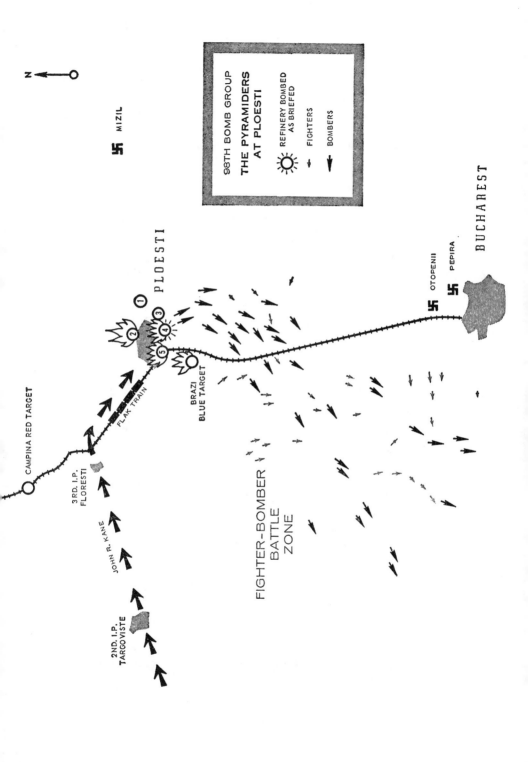

N

MIZIL

98TH BOMB GROUP
THE PYRAMIDERS
AT PLOESTI

REFINERY BOMBED
AS BRIEFED

FIGHTERS

BOMBERS

PLOESTI

① ② ③ ④ ⑤

CAMPINA RED TARGET

3RD. I.P.
FLORESTI

FLAK TRAIN

JOHN R. KANE

2ND. I.P.
TARGOVISTE

BRAZI
BLUE TARGET

FIGHTER-BOMBER
BATTLE
ZONE

OTOPENII

PEPIRA

BUCHAREST

say Potts's attack twenty minutes earlier. Group commanders had been instructed before take-off that if they could not reach their objectives they should radio the word "crabapple" to Benghazi, announcing that they were turning away. Killer Kane would not send the signal. He sped on toward the volcano. In *Tagalong*, a plane on his left flank, a shell from the flak train killed radioman Paul Eshelman. The Q-train scored a direct hit on Kane's wingman, *Hadley's Harem*, blowing off most of the greenhouse, killing bombardier Leon Storms, and wounding navigator Harold Tabacoff. Pilot Gilbert B. Hadley was unable to deliver his bombs because of the death of his bombardier and the destruction of the bombsight. Hadley ordered his engineer, a Rygate, Vermont, cattle buyer named Russell Page, to release the bombs manually. The combination of air currents through the open nose and a new strike from the flak train on No. 2 engine almost spun *Hadley's Harem* into the ground, but Hadley and co-pilot James R. Lindsey held the ship up.

Manfred Spenner, leading ten Me-109's of Yellow Wing over the northern outskirts of Ploesti, happened upon Killer Kane's target run. It was one of the few occasions in the battle on which the Germans were able to locate bombers before they reached the target. "The bombers were about seven hundred feet high," said Spenner. "I started to attack the lead Liberator, closing at less than a right angle with a dive. I would not say it was the lead of all the desert-colored planes, but it was at the head of a wave. The bomber I intended to attack suddenly exploded and disintegrated in front of me, hit by flak, not by me.*

The first wave of the Pyramiders dived into the smoke, Kane so low that *Hail Columbia* was wrapped in flame that singed the hair off his left arm. His co-pilot, John Young, called, "Number Four is hit." Kane feathered the engine and stepped up power on the other three. The bombardiers delivered their bombs into crackling flame. The cyclonic updrafts from White Four wafted thirty-ton bombers like cinders of paper. Samuel R. Neeley's B-24

---

* The sole Pyramider flight leader shot down was Wallace C. Taylor, fronting the fifth wave.

hit a balloon cable, which did not break. The bomber climbed the cable until it struck a contact bomb which removed a wing. The plane fell and the balloon soared.

Neeley's companion ship, *Tagalong*, piloted by Ralph V. Hinch, plunged on with its dead radio operator. As Stanley J. Samoski dropped his bombs, German shells hit *Tagalong*. Waist gunner Delmar Schweigert said, "They knocked out one motor, then got us in the tail, and another motor was gone. We crashed in a cornfield." He and gunners Robert E. Coleman, Harry G. Baughn, Robert Mead and Donald G. Wright left by the rear bottom escape door. Schweigert found the co-pilot, Charles Barbour, on the ground with his clothes completely burned off, and dragged him away before *Tagalong* exploded. German soldiers marched the sergeants away. "I never saw Lieutenant Barbour again," said Schweigert. The co-pilot died, along with Lieutenant Hinch, bombardier Samoski, and navigator James G. Taylor.

Major Herbert Shingler led the second Pyramider wave over White Four, with Robert Nicholson piloting the B-24 on his left. Nicholson's bomb-aimer, Boyden Supiano, was hit in both legs as he dropped his bombs, and his companion, navigator Oscie K. Parker, was wounded in the arm. Shattered pipes showered hydraulic fluid into the forward compartment, and a fire started. Supiano and Parker thrashed around in the slippery fluid and their own blood to get the fire extinguisher working. They doused the fire but could not stop the flow of CO^2 and nearly smothered in rising billows of foam.

Dwight Patch, on his third combat mission, flew *Black Magic* in the second wave, with co-pilot John C. Park. They neared the burning refinery in propeller-wash so turbulent that "it was all we could do to keep from flying into the ground," said Patch. "We had full control cranked in, everything shoved to the firewall." *Black Magic* had been ordered to bomb from an altitude of 200 feet, but Patch saw planes at that height being blasted to bits. He chose to go in at flame level instead. *Black Magic* bombed and came out of the conflagration. Patch saw John B. Thomas' plane directly ahead. The positions of the two ships exemplified the buffeting that the formations took over the refineries. Thomas had gone into the target two waves behind Patch and came off of it ahead of him.

Thomas received a direct hit in the cockpit and his craft began a faltering climb, drifting back into Patch's flight path. It slid by so close that Patch glimpsed "in the black, smoke-filled turret, ammunition exploding like popcorn." Thomas's ship crashed left wing first and disintegrated. Its co-pilot, David M. Lewis, was one of Patch's closest friends. One man got out of the crash alive —the navigator, Robert D. Nash.

The flak men hit *Black Magic* heavily. Patch still had good control, so he went as low as he dared. "I almost knocked a machine gunner off a hay wagon," he said. From his fuselage three wounded gunners, John A. Ditullio, Joseph J. McCune and Ellis J. Bonorden cried for help. Navigator Philip G. Papish, who had been a veterinary surgeon in peacetime, expertly treated them and administered morphine. Bombardier William Reynolds took up a post between the waist guns, ready to defend *Black Magic* from fighter attack on either side.

During the bomb run the Q-train knocked out an engine on *Boilermaker II*, piloted by Theodore E. Helin and Charles E. Smith. Another motor caught fire. On reduced power, with his heavy load, Helin realized he could never clear the high stack of the cracking plant. He ordered the crew to throw out a full bomb bay tank. Four hundred more gallons of gasoline entered the conflagration. Helin's quick decision paid off in every way. He managed to bomb and the lightened ship heaved over the chimney. Radioman Harry C. Opp phoned the pilot, "Number Two and Number Three are shot out. I believe another is running wild. The left wing tank is on fire." There was no reply. The interphone was destroyed. Opp went forward and yelled the news to the pilot. Without brakes, ailerons or nosewheel, Helin and Smith put *Boilermaker II* down on two wheels in a cornfield. The wing tank flames crackled toward the fuselage, but there was no longer a full Tokyo tank there to turn the plane into a ball of fire. Every man in Helin's ship got out alive, with only one wounded. The thing was done so neatly that engineer Arthur W. White described his Ploesti experience in full as "nothing remarkable."

However, another flier in the second wave went through a spate of remarkable events that day. He was a good-looking, perceptive native of Chattanooga, Tennessee, named Lewis N. Ellis, the pilot of *Daisy Mae*, an old war horse with 56 missions by previous crews. As he neared the ignited refinery looking for his aiming point, the left end of the boiler house, Ellis heard his bombardier, Guido Gioana, say, in a matter-of-fact fashion, "We're headed straight for our building. Be sure you pull up in time." Ellis and co-pilot Callistus E. Fager drew back their control columns, held the climb for a few seconds, and pushed forward, barely clearing the chimneys. As *Daisy Mae* entered the smoke, Gioana bombed, and Ellis felt things clutching at his wings. He was probably snapping guy wires on refinery stacks. In a patch of better visibility he saw a ship on his left smashing into a storage tank. It had waited too long to pull up. Burning pieces of the plane flew around, and among them Ellis saw men sailing through the air.

Ellis burst from the black clouds into the light. "It's a miracle!" he thought. Tail gunner Nick Hunt had a more mundane reaction. "Look at that oil burning!" he phoned. "And to think this time last year I was working a gas station!" The crew reported the damage to *Daisy Mae*: No. 3 engine smoking, nosewheel destroyed, hydraulic fluid pouring into the bomb bay, top and tail turrets wrecked, and flak holes spread over her. Yet no one had been seriously injured and the plane was still flying.

Ellis looked around for his sister ships. "The *Cornhusker* is gone," he said. "*Lil Joe* isn't here, or *Semper Felix*. I don't see *Old Baldy* or *Air Lobe*. Where's *Vulgar Virgin*?" He could guess their dispositions from planes falling before his eyes. One climbed, stalled, and spun in. Another erased itself in a long flaming skid. A twin-engine fighter dropped in flames.

Major Julian Bleyer took the third wave into the smoke, carrying the only trained motion picture cameraman to fly Tidal Wave, Sergeant Jerry J. Joswick. Other members of his combat camera unit had been ordered from the ships before take-off. Many planes carried automatic cameras, which were started, if at all, by busy untrained gunners, so that professional annotation of places and events in the pictures was not brought back except by Joswick. As Bleyer's ship vaulted through the target smoke, his right waist gunner, Frank B. Kozak, dimly saw Clarence W. Gooden's plane lurch toward him. "I could see Gooden working the controls," said Kozak, "and power his plane into a refinery building to shorten the war. The building, the plane and the crew exploded together."

A moment later Kozak saw Lawrence E. Murphy's Liberator crash into a cracking plant. All three right-hand ships in Bleyer's blinded wave were wiped out. The last was the extreme wing ship, piloted by Lawrence Hadcock, which plunged into a refinery building, raising fresh flame and showers of rubble. A top turret gunner of third wave, James E. Callier, left the target unable to see out of his dome for smoke. "It took some time before it cleared," he said. Air pouring through the shell holes cleared the fuselage. The gunners stared at each other. Their faces were blackened like minstrel men and the tawny planes were painted with oil smoke.

The fourth wave, led by Delbert H. Hahn, flew into the black boil over White Four and again the three right-flank aircraft were destroyed—the machines piloted by John J. Dore, Jr., John B. Thomas and Lindley P. Hussey.

Hussey's men of *Lil Joe* had gone to the target aware that they would not get back to Africa because of the gas leak during the sea leg of the journey. They had tried to get rid of the fume-filled tank, but it was too big for the smaller bomb doors of the old model B-24 they were flying. A German shell hit the perverse tank and *Lil Joe* burst into flame. Hussey climbed steeply to let men parachute. *Lil Joe* got up to 75 feet and stalled. Eight men bailed out at that altitude. Three landed alive with many fractures: Sergeants Ray Heisner, Joseph Brown and James Turner. Pilot Hussey and his radioman, Edmond Terry, a former golf professional from California, remained in the falling plane. After two days of unconsciousness Hussey awakened in a hospital. He had a fractured skull, seven broken ribs, a broken shoulder, flak wounds in his legs, and one side of his face was caved in. Sergeant Terry was almost as badly battered, but also alive. Hussey was told that Romanians had marched him and Terry three miles to an aid station in this condition, but he remembered nothing of the walk.

The plane next to the three right-flank victims was an old pink one named *Wahoo*, manned by novices from the Sky Scorpion group who had arrived at Benghazi by Air Transport Command and begged for a plane. On the target run, radio operator Anthony T. Fravega of Memphis, Tennessee, stood in the open bay to see that the bombs fell. He climbed up behind the pilots for a moment to see what was ahead. He said to himself, "We can never get through this." He wordlessly touched the pilot's shoulder and got back down. The pilot was his brother, Thomas P. Fravega. Since enlistment they had insisted on going to war together.

Anthony saw *Wahoo*'s bombs drop out. His brother hurdled the refinery stacks, pressed low and ran at top speed across the ground. Anthony put on his headset and heard, "This is Killer Kane. Anybody that's hurt, go to Turkey!" However, Thomas Fravega was not ready for that remote decision. He merely wished to put Ploesti behind as rapidly as possible. He drove *Wahoo* at 225 mph, so long that Anthony called to him, "The engines are going to blow their heads off!" Thomas climbed to 3,000 feet and reduced his power settings. One of the slow German biplanes that had been sent up to avoid being bombed on the ground had the misfortune to be in his path. *Wahoo*'s gunners shot the old crate down.

Fravega joined two other Liberators and asked his crew for an assessment of their damages. Flight engineer Oscar McWhirter reported, "Lieutenant, I can't find a dang thing wrong with this ship, except that we got four hundred gallons of gas in a Tokyo tank that we can't get at. The fuel transfer pump is out." The pilot said, "Well, we've got to have that gas or we won't get back." Anthony Fravega and McWhirter tinkered with the transfer pump but could not repair it. They disconnected the hose and let the engine suck at the tank. This seemed to work. *Wahoo* took up course for Corfu.

The bloody business at White Four was not over. The fourth Pyramider wave passed out of the flickering night over the target into the sights of Manfred Spenner's Yellow Wing of Messerschmitts. The German ace saw "fighters and bombers flying in all directions, flak coming up, balloons going down." He spotted a Liberator whose pilot had not yet appreciated the security of the earth and was leaving the target at an altitude of 1,300 feet. Spenner circled for his tail and attacked through heavy fifty-caliber fire from its top and tail gunners and those of another bomber. "I hit mine good," said the German. "As I passed him I could plainly see the gunner at the right waist window. I looked back and saw the plane settle down without wheels, bump along and explode." Circumstantially, his victim would seem to have been a fourth wave Pyramider piloted by John V. Ward, which left no survivors.

Pilot Robert W. Sternfels of the fourth wave plunged into the target smoke yelling, "Here we go!" Gunner Harry Rifkin said, "We tore through a balloon cable and skimmed through the flames so fast we had no time to be scared." Their wingmate, a Colton, California, railway shopman named Leroy B. Morgan, came out with part of a wing ripped off by a cable. "The anti-aircraft made good with six direct hits on my ship," said Morgan, "which left about two hundred fifty holes and knocked out my hydraulics, oxygen, electricity and radio. I decided closest to the ground was safest." Both of these planes returned to base.

The fifth and last of Kane's waves over Ploesti had a short history. Six went in. One came out. It was the heaviest toll of any echelon in the battle. Only Francis E. Weisler's Liberator got home. Edward T. McGuire's wreck deposited three living men on the ground—Clark Fitzpatrick, James Waltman and Robert Rans. When James A. Deeds crashed, his co-pilot, Clifton Foster, and radioman James Howie were left among the living. Radio operator William Treichler was the only man delivered of August W. Sulflow's demolished B-24. Pilot Wallace C. Taylor alone survived his ship and the first question the Germans asked him was, "Where is Killer Kane?"

The remaining victim of the fifth wave shambles was piloted by John J. McGraw and Charles Deane Cavit, on their first combat

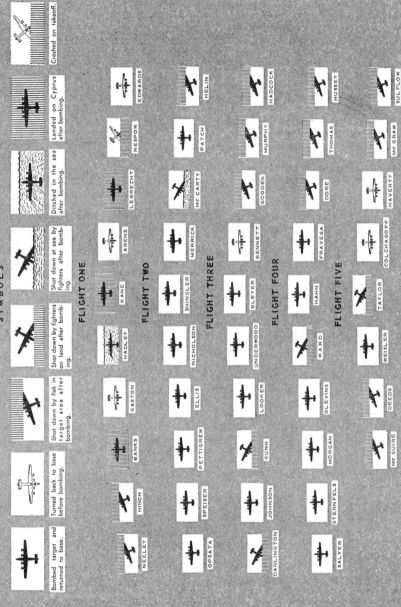

THE PYRAMIDERS ON TIDAL WAVE

Adapted from a sketch by Col. John R. Kane

SYMBOLS

Bombed target and returned to base.

Turned back to base before bombing.

Shot down by flak in target area after bombing.

Shot down by fighters on land after bombing.

Shot down at sea by fighters after bombing.

Ditched in the sea after bombing.

Landed on Cyprus after bombing.

Crashed on takeoff.

FLIGHT ONE

NEELEY | HINCH | BANKS | GASTON | HADLEY | KANE | ARENS | LEBRECHT | NESPOR | EDWARDS

FLIGHT TWO

OPSATA | SPEISER | PETTIGREW | ELLIS | NICHOLSON | SHINGLER | MERRICK | MC CARTY | PATCH | HELIN

FLIGHT THREE

DARLINGTON | JOHNSON | GUNN | LOOKER | UNDERWOOD | BLEYER | BENNETT | GOODEN | MURPHY | HADCOCK

FLIGHT FOUR

MORGAN | BLEVINS | WARD | HAHN | FRAVEGA | DORE | THOMAS | HUSSEY

FLIGHT FIVE

SALYER | STERNFELS | MC GUIRE | DEEDS | WEISLER | TAYLOR | COLCHAGOFF | HAVERTY | MC GRAW | SULFLOW flight. Like the Fravega crew, they were Sky Scorpions who had hitchhiked from England by Air Transport Command a few days before Tidal Wave and demanded a plane to fly to Ploesti. The Pyramiders gave them "an old junk heap" called *Jersey Jackass*. The proud fledglings removed old pieces of flak imbedded in her and scrubbed away dried blood. A tall lad from Philadelphia, Jack Ross, cleaned up the tail turret for his first war adventure and his last.

They got their bombs into the target, but the flakmen knocked *Jersey Jackass* to pieces. The pilots crash-landed the flaming heap and broke free. Farmers with pitchforks drove them to a German field dressing station. Cavit said, "Our uniforms hung in smoky tatters, and the medics thought we were Germans or Romanians until we spoke." Then the doctor in charge yelled in English, "You killed my wife and daughter on a raid in Germany! I order my men to do nothing for you." He gave his people a passionate speech in German about the bestiality of the two fainting Americans. In the midst of it tail gunner Jack Ross was brought in, hairless and seared black, but still on his feet. He held out his burned hands to be treated. The doctor grabbed a knife and said, "I'll cut them off." Ross jerked his hands behind his back and said to Cavit, "What have we got into?"

The pilot fell unconscious. When the doctor turned, Cavit snatched a bottle of ointment and treated McGraw's burns. A German sentry sidled over and handed him a bottle of water. "He was scared of the doctor," said Cavit, "but he wanted to help us." McGraw died, perhaps, as Cavit and Ross think, from lack of medical attention.

With one engine out, Killer Kane flew off target into the fighter battle, feeling "like a crippled fish in a school fleeing from sharks. My eyes burned from salty drops falling from my eyebrows." Co-pilot Young reduced power. "Why?" yelled Kane. Young said, "We must save the engines." Kane roared, "We'll save them after they save us!" He pushed his settings up full, but could make only 185 mph. Kane's was the last plane in a collection of about eighteen and he was falling farther behind. He could not hear any noise from his turret gunner and asked why. The bombardier,

Raymond B. Hubbard, said, "He shot all his rounds. He's sitting up there oiling his guns." The gunner, Harvey I. Treace, his features petulantly contorted, was trying to pull a stuck oil can out of his pocket. "And Hubbard and me laughing like crazy," said Kane. "It beats me how men can laugh under those circumstances, but, by glory, they do!"

Kane's other gunners were busy with fighters. "We took everything they had," said Kane "—five hits on an inboard engine and the underside of the right wing. The main spar was buckled." The Germans shot the tip off one propeller and put a two-inch hole through the blade of another. "The fighters were hanging on us like snails on a log," said the Pyramider leader. Three corporals who rode with Kane passed through gunnery school that day: Harry G. Deem, Jr., Yves J. Gouin and Thomas O'Leary.

Kane headed south, knowing that his afflicted machine could not get back on the planned withdrawal course. The distance to Libya was too great, the mountains too high. To the south there was a chance for *Hail Columbia*, in the lower passes of the Balkan Mountains. Navigator Whalen gave him the heading for Cyprus. Three other ships accepted Kane's radio appeal to make for Cyprus and followed him. One was *Hadley's Harem*, with nose shot off and a feathered engine. Another was *The Squaw*, piloted by Royden L. LeBrecht, which had come through little damaged from the flak devastation on the right column of the first wave, but was short of fuel. The third craft, piloted by William D. Banks, was in fairly good flying condition. Kane's *Hail Columbia* seemed the worst damaged. He diminished his airspeed to 155 mph and ordered his crew to unburden excess cargo. LeBrecht saw the air filled with objects and radiophoned, "What is this— spring housecleaning?" Kane was not amused. He was facing a 6,600-foot climb over the southern hook of the Balkans, and on the ascent could produce an airspeed of only 135 mph, which was close to stalling speed for an aircraft as hard hit as *Hail Columbia*. Kane told his men, "Throw everything out!" Into the slip stream went ammunition belts and cans, rations and precision tools. "Dammit, I said throw *everything* out!" roared Kane. The corporals ripped out oxygen bottles and gun mounts and pantomimed grimly at the windows with their parachute packs. *Hail Columbia* trudged up a mountain pass, clawing for altitude, feeling for updrafts. She seemed unequal to the climb. The plane heaved on, 200 feet lower than the top of the Balkan Mountains.

Kane's force had destroyed half the productive capacity of the largest oil refinery in Europe at the appalling cost of 22 heavy bombers. And a dozen other Pyramiders were, like himself, struggling hard to remain airborne.

Long, too long America,

Traveling roads all even and peaceful you

    learn'd from joys and prosperity only,

But now, ah now, to learn from crises of

    anguish, advancing, grappling with direst

    fate and recoiling not,

And now to conceive and show to the world

    what your children en-masse really are,

(For who except myself has yet conceiv'd

    what your children en-masse really are?)

            WALT WHITMAN, "Drum-Taps," 1865

11

RED TARGET IS DESTROYED

The last Tidal Wave group over the targets was the 389th—the Sky Scorpions, who had found their style in the stinging sands and clear skies of Africa. They made up a fervent, close-hauled, con-

179

fident organization. New to battle, they were the second generation of U. S. bomber schools, instructed by retired combat fliers
from Europe. The Scorpions doted on tight formations and equipment maintenance. Despite the fact that most of their ground
mechanics still languished in Britain, the air echelon, in its half-
dozen short raids in the Mediterranean prior to Tidal Wave, had
always put up more planes than were called for in the field order.
For Ploesti they lent nine crews to Kane for pink ships he could
not man.

Their objective was the isolated Steaua Romana refinery,
owned by the Anglo-Iranian Oil Company and located at Câmpina, nestled in a valley of the Transylvanian Alps, eighteen miles
northwest of Ploesti. It was known as Red Target. The assignment had drawn razzing from other groups. "You guys get the
soft one. . . . Away from the heavy flak . . . They must think
you can't find Ploesti." The fact was that Timberlake and Ent had
given the newcomers the separate target because the Scorpions
were flying new Liberators with a slightly greater range and Red
Target was the farthest objective of the seven. Some of Colonel
Jack Wood's planes carried ball turrets which set up a slight drag,
so that if they could not keep up with the simultaneous bombing
front over Ploesti it did not matter. He could bomb Red Target a
few minutes later without affecting the timing of Tidal Wave.

The ingenious Scorpions had devised their own bombing plan,
which Timberlake had approved. The critical part of Red Target
was only 400 feet wide. Its four vital buildings—boiler plant,
power plant and two still houses—lay in a diamond pattern. Jack
Wood proposed to cross in three waves, hitting each objective
three times with bombs graduated from one-hour delay on the
first wave to 45 seconds for Tailend Charlie. The first wave would
drive up over the diamond, hitting the lowest and side aiming
points and dumping overages into the top point. A second wave
would cross obliquely, hitting bottom and side AP's, and crash
overages into the remaining two. The third wave would repeat the
tactic from the opposite angle.

As the Scorpions descended to the Danube, Pilot Harold James,
survivor of the low-altitude training crash in England, asked his

flight engineer, Harold M. Thompson, for an estimate of remaining fuel. Thompson checked the gauges and reported privately to the radioman, Earl L. Zimmerman, the other man left from the training collision, "Even if we turn back right now, we don't have enough gas to reach base." Zimmerman said, "Don't tell the pilot until we get off the target. He has enough worries." The plane went on, burning up its chances of return. James was flying with a substitute co-pilot—his customary seatmate was one of the three men who had refused to fly to Ploesti.

The Scorpions trailed Johnson and Kane to the First Initial Point, Pitesti, where they swung out a few degrees northeast, as briefed, to climb the foothills above Red Target. Their turning point was going to be extremely difficult to pick out in the washboard of wooded ridges and ravines ahead. Wood's people had to lower into bombing altitude while the foothills were rising under them, a tricky matter of pilotage. Small mistakes in judgment of height could leave wrecks in the trees.

Wood's flagship was piloted by Captain Kenneth M. Caldwell, a senior command pilot with ten years in the service, but only recently come to war. Wood crouched behind him with a map spread on his knees, peering intently ahead for recognition points. The group navigator called up, "Can't see a single peak ahead, sir. There's a complete cloud cover on the mountain tops." Wood said, "Look for the monastery." They had been briefed thus: "When you pass north of Targoviste, the ancient capital of Romania, look for Monasterea Dealului [The Monastery on the Hill], a landmark that can be seen for miles around in clear skies." The navigator said, "Yeah, if we only had clear skies."

The miles were fleeting by. The monastery was nowhere in sight. Wood could not delay decision any further. In fear that he was overshooting the I.P., he decided to turn into a ravine that had to be the right one according to his time computations. As he turned into the valley he saw with relief that it extended along the correct target heading and that near the mouth there was a huge plant and town.

His deputy, Major Brooks, leading the second element, saw Wood turn and his heart sank. "They're going down the wrong valley," he said to his navigator. "We're short of the I.P. Colonel Wood has made a mistake." The meticulous Scorpions had fallen into the same error as the Liberandos and were turning short of their I.P.

Brooks had to decide instantly whether to obey standing orders and follow his leader on the wrong course or to continue straight on to the proper turning. He decided to stick with Wood. A few miles from the big plant, which was a cement factory in Targoviste, Wood recognized and rectified his error by an immense and perfectly executed maneuver. He doubled his twelve Liberators back in their tracks and S'ed over the next ridge, Brooks leaping behind him with his seventeen ships. Brooks said, "I learned a lesson in discipline. If I had left the formation, after he jumped the ridge my force would have collided head-on with his."

The tricky, miniature weather changed like a magic-lantern slide. The skies became transparent and the tail gunners saw the monastery gleaming in the sun. Down the next ravine lay the stacks of Red Target. The Scorpions tucked in tight and low, each ship in its slot in the three-wave surprise for Steaua Romana.

Hurtling down the valley, propellers threw up chopped leaves like lawn mowers. The fliers saw picnic parties; three richly caparisoned horsemen sitting like statues as the prop-wakes tossed their horses' manes; a small boy bolting in terror, then stopping and hurling a stone at them.

The flak batteries opened up. Machine-gun volleys poured into the first wave. Captain Caldwell steered Wood's ship toward the boiler house at the bottom of the diamond. He put the nose down and his co-pilot fired the fixed forward guns at flak positions. The top turret joined in. Its vibrations jarred bits of things down on Caldwell's head. Leveling for the bomb run, he wiped dust from his eyes. "Push up over the chimneys!" Colonel Wood commanded. "Go down to altitude!" pleaded the bombardier, John Fino. Caldwell went in thirty feet from the ground, helplessly looking at two guns firing into him from the top of a boiler house. He was thinking of nothing but delivering the bombs. His gunners shot the flak men off the boiler house, and Fino crashed a a thousand-pounder into it. The bomb, fused for an hour, did not

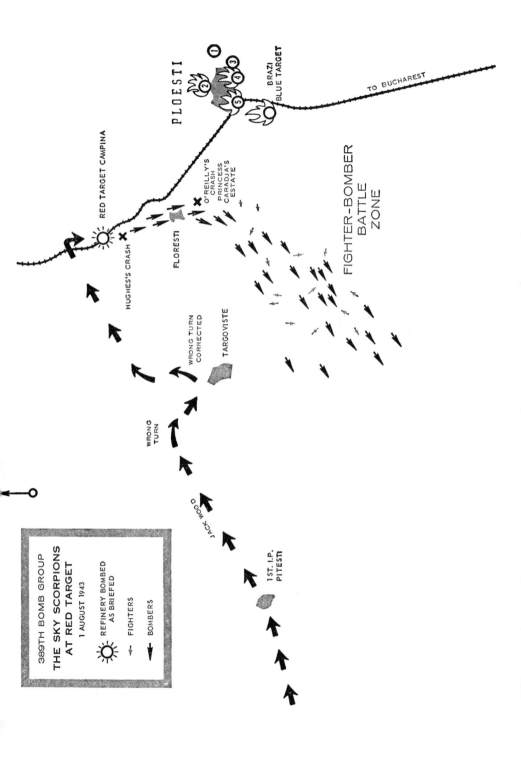

389TH BOMB GROUP
THE SKY SCORPIONS
AT RED TARGET
1 AUGUST 1943

☼ REFINERY BOMBED
AS BRIEFED

← FIGHTERS

↑ BOMBERS

PLOESTI

BRAZI
BLUE TARGET

TO BUCHAREST

RED TARGET CAMPINA

O'REILLY'S CRASH
PRINCESS
CARADJA'S
ESTATE

FLORESTI

HUGHES'S CRASH

FIGHTER-BOMBER
BATTLE ZONE

WRONG TURN
CORRECTED

TARGOVISTE

WRONG TURN

JACK WOOD

1ST. I.P.
PITESTI

need to explode. The boiler burst and the plant blew out, flinging up a fountain of debris.

Caldwell saw flames shooting out of the tallest chimney in the refinery. Fino put his remaining bombs in the secondary aiming point and began firing his nose gun, feeding it belts loaded successively with two armor-piercing, two incendiary, and two tracer bullets. "I saw a tracer carve a little hole in a storage tank," said the pilot. "It was a funny thing. A squirt of oil came out. It became solid flame, hosing out in a neat stream and spreading a big pool on the ground like molten iron. The tank got white hot and buckled. Then I lost sight of it."

Captain Emery M. Ward's Liberator, carrying B Force Leader, Major Brooks, whizzed across the burning target bearing the most secure and contented man on the mission—the tail gunner. He had been terribly airsick during the low-level rehearsals and *mal d'air* had returned as they reached low at the Danube. A sympathetic comrade, tunnel gunner Brendon D. Healy, said, "I'll take care of your guns till we get near the target." The sick man staggered forward and lay retching in the bomb bay. Healy became preoccupied with flak gunners and forgot to change places with him until they were well past bombing the power-house and boiler plant. He found the tail man snoring soundly in the bomb bay. Healy said, "I guess he's the only guy who got the D.F.C. for sleeping over Ploesti."

Lieutenant Stanislaus Podolak flew *Sweet Adeline,* named for his sweetheart in the Army Nurse Corps. He carried two gunners from Columbus, Ohio: Paul F. Jacot and Herman Townsend. A former aircraft welder, Richard Crippen, knelt in the rear escape hatch and photographed the target as they bombed the rear of a distillation unit. In the ball turret was Robert McGreer, one of the three privates who flew to Ploesti. Podolak was low on fuel. He asked navigator Gilbert Siegal to give him the heading for Cyprus.

Crews coming off the target saw Robert W. Horton's Liberator crash-land with wings aflame, and later reported, "there seemed no possibility that anyone survived." Yet, top turret gunner Zerrill Steen was alive. His turret remained in place on the impact and

Lt. Gen. Alfred Gerstenberg (left foreground) creates at Ploesti the strongest flak and fighter defense in the world.

Forty batteries of antiaircraft guns ring the oil refineries, awaiting the Americans.

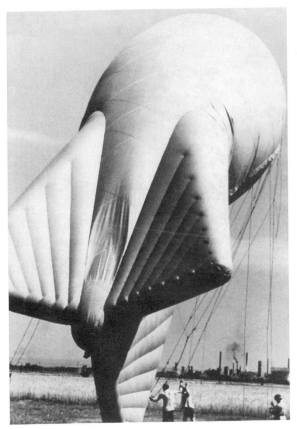

Part of the defenses at Ploesti are a hundred blocking balloons. Their tethering cables are strung with contact explosives.

Col. Bernhardt Woldenga commands Luftwaffe fighters in Romania.

Axis aces: From left, Romanian fighter chief Captain Toma with Luftwaffe pilots Hans "Gamecock" Hahn, Jack Rauch, and Werner Gerhartz.

In a ceremony to bless a new Romanian Me-109, German Gen. Otto Dessloch serves as altar boy. Flak defenses in Romania were nominally under his command.

Capt. Manfred Spenner commands the Luftwaffe's 3rd Fighter Wing at Ploesti.

Capt. Wilhelm E. Steinmann, German fighter ace, is the only German pilot to shoot down two B-24s over Ploesti on Black Sunday.

Left: Maj. Douglas Pitcairn was the Luftwaffe air traffic controller who identified the air raid and sounded the alarm.

Above: Lt. Hans Schopper, commanded Luftwaffe's Black Wing.

Left: Bulgarian fighter pilot 2nd Lt. Stefan Marinopolsky was unsuccessful against the Ploesti raiders.

Col. Jacob E. Smart (*left*) is given the assignment to bomb Ploesti by Gen. Henry H. "Hap" Arnold, chief of staff of the U.S. Army Air Forces.

THE ATTACK'S LEADERS

Brig. Gen. Uzal G. Ent is mission air commander.

Commander Lt. Col. Addison E. Baker briefs his 93rd Bombardment Group before the takeoff for Ploesti. His heroism would win him the Medal of Honor and cost him his life.

Col. Keith K. Compton of the 376th Bombardment Group, whose wrong turn would lead the bombers of Operation Tidal Wave into the teeth of the German defenses.

Lt. Col. Addison E. Baker, 93rd Bombardment Group commanding officer, promises he'll lead "The Circus" to target. He does and wins the Medal of Honor, but he and the crew of *Hell's Wench* die in the process.

Below: Col. Leon W. Johnson leads the 44th Bombardment Group— "The Flying Eight Balls." Another Medal of Honor recipient.

Above: Col. John R. "Killer" Kane, commanding officer of the 98th Bombardment Group, sets the pace for the three groups in trail. He wins the Medal of Honor.

Col. Jack W. Wood will take his 389th Bombardment Group, "The Sky Scorpions," to a target north of Ploesti—the refinery at Campina.

Maj. John L. Jerstad was Addison Baker's copilot in the *Hell's Wench*. He also received the Medal of Honor for his heroism at Ploesti.

One of the leaders of the low-level strike, Ramsay Potts, who rose in nine months from lieutenant to major and ended the war a colonel.

B-24 Liberators en route to Ploesti.

Erich Hanfland, 20, needs just seventeen seconds to reach his 20mm gun emplacement after the alert is sounded.

Left: Maj. Norman C. Appold recovers from the wrong turn by the 376th and leads a five–plane section that bombed an undisturbed refinery.

Right: 1st Lt. John D. Palm would break his *Brewery Wagon* from the errant formation and head for the target alone.

Below: A low-flying B-24's silhouette on the outskirts of Ploesti.

Euroclydon is the first ship to go down. Its navigator, Jesse D. Franks, bails out and is killed when his parachute does not open.

Over the flaming refinery at Ploesti, a B-24 is framed in smoke at the upper right.

Lt. Lloyd D. "Pete" Hughes kept his plane in formation although it was streaming torrents of gasoline. He "got off his bombs just fine" and nearly pulled off a crash landing. His Medal of Honor was awarded posthumously.

Photo taken by German medic Ewald P. Wegener of a burning refinery. Wegener, a Catholic priest who had been drafted, would attend many wounded American airmen and deliver last rites to some.

For pilot 1st Lt. Nicholas Stampolis and the men of the *Jose Carioca*, Ploesti was their first and final mission. Although their plane caught fire five miles from the target, Stampolis kept it on course, finally crashing in the refinery area but into a women's prison.

A B-24's sister ship crashes in flames.

Utah Man was sole survivor of the lead wave. Kneeling, left to right: Richard E. Bartlett, Ralph W. Cummings, Benjamin Kaplan, William Major, John E. Connolly. Standing: Paul E. Johnston, Joseph R. Doyle, Walt Stewart (pilot), Robert Timmer, Loran Koon (copilot), Robert L. Cox.

Hubert H. Womble's *Honky Tonk Gal* crashes into a field. All its crewmen become prisoners of the Romanians.

A wooden flak tower seen from a B-24.

Despite the difficulty of flying a bomber in tight formation at tree-top level, there were no collisions in the target area.

Blast walls protecting the refineries' vitals can be seen in this
photo taken from an attacking Liberator.

The Sandman barely clears the stacks of the Astro Romana
refinery.

In an epic flight, 1st Lt. Lew Ellis brought *Daisy Mae* home through three fighter battles.

The B-24 to the left of the smoke pillars is on fire.

Ploesti burns.

The Creditul Minier refinery, on Ploesti's outskirts, is hit by Eight Ball's B Force. It is Tidal Wave's most successful strike.

Liberators force their way through a tunnel of smoke and fire.

A distillation plant goes up.

1st Lt. Henry A. Lasco, Jr., pilot of *Sad Sack II*, and Sgt. James A. Brittain go down in the target area but survive.

Pilot Capt. Philip P. Ardery.

The view from the cockpit of a fourth wave plane as it plunges into the fight at Astro Romana.

Jack Wood's fledgling Scorpions sweep down an alpine pass to attack the Steau Romana refinery at Campina.

Chattanooga Choo Choo crash-landed on the estate of Romanian Princess Caradja, who helped rescue the nine survivors and kept them from the Germans.

Princess Caradja took care of "her boys."

Flames erupt from the distillation plant at the
Steau Romana refinery.

Germans survey the wreckage of a B-24.

Prince Charming's pilot James A. Gunn (*left*) dropped back to aid Julian T. Darlington's *The Witch* and paid for it with his life.

Greece-based Me-109s ambush four B-24s over the Ionian Sea, including *Here's to Ya* pictured here. Ralph McBride and all his crewmen are killed. Sixteen other Tidal Wave men downed at sea survive.

Liberator gunners strafe gun sites on the way out of the inferno.

Douglas Collins, "escapologist." A British sergeant imprisoned with Tidal Wave POWs in Romania, he had escaped eleven times since Dunkirk.

An enlisted men's volleyball game in a Romanian-run prisoner-of-war camp. The 121 Tidal Wave crewman captured in Romania found conditions in camps there to be relatively good, as many Romanians were not unsympathetic to the Allied cause.

Some of the officers held in Romania.

Finally back in Italy, Ploesti men are deloused: "You're back in the Army, bud."

Steen stayed in it, firing his machine guns at flak towers after the crash. He used up all his ammunition while flames converged on the turret. Steen broke out of the plexiglass dome between his guns and jumped through the fire. He ran, stripping off his flaming clothes. Romanians found him lying in a stack of hay and took him to a hospital. He was the only survivor of Horton's craft.

An American of Greek extraction, John T. Blackis, took *Scheherazade* toward a boiler house. His bombardier, Milton Nelson, phoned, "The bomb bay doors are jammed. The Tokyo tanks are stuck against them and they won't roll up." Blackis told engineer Joseph Landry, "Clear the bomb doors." Landry got down from his turret just as the flak opened up. Radioman David L. Rosenthal impulsively climbed into the turret, although he had no experience with machine guns, and started hammering the flak towers. Navigator Arthur H. Johnson reported to the pilot, "We can't get the doors open." Blackis said, "Okay, drop them right through the damn doors." Landry manually disengaged the bombs from the slings and they plunked through the bottom. Johnson said, "Coming off target we picked up cornstalks on the hanging parts of the doors." Landry found himself an unemployed top turret gunner. The radio operator was firmly in charge, by now dueling with fighters. Rosenthal was credited with destroying a Messerschmitt in his first gunnery lesson. *Scheherazade* flew the whole way home alone.

As Captain James rode away from a flaming cracking plant, radioman Zimmerman saw only one other B-24 going with them. "His bomb doors hung open and Number Three was stopped. It was Captain Bob Mooney. We flew right wing on him for many miles at low level. We gained a little altitude and Mooney's ship sent me an Aldis lamp signal: 'Pilot dead. Wounded aboard. Trying for Turkey.' I blinked him, 'We're short on gas. Will join you for Turkey.'"

In the other ship the pilot's head had been shot off by a 20-mm. shell. A long, gawky co-pilot, Henry Gerrits, was flying it while helping the bombardier, Rockly Triantafellu, pull the body from the left-hand seat. Gerrits was flying on three engines, and with five sergeants prostrated by wounds. Gas streamed from a hole in a Tokyo tank. Triantafellu covered the pilot's body and stuffed his leather flying jacket into the rift in the tank.

Crossing Red Target were a pair of fledgling second lieutenants, Pilot William M. Selvidge and co-pilot Bedford Bruce Bilby, on their fifth sortie. Selvidge remembers the mission as a "rather long day, most of which I spent looking at the flight leader on whom I was flying formation." Bilby did most of the close flying, since the element leader was on his side. "I think I was less concerned with getting shot," said Bilby, "than I was with keeping closed up. I was bucking to get my own crew, and I was scared to death I would be chewed out if I didn't keep it tucked in. I never did see our target, the left rear of a distillery, or where our bombs hit. My eyes were glued to the element leader during the bomb run." Scrupulous formation-keeping had its reward; they were not hit, and Bilby got his own crew five missions later.

Lieutenant Kenneth Fowble led the second wave into Red Target. Sitting beside him was the command pilot, Major Ardery, who had bumped Fowble's regular co-pilot, Robert Bird, out of his seat. However, Bird had insisted on going with Fowble to Ploesti and was riding in the rear, coiled in the ball turret.

The two planes bracketing Fowble were captained by devoted friends, Robert L. Wright and Lloyd D. ("Pete") Hughes, the last pilots to join the Scorpions before leaving the States. Before missions they would flip a coin to see which would fly the favored left-wing position on Fowble. The winner that morning was Hughes, a slight, dark-complexioned youngster with a gay smile.

As antiaircraft fire laced into them on the target run, Hughes was hit in the bomb bay tanks. In *Old Buster Butt*, navigator James H. McClain saw "a stream of gas about the thickness of a man's arm coming from Hughes's bomb bay tank. The lead aircraft of the flight ahead bombed a boiler. It exploded in front of us. Hughes stayed in formation." Ardery noted "raw gasoline trailing from Hughes's plane in such volume that his waist gunner was hidden from view. My stomach turned over. Poor Pete! Fine, conscientious boy, with a young wife waiting for him at home. He was holding formation to bomb, flying into a solid room of fire, with gasoline gushing from his ship. Why do men do such things?"

The waiting flames touched off the geyser of gasoline and Hughes's ship became a blowtorch. Fire streamed from the trailing edge of the left wing and from the top turret and waist windows, Hughes's comrade, Wright, said, "Pete got his bombs off just fine."

Beyond the target the burning ship slowed to about 110 mph, seemingly under control. The witnesses had the impression that the pilots were steering for a belly-landing in a dry river bed. McClain said, "Pete was doing a good job. The flaming plane came to a bridge and actually lifted over it. He came down beyond the bridge to land. His right wing caught the riverbank and the plane cartwheeled to its flaming end."

The other B-24's settled beyond the trees too quickly to see what was happening in the blazing creek bed. Hughes's last exertions had cheated death of two of his crew. Out of the fire came gunners Thomas A. Hoff and Edmond H. Smith and bombardier John A. McLoughlin. The officer died of burns but the sergeants lived.

Hughes was later awarded a posthumous Medal of Honor. The citation said, "Rather than jeopardize the formation and success of the attack, he unhesitatingly entered the blazing area, dropped his bombs with great precision, and only then did he undertake a forced landing."

The final bombs of Tidal Wave were deposited in the powerhouse and boiler of Red Target by *Vagabond King*, piloted by John B. McCormick. Sergeant Martin Van Buren* was kneeling on his chute to activate the K-2 target camera, when a shell burst under him. The chute stopped most of the fragments. As crewmen gave him first aid, Van Buren crowed, "Now I'll have one more medal than you guys."

Vagabond King bombed amidst exploding kettles and the crumble and crash of a high smokestack. Pilot McCormick thought that

---

* Not related to his namesake, the bachelor fifteenth President of the United States.

"from an esthetic point of view, the best thing was the incendiaries flickering up and down in the smoke like fireflies." Tail gunner Paul M. Miller, the last man in the Tidal Wave force, looked back at *Vagabond King*'s 45-second bombs exploding, and phoned the pilot, "They didn't give us too much time for the getaway." McCormick had this topic much on his mind. "I didn't know whether we were going to get back," said he. "My crew was prepared for a crash-landing before we left Africa. We had everything with us that we would need for a month—clothes, hiking boots and rations. Our plane was in bad shape. We got into formation on the treetops with another wounded ship and three good ones that stayed outside to protect us, and got a heading for Cyprus."

Coming off the target, Philip Ardery entered "a bedlam of bombers flying in all directions, some on fire, many with smoking engines, some with gaping holes or huge chunks of wing or rudder gone; many so riddled their insides must have been stark pictures of the dead and dying or grievously wounded men who would bleed to death before they could be brought to land; pilots facing horrible decisions—whether to crash-land and sacrifice the unhurt to save a dying friend or to fly on and let him give his life for the freedom of the rest."

The Sky Scorpion strike on Red Target was one of the two classically executed performances of the day. The Steaua Romana refinery was totally destroyed and did not reënter production for six years. Colonel Wood's group lost six of twenty-nine planes.

Few people in the target area realized what was happening that Sunday. Many who saw the Liberators thundering close above thought it was a supernatural visitation. Romania was steeped in illiteracy and fascist-controlled ignorance. War was an unseen, bloody maw in the east into which its men vanished, but this apocalyptic event in the air did not seem related to war. Even the German technicians found the raid hard to believe. Werner Nass's impression of the charred and shrunken corpses of a B-24 crew as "men from Mars" typified the reaction. Werner Horn, seeing the colossal machines sweeping over, had the initial notion that "the Americans were out joy riding," as though they had come a thousand miles to amuse themselves by buzzing the country. Most Romanians, obsessed with the death mill in Russia, assumed the planes came from there. One who thought so was Princess Caterina Caradja, *doyenne* of the ancient house of Cantacuzene. She lived on a thousand-acre estate at Nedelea, ten miles northwest of Ploesti.

That Sunday she was lunching in her manor house under a cartouche of the double-crowned eagle of Byzantium, the armorial bearings of her family. Since early Christian martial history in Wallachia, generations of Cantacuzene princes had ridden against the Saracens to win or die—the latter fate often produced by the axe of the Sultan's headsman. However, the family fortunes had improved in recent times, and the arms could have been brought up to date by perching the double eagle on an oil derrick. The first engineered petroleum well in the world had gushed forth on this domain of her grandfather, Prince George Cantacuzene.

Princess Caterina was a handsome, robust, blue-eyed woman of fifty with a managerial ability equal to that of any man in the kingdom. She had been educated in England. Her chosen occupation was the care of 3,000 war waifs and orphans in institutions and foster homes in the region. At this Sunday lunch the princess had as her guest a thirteen-year-old polylingual Polish countess whom she had rescued in 1939 from the Nazi smash-up in Poland. They were chatting in English when the talk was drowned by roaring engines. They ran out on the terrace and were nearly bowled over by air blasts from Colonel Posey's force, bound for Blue Target. "They looked like they were falling out of my attic," said Caterina. She assumed they were Russian planes. That summer Romanian insiders were in dread of a Soviet offensive striking through Romania to climb the Transylvanian passes before the snows.

After Posey's ships disappeared, another roar came from the north—the Sky Scorpions were coming off Red Target. They passed over, some planes trailing smoke and flame. The princess saw one sinking toward her with an engine smoking. It streamed silvery cascades across the fields, like a crop duster. Caterina, who had lived aviation with two generations of flying Cantacuzenes, said to the child, "The pilot is dropping petrol so the fire will not be so bad when he lands. Now, my dear, you must go inside and not come out until I return." She drove her 1939 Plymouth, which had white-wall tires, through roundabout lanes toward the falling B-24.

Pilot Robert O'Reilly was coming down in the luckiest spot in Romania; the princess' farm hands and orphan boys were trained in fighting oil-well fires. The plane crashed a mile from the house and bounced. The burning motor came out of its seat and flew away. The B-24 stopped with its fore section crushed and the tail in the air. Eight airmen emerged and ran.

The princess found a squad of orphans with foam bottles quenching the fire in the engine casing. A farmer touched his fore-lock and said, "Your Honor, the Russians have come." The crumpled flank of the plane bore a large white star. He said, "There are two dead Russians in the front." As she went to look she noticed in large lettering under the pilot's window: *Shoot, Fritz, You're Faded.* A wide-eyed orphan clutched her, crying, "One of the dead Russians is moving." The man farther back in the fuselage was crushed to death under the fallen top turret. He was the flight engineer, Frank Kees. As *Shoot, Fritz* was falling he had gone into the bomb bay to parachute, found the plane too low, and could not get out from under the turret before the crash.

The man entangled in the nose was soaked with gasoline trickling down from the wing tanks. Caterina saw his eyes open and said, "Boy, are you an American?" Navigator Richard Britt of Houston, Texas, replied, "Yes, ma'am." She addressed the crowd: "*Lunt aviator Americani!*" Farmers ran for tools to extricate Britt. A woman handed the princess a bottle of plum brandy. She passed it and a glass of water through the shattered greenhouse to Britt. The farm hands plied axes and crowbars to free him. The foreman said, "We'll have to cut off his shoe." Caterina said, "Be careful! Don't ruin it. We'll never be able to find American shoes for him." She kept the shorn G.I. boot to be repaired in the orphans' shoe shop.

They lifted Britt out and he fainted on the ground. Two German soldiers took his feet and began dragging him away. The princess grabbed his shoulders and dug in, yelling in German, "Oh, no, you don't take him. He's *our* prisoner." The large, unconscious American was the medium of a tug of war between supposed Axis allies. The princess won. She put Britt in the Plymouth, concealed him with a crowd of orphans, and drove him to a clinic in the village of Filipestii de Targ to treat him for skin burns received in the gasoline bath.

The episode was witnessed from a tall stand of corn by two sergeants from O'Reilly's crew, Troy McCrary and a wounded shipmate, Clell Riffle, whom McCrary had dragged there and covered with pumpkin leaves. The stunned men looked out through an American harvest scene at an English-speaking woman driving away in a Detroit automobile. McCrary said, "Looks like we're home." The illusion was dispelled by German soldiers, coming toward them, firing into the corn. McCrary tried to carry Riffle away, but escape was impossible. They gave themselves up.

The retainers took O'Reilly and three crewmates to the manor house. (The remaining three crewmen were at large three days, eating turnips, before they were bagged.) The princess came back from the clinic and found O'Reilly's party was gone. Her major-domo said, "People took them to Nedelea." She said, "Idiots!" and drove into the village, where an elder lamely told her, "For safety's sake we hid the Americans in a cellar." She called down into the dark, "Boys, there are only friends here. Now come up and let us help you." O'Reilly emerged with his co-pilot, Ernest Poulsen, bombardier Alfred Romano and gunner Louis Medeiros.

In Romania arrivals are festive occasions. This extraordinary visit of friends of the princess brought the villagers out with pitchers of fresh milk, peaches, cheese and apples, and two things rarely seen on wartime tables—white bread and sugar. The ravenous airmen tore into their finest meal since the States. O'Reilly said to Caterina, "We have just been shooting this place up and yet they give us this wonderful food." She snorted, "My boy, we Romanians never hit a man when he is down, and besides, we like Americans very much. Your chaps used to work here in the refineries." She had already decided to keep these young men out of German hands.

ODYSSEUS: It is time that I told you of the disastrous voyage
Zeus gave me when I started back from Troy.

The Odyssey, Book IX

12

THE STORMY RETURN

The battle of the target ended when the Liberators passed beyond the outer flak ring and the fighters turned away with fuel warnings. The Tidal Wave plan called for orderly withdrawal in massed formation on a course paralleling the inbound journey. But now a general formation was out of the question, after the divisive fates of the mission in which the groups had been parted from each other in the Balkan clouds, further split by the unplanned target turns, and subdivided in the witches' Sabbath around the burning refineries. Instead of hitting the objectives simultaneously, as had been demonstrated in the desert rehearsal the day before, the attack had taken 27 minutes from Walter Stewart's first bomb on White Five to John McCormick's last on Red Target.

The retreating Liberators were flung out for a hundred miles over the Danubian plain. More than half of them were seriously damaged. The situation had aspects of a rout, one that was very likely to be followed by deadly pursuit along the thousand weary miles to Benghazi. Half the planes had expended their ammunition, had too little left to fight long, or carried dead and incapacitated gunners, wrecked turrets and weapons. The crews were surveying airworthiness, counting their remaining gas and bullets, and estimating the chances of wounded comrades to remain alive six or seven hours more. Their pilots were weighing these factors to decide what course to take.

The shortest way out of Gerstenberg's web was to Chorlu on the European tail of Turkey. The next escape possibility was the Turkish mainland in Asia Minor. This southerly direction offered the possibility that a ship could stay in the air across Turkey and reach British bases in Cyprus, thereby avoiding internment in the neutral country. On the briefed southwestern route home, the first possible haven was in partisan-held regions of Yugoslavia. Beyond Corfu there were five hundred miles of sea. From that island, if a plane did not have enough gas to reach Libya, it had two slightly shorter refuges, Malta and the southern tier of Sicily recently conquered by the Allies.

The majority of pilots followed the planned route. The two least-damaged groups, the Liberandos and Sky Scorpions, resumed formation for Corfu, but they were seventy miles apart. Most of the Pyramiders gathered behind Julian Bleyer on this course; so did many of the 26 survivors of the 37 Eight Ball ships. George Brown rallied those Circus ships he could find. Appold's raiders, parted from all the rest by their withdrawal in the stream bed, flew home alone, as did five or six more bands made up of ships from various groups.

In the summer sky there were nearly a dozen Liberators that could find no one else to tack on to. Minutes after maneuvering to avoid collision with many others over the target, these waifs were in empty air and never found a friend during the thousand-mile adventure ahead.

Dramas of courage were taking place among the crews trying to save the ships. A gunner severely wounded in the leg, arm and back had continued to fire at fighters as his shipmates bound up the wounds. Another plane took fire in the nose, and the pilot rang the bail-out gong. From the nose the bombardier and navigator asked the men not to jump, while they fought the fire. They could not get at it with an extinguisher, so they ripped out fuselage padding to smother it. One took off his parachute to get closer to the fire. They put it out and the ship got home. In a Liberator whose Tokyo tank had been holed over the target, crewmen caught the fauceting gasoline in their steel helmets. By another perforated bomb bay tank a radioman lay on the catwalk and held his fingers in the hole until the engineer could transfer the contents to a wing tank.*

Old Buster Butt, completely undamaged, ran away from Ploesti across the harvest fields. From the nose McClain called, "Smoke over the treetops at eleven o'clock. Top turret and left waist get ready." As the plane jumped the trees, the guns rattled. "Cease fire!" yelled pilot Wright. The smoke was rising from a locomotive pulling a holiday passenger train with people riding on top and clinging to the sides of cars.

The tail gunner reported, "There's a ship behind us with an engine feathered." Wright said, "Maybe we ought to give him some help, hey?" Co-pilot Fred E. Sayre said, "Why not?" *Old Buster Butt* circled back. McClain said, "We had a lonely feeling as we saw the other planes in our formation disappear in the southwest. We came up on the straggler's wing. It was Frank McLaughlin from our group. We felt good that we decided to go back. We slowed down and escorted Mac."

Racing across the fields, a shout went up on Colonel Posey's intercom, "Hey, look on the ground at one o'clock!" A farmhouse door burst open and a peasant in red flannel underwear ran out and fired a shotgun at the bombers. None of the air gunners replied. They were laughing too hard. Anyway, they were under orders not to harm civilians.

---

* The men who did these things are not known. The incidents are recorded in secret morale report to Washington by the Office of Theater Censor, drawn from letters by survivors, none identified. Other acts of heroism were lost to record or award by the deaths of whole crews, the incredulity of base officers about what had taken place, and the traumatic state of the airmen when interrogated. One of the five Medals of Honor given for Tidal Wave, that of Lloyd Hughes, was awarded only because of the persistence of a man from the Office of War Information who took the trouble to collect eyewitness evidence of Hughes's deed.

K. O. Dessert brought *Tupelo Lass* out with hardly a scratch. This was the ship in which the grounded mission planner, Jacob Smart, was to have flown. *Tupelo Lass* crossed a village in which the inhabitants were out in their Sunday best, waving gaily to the planes. K. O. appreciated their attitude and could not resist an acknowledgment in kind. He made a tight 180-degree turn and scribbled: "This food is from the United States Army Air Forces who came to Romania to destroy German installations and not to harm Romanians." The crew fastened the note to the plane's K-rations and dropped them into the village square. *Tupelo Lass* resumed the return voyage. K. O. had added his bit to the larder of the best-fed people in Europe.

Winging away from Red Target, John Brooks saw a Liberator hit a haystack, blow it "all over hell and gone," and continue its flight.

The first Tidal Wave bomber to escape Axis territory and land safely was that of Hughes and Hunn from the last wave of the Eight Balls. They came into a Turkish air base at Chorlu without hydraulic power. The pilots landed nose-high to brake her by dragging the tail. The tail stayed on but the runway collapsed under it. People ran along the furrow of broken concrete to admire the monster that had made obsolete the specifications of Turkish airdrome engineers. A Turkish general greeted the pilots effusively with, "Soon I hope we can join you in an attack on Bulgaria!" The exhausted Americans noted that he did not mention accompanying them to nasty places like Ploesti.

Along the Turkish distress route *Sweet Adeline* came upon a badly shot-up pink ship, dragging along alone. Pilot Podolak phoned, "Hey, you from the 98th. What's your situation?" There was no reply. Co-pilot James Case flashed a lamp signal: "Heading Cyprus. Come on radio." The pink one winked back, "Radio shot out. Will you stay with us?" Podolak said to Case, "Tell 'em we sure will." *Sweet Adeline* slowed down and the two ships crossed the Turkish border, wing to wing. Three U.S.-built Warhawks, wearing star-and-crescent livery, climbed alongside and radioed, "You come land with us." Podolak told his crew, "To hell with landing in Turkey. Everybody level guns on them but don't shoot. You okay, Junior?" From the ball turret young Private McGreer replied, "Yeah. Got 'em right in my sights." The Turkish pilots saw the guns and dived away. *Sweet Adeline* and the pink cripple continued toward Cyprus, where they landed safely.

Another pair on the southern heading were Harold James's Liberator and that of the dead Captain Mooney, whose co-pilot, Henry Gerrits, was flying the machine beside the empty seat. James asked radioman Earl Zimmerman to code a message to Benghazi saying they were heading for Turkey. Before sending it Zimmerman warmed up on the group frequency and phoned the pilot, "I hear an S.O.S. and another ship calling for a QDM [bearing]." James said, "Turn it off. Don't send anything. It would interfere with planes in worse shape than we are."

Two Turkish Warhawks came alongside and lowered their landing gear, the summons to surrender. Gerrits and James were very low on fuel. They dropped their wheels. Gerrits landed his dead and wounded in a wheat field. A Turkish fighter came in with him, hit a ditch, and broke up. The pilot got out, but he was court-martialed and sentenced to twenty years for destroying government property.

James landed on a fighter strip and burned his brakes out on the short run. His crew was surrounded by soldiers with fixed bayonets. A Turkish officer arrived, gave the Americans a smiling hello, then turned and knocked the nearest soldier flat on the ground. Turkish officers got into the plane, berserk with curiosity. They pulled the rip cords on the parachutes, emptied the first-aid kits, and unrolled the bandages. "They even squeezed the ointment from the tubes," said Zimmerman.

Crossing Turkey, the engineer of *Vagabond King*, the last plane to bomb during the mission, was transferring gas when all four engines cut out at once. Pilot McCormick said, "Ringing the bailout gong was out of the question because of Van Buren's shot-up parachute. We just stuck with it. The motors came back in. We landed at Cyprus on an uphill runway, feeling very good. I turned off to find a place to park and a truck hit us. We were on a highway." *

On the southern route Killer Kane was trying to lift his airborne wreck over the lowest pass in the Balkan Mountains in Bulgaria. *Hail Columbia* was 200 feet too low. The controls were pulling the pilots' arms out of their sockets, and the harness was binding into their chests. Kane gasped, "Hey, navigator, what's the altitude?" Whalen replied, "I guess we'll get over it." Kane howled, "Guess, hell! You'd better be right or it'll be everybody's ass!" The sluggish moloch sailed slowly toward the peak.

There was a tiny favor of weather. A small thermal flicked up under *Hail Columbia*. She was over the top and free. The tail gunner said, "Killer, I swear I felt the belly scrape the mountain." White Four Leader replied, "You can get good and plastered, boy, when we land. And that goes for all of you." He kept the intercom open to pay tribute to the Kane-deafened Whalen: "That was one hell of a swell job of navigation, fella." Kane was bluffing to give his men hope. He thought, "we have about as much chance as a snowball in hell to come out of this." He was short on gas, with one engine gone and another turning a buzzing prop with two shot-up tips. He had a warped main spar and hundreds of flak holes. Yet the astonishing B-24 still flew.

Fred Weckessler, the flight engineer, phoned Kane, "There might be some gas in the left bomb bay tank. She indicates zero. All the same I think there's juice left in her." Kane said, "Get to work." Weckessler cleared a clogged outlet and pumped the bonus into a wing tank. The corporals dropped the auxiliary tank through the bomb bay, hoping not to go down like that.

Kane clattered across Turkey, eking out the miles to avoid internment and reach Cyprus, a half hour beyond the Turkish coast. He radioed his position to Benghazi via the R.A.F. stations at Cyprus and Cairo. R.A.F. Station 73B at Nicosia, Cyprus, called Kane: "We can receive you. If after dark, we shall make a green light. Reply with same and we'll give you a flare path." The Liberators crossed the last mountains of Turkey in the set-

* McCormick and his crew were shot down three months later in the North Sea.

ting sun and sighted the twilight blue of the Gulf of Antalya. *Hadley's Harem* phoned Kane, "We've lost another engine. Going to try landing on the beach."

Gilbert Hadley still had a mile-high column of air between his plane and the wine-dark sea. His last two engines started to kick. He polled his crew: "Do you want to bail out or ride her in?" They voted for a crash-landing. Radioman William Leonard broadcast their position as Hadley banked around, and the *Harem* faltered toward the Turkish shore near Alanya. The crew removed clothing and opened the top escape hatch in the radio compartment. Hadley tried to will his ship as far as the beach. He pushed up all the power he had. The last two engines failed. A wing hooked into the water. The plane sprawled and sank. A wave slapped shut the escape hatch. The pilots and engineer Page shoved at the hatch, but water pressure sealed it beyond their strength. The pilots swam toward the hole in the nose. Page popped back up in his turret and breathed from a sweet pocket of air. He filled his lungs and dived again, feeling his way back to the crash opening. He bobbed out to the sea surface. The world was pink and glorious and he heard angel voices. Afloat in the still, warm water were the wounded navigator, Tabacoff, radioman Leonard, and Sergeants Pershing W. Waples, Leroy Newton, Frank Nemeth and Christopher Holweger. The wreckage sank, sucking and gurgling, carrying down Hadley and his co-pilot Lindsay and bombardier Storms's body.

The survivors inflated their life vests and swam for the darkening shore. Hadley had stretched his last flight to within a half-mile of land. The seven castaways fell exhausted on the Turkish beach. Fisherfolk coming with ancient rifles recognized them as miserable, harmless souls and built a driftwood fire. The naked airmen crawled to the warmth, and the fishermen squatted around all night watching them.

Air-Sea Rescue at Cyprus had heard Hadley's last position on the radio. In the morning a Wellington spotted the beach bivouac and dropped a note. The survivors confirmed that they were U. S. airmen by spelling out a message on the sand with stones. A high-speed rescue launch arrived from Cyprus, anchored offshore, and its captain and an interpreter came to the beach in a dinghy. The British skipper addressed the local pasha: "These men cannot be interned. They sank at sea. Is that not so?" The fishermen nodded. "Therefore they are shipwrecked mariners! And we have come to rescue them." This invocation of Admiralty Law touched the Turkish sense of justice and humor and Air-Sea Rescue was allowed to take them off.

After *Hadley's Harem* sank, Killer Kane's trio continued for Cyprus in complete darkness. Kane saw a green dot—the promise of Nicosia—and saluted it with a green flare. R.A.F. men lighted the runway flare path. Unknown to Kane, at either end of the runway there were ditches, which the R.A.F. customarily placed to encourage precise landings. In the feeble light, "exhausted, too tired to fight the unbalanced pull of the engines any more," Kane saw that he was landing too short, his wheels headed for the ditch. "I tried to stretch the glide and float the plane those extra yards," he said.

Hail Columbia's undercarriage snagged the ditch and she bounced with her tail rising. Kane saw the flare path climbing his windshield and glowing through the astradome. He was coming in standing on his nose. He and Young braced their feet on the instrument panel and pulled the control columns hard against their chests. Slowly the tail fell back and hammered the ground. In the B-24's landing beams Kane saw "amazing things rolling ahead of us—the prop from the dead engine and our two main wheels." *Hail Columbia* screeched along the tarmac, slewed around, and stopped, facing backward. The tower shot a red flare to warn the other incoming B-24's of a ship wrecked on the runway. The light glared into Kane's flight deck. Young yelled "Fire!" and leaped for the top hatch. Kane switched off the engines and electricity. Young dropped back and said apologetically, "After you, sir." Kane shoved the co-pilot's rump through the escape hatch and unbuckled his seat belt. He got up, and fell back into the seat. His legs were numb after thirteen hours of pedal-tramping. On the second try he gained his feet. He climbed out on top of *Hail Columbia* and sat there, a red man in the dying flare. Below, his men were kissing the ground and contentedly sifting handfuls of sand over and over. Kane slid down and pawed the earth.

The R.A.F. brought LeBrecht and Banks in on a transverse runway, followed by five more Liberators. Two had arrived ahead of Kane. An R.A.F. flight surgeon said, "We didn't know you were coming, Colonel, and our mess is closed. Could I give you dinner in town?" Through the blackout curtains of a Nicosia night club, into a brilliantly lighted foyer, came the crew of *Hail Columbia*. Killer Kane caught sight of himself in a pier glass. One arm was sooty from the fires of White Four. His suntans were lace-white with encrusted sweat. Red eyes stared at him from a harlequin face caked with salt and soot. At dinner the crew fell asleep with their heads on the table, oblivious to flimsily clad Cyprians kicking high.

While Killer Kane and the Cypriot and Turkish refugees were unwinding their destinies, the majority of ships, still widely strewn over the sky, were crossing western Bulgaria on the planned withdrawal course. Lewis Ellis, who had felt "enormously tired" on the way to Ploesti, suddenly felt "fresh and almost completely rested. In spite of everything that happened, I thoroughly enjoyed flying." Crossing low over a village, he glanced at the plane at his side. "I was horrified to see the bombardier fire his nose gun, knocking two men flat," said Ellis. "We had been specifically briefed against firing at civilians." *

Since his mortification in the forenoon, which found his best pilots off post, Colonel Vulkov, commanding the Bulgarian Sixth Fighter Regiment, had pulled his four bases into readiness for the return voyage of the bombers. From Karlovo and Asen, 46 Avias and six Messerschmitts climbed to intercept the southbound American convoys, while the two squadrons of Avias near Sofia went up to block the bombers in the Osogovska Mountains. This time the B-24's were low enough to be reached by the oxygenless Avias.

* Later, during interrogation, Ellis hung around the bombardier to see if he would report the incident. The bombardier said, "Oh, yes, on the edge of a town there were two German soldiers firing at us with rifles, and I knocked them out." "Furthermore," said Ellis, "his crew had taken pictures of the two men that proved they were soldiers."

Climbing between Pleven and Sofia, *Daisy Mae* was passing through dark thunderheads when top turret gunner Owen Cold-iron called, "Fighters at three o'clock and a little high. I think they're Italians." Lieutenant Rusev of Squadron 622 drove at Ellis. The B-24's threw brilliant tracers across the somber clouds and collected a few more rents in their hides. The Bulgarian fighters got on Ned McCarty's Pyramider Liberator and hit him hard in both left engines. They streamed white smoke, but he kept them turning. His plane sank, threading its way through the hills, barely matching the air speed of the formation. The Bulgarians had only one sting in them. After one pass their old machines could not overtake the bombers. Rusev broke off with little result.

As the brush ended, Ellis was overjoyed to see his close friend, Julian Darlington, sailing along in *The Witch*, close to the wing of James A. Gunn in *Prince Charming*, both planes seemingly in good fettle. The three formed a diamond with another plane. As they ascended through clouds, Lieutenant Petrov's Bulgarian Squadron 612 located the diamond and attacked. Again the Bulgarians failed to inflict serious damage. The Liberators disappeared in a cloud, and the second Bulgarian squadron had lost its chance.

At that point the Bulgarian fortune improved. By an eerie, intuitive stroke, Lieutenant Stoyan Stoyanov showed up leading the Karlovo Messerschmitts, the only six planes in the Bulgarian *polk* that were faster than the bombers. Stoyanov drilled into a cloud top and destroyed the No. 2 and No. 3 engines on *The Witch*. In the next patch of visibility, Stanley Horine, the tail gunner of *Prince Charming*, phoned his pilot, "*The Witch* has been hit bad. She's falling behind." Without temporizing, James Gunn throttled back to take Darlington's side against the foe. As he drifted back, the Bulgarians struck *Prince Charming*, which began to emit white smoke. By the time Gunn had come abreast of Darlington, flame was coming out of his waist windows.

The Messerschmitts swooped again on the pair of cripples. Lieutenant Peter Bochev gunned *Prince Charming* and saw Gunn turn over and fall in flame. Several burning parachutes came out of the ship. The fighter pass wounded four men in *The Witch* and fatally damaged her mechanisms. Darlington nosed down, rang the emergency bell, and looked for a place to crash-land. Three of his sergeants bailed out on the way down. Darlington skidded *The Witch* into a mountain wheat field without further injuring anyone. His conscientious bombardier, Lieutenant Major R. Gillett,* destroyed his ten-cent bombsight, while the other lifted the wounded engineer, Lloyd M. Brisbi, from the turret. Bulgarian border guards seized Darlington and navigator Joseph N. Quigley while they were assisting the wounded man. Darlington's other four men—co-pilot Daryl Epp, bombardier Gillett, and gunners Dale G. Hulsey and Walter D. Hardiek—ran for the woods. The Bulgars sent a corporals' guard to chase them. Epp's bolters had little chance. They were in a heavily patrolled border area; Hitler's Bulgarian ally claimed that part of the woods from indomitable Yugoslavia.

Darlington's trio was decently treated and taken to jail in Sofia, where a surprise awaited them: three living men, the parachutists from their plane—Ned A. Howard, Anthony J. Rauba and Joseph J. Turley. Presuming that co-pilot Epp and the other three runaways had not been slaughtered in the forest, Julian Darlington's entire crew was alive!

In the morning the Bulgars brought in a burned man with bandaged head and hands. He was Stanley Horine, the tail gunner from *Prince Charming*, who had reported the plight of *The Witch*, bringing the gallant Captain Gunn back to his doom. Somehow Horine had bailed out of a ship spiraling down in flames. He was the only survivor. In the crew of many a crashed plane there was this tithe of one living man.

In the meantime Daryl Epp's fugitives had outrun the Bulgarian guards and were at large in the border region with many armed men looking for them. Epp had one thing on his side. Three months before, British Intelligence had had such misgivings about Mikhailovitch, the supposed leader of Yugoslav resistance, that British agents were parachuted to his adversary, Tito. Shortly before Tidal Wave, the British cabinet decided to

* His Christian name was Major.

support Tito instead of Mikhailovitch. Consequently some of the
U. S. fliers had been orally instructed to ask for Tito should they
land in Yugoslavia.*

Epp's men scrambled over mountains, headed west for the land
of the mysterious Tito. They got up nerve to approach some
mountain folk and pronounced the password, "Tito." The peasants
took in the sore, half-starved airmen, fed them, and gave them a
long sleep. Mountaineers passed them along a chain of patriots
to a man who spoke English. He offered a toast in *raki* to Allied
victory, and handed them a photograph. It showed their plane
belly down in the Bulgarian wheat field, surrounded by German
and Bulgarian officers. Tito's man, in the role of an innocent
bystander, had snapped it himself. He gave the picture to Epp.

Tito's man explained that it might be some time before he
could arrange to send Epp's rangers back to their outfit—such
movements were difficult for the partisans. The Americans made
themselves useful and were absorbed into the underground. The
Yugoslav partisans had no way to report that Epp's men were
safe, and the Bulgarian Red Cross did not bother to advise
Geneva on the Sofia prisoners, so that the survivors of *The Witch*
and *Prince Charming* were written off as dead by the U. S. War
Department. They were in limbo for more than a year.

The rear elements of the Tidal Wave retreat were still crossing
Bulgaria when two new Messerschmitt 110G's, on a ferry flight
from Wiener Neustadt to Sofia, picked up chatter on the radio
about the bombing of Ploesti. One of the pilots was Cadet Sergeant Zed,** a veteran of sixty air battles, who was delivering
aircraft while recuperating from wounds. He phoned his wingman, Cadet Sergeant Richter: "Would you like to go hunting
bombers?" Richter said, "I'm for it. Let's go." Each of the fast
new fighters was full of ammunition for its four fixed machine
guns, two cannons and two swiveling machine guns in the radioman's rear compartment. Near Vratsa, Bulgaria, the hunters
sighted luscious prey, a single B-24 with No. 4 engine dead and

* The printed escape instructions advised contacting "the Communists"
but did not mention Tito by name.
** Name disguised by request. He now lives in East Berlin.

smoke issuing from No. 3. The Messerschmitts fell on the tail of the bedraggled Liberator. The American tail gunner was wide awake. He hit Zed's right wing tank. The fighter pilot said, "I began losing gas and, for fear of fire, had to stop my right engine." He pulled away on his remaining engine, leaving the kill to Richter, but the U. S. tail and top turret gunners drove off the second Messerschmitt.

Zed was worried. New Me-110G's were jewels, and for a ferry pilot to lose one meant a court-martial. "The American pilot was resourceful," he said. "As Richter made his second pass, the American headed as fast as he could for a cloud. Richter did not get him. The cloud swallowed him." Zed called his comrade and the two chastened ferry pilots made for Sofia.

Colonel Brown of the Circus led his homing "Romanian remains" into a mountain valley with antiaircraft ranged along the ridges. The deep ravines they had feared before the raid were now their best friends. The flak crews faced a problem not in the books. They had been trained to compute, track and pick away at tiny black stars inching across the zenith. Now these same targets, suddenly grown to seventy-foot green monsters, reeled past beneath them faster than they could traverse the guns. And the planes spouted something the ground gunners had never dreamed of—flails of machine-gun fire ripping along the hillside, chipping up cement, and hurling men down in splatters of blood. Rustling the treetops, the Circus ships passed up the valley. Joe Tate, the mild, green-eyed West Pointer, who had come off the target without damage, sat in his cockpit in his British battle jacket, smoking his pipe, and looked up at the rippling surface of tracers. He took his plane up a hundred feet, like a submarine raising a periscope through bright waves, and then submerged again to his place in the Pratt & Whitney riptide.

Many miles behind, in ramshackle *Utah Man*, Stewart heard his gunners cheering. "Hugh Roper, my old and dear friend, passed under us in *Exterminator*, doing about a hundred seventy," said Stewart. "We tried to catch up and fly with him, but it was no use. Then we saw *Thundermug* and *Let 'Er Rip* closing up to *Exterminator*. The three of them left us and flew a beautiful tight formation into the clouds over the mountains. We were immensely happy for Roper. Six of the men in his plane were on their twenty-fifth mission: Hugh, John White, Walter Zablocki, Earl LeMoine, William Defreese and Hank Lloyd. Also headed home for a rest was Captain Jack Jones, who was flying as an observer with Roper. As soon as they got over a few miles of enemy territory and the sea, they'd all have a ticket to the land of the free."

From *Let 'Er Rip*, waist gunner Clifford E. Koen, Jr., looked over at Roper's plane. "Wires were hanging from the vertical stabilizers," he said. "They must have been guy wires from refinery stacks. The gunners in the other ship kept pointing to different spots on our plane that we couldn't see from the inside. We never learned the extent of this damage."

The three ships caught up with Brown's main Circus formation and sat on top of the flying slum. Clouds soon forced the planes to space out, but Hugh Roper and Vic Olliffe remained close together. They had flown the whole mission tight as a team of aerobats. Russell Longnecker was not as confident as they. As they entered a cloud top he would hold on Roper until the lead ship became invisible, then make a fifteen-degree turn away from him, hold it for a half minute, and resume the original heading. When they got out of the cloud Longnecker would slide *Thundermug* back on Roper's wing. "We passed through a lot of clouds," said Longnecker, "then I came out of one and glanced to the right for Roper and Olliffe. They were not there. I never saw them again."

Below them, men in the main formation saw two B-24's falling out of the cloud. A tail turret fell separately. After surviving Ploesti, the good comrades, Roper and Olliffe, were lost in a banal cloud collision. But the great adventure was not over for three sergeants in *Let 'Er Rip*. Harold Murray had seen the badly damaged *Exterminator* floating in on top of them, and the collision cut off her tail. "We broke away and went into a steep dive," said Murray. "In the fuselage we hardly knew what was happening. It was full of red dust and floating ammo boxes. We could scarcely move because of the force of the dive."

Exterminator crashed, killing everyone on board. *Let 'Er Rip* grazed a mountaintop and went into a flatter glide. Koen snapped on his chest chute and went out the window amidst falling debris. Gunners Edgar J. Pearson, Eugene Engdahl and Murray followed him. Pearson's parachute collapsed and he died in the fall. The other three parachutists landed alive, not far from the burning wreckage of their plane. Bulgarian border police trussed their arms behind their backs and took them to a field into which peasants were bringing bodies and paraphernalia from the crash. The sergeants were unable to identify the bodies. They were marched 25 miles to the nearest road.

After the cloud collision the orphaned *Thundermug* continued on alone. Her pilots, Longnecker and Jones, glimpsed ships far ahead. Longnecker said, "Deacon, if we pour it on to catch up with them, we might not have the gas to get home." Jones said, "I'm for saving gas, even if we have to fly it alone, Russ. We haven't been hit. There's plenty of ammo." Longnecker called on navigator Stanley Valcik to give a heading and prediction on a landfall at Benghazi. The navigator handed him a chart and said, "Just follow this course exactly and it'll take us to Benghazi." With that Valcik sat down on the flight deck, yawned, and opened a magazine. In this relaxed atmosphere the gunners came forward to tell the pilots how it had gone with them. Pinson, the top turret man, said, "There I was with the guns turned to the rear, expecting to get shot any minute. There was a crash behind my head. I wheeled around. The plexiglass was cracked and covered with blood. I thought, 'Boy, I've had it!' I felt the back of my head. It was still there. Then I saw feathers in the blood. A bird had crashed into the turret."

Longnecker now had time to return to his main worry— whether he could hold his new first pilot's job. Yesterday the CO had told him, "Any pilot who fails to keep tight formation on this mission will be a co-pilot the day after tomorrow." "Now," reflected Longnecker, "I have my big opportunity to prove I can handle a plane of my own, and here I am all alone and probably going to get in much later than the others. That is, if I make it at all."

Pilot Kenton D. McFarland, a 31-mission veteran of the Circus, was trying to bring *Liberty Lad* home with a No. 3 engine "sick" from a flak hit. He called his flight engineer, John J. Hayes: "The wing tanks ought to be plenty low. Let's begin transferring gas from the bomb bay tanks." Hayes reported, "I can't pump into Number One or Number Two. The fuel lines are cut or clogged."

McFarland was confronted with the imminent failure of two engines, both on the same side. On the other wing, No. 3 was in bad shape. He wondered whether to turn back while he still had power, and bail out to become a POW, or take a chance and continue out over the Mediterranean, where bailing out was usually fatal. He decided he did not want to be a prisoner of war. He would try to make it to base.

McFarland's reasoning was bolstered by the presence beside him of the pilot with the most combat experience of any man in the air at the battle of Ploesti, Flight Officer Henry A. Podgurski, an American transferee from the Royal Canadian Air Forces. Podgurski had flown 127 raids with the R.C.A.F. He did not like the Liberator because the book said you should not try to fly it upside down.

The No. 1 engine in *Liberty Lad* sputtered out. Podgurski feathered it and he and McFarland pressed more heavily on the left rudder pedals to hold on course. The distorted rudder position dragged *Liberty Lad* out of the formation into a slow and steady descent. The pilots dared not waggle their wings to signal distress lest they lose airworthiness. They watched the formation disappear ahead. Fifteen minutes later No. 2 engine went dry and out. McFarland and Podgurski stiffened their legs on the left rudders to keep the ship in the air and pushed the throttle on the two remaining left-wing engines. They were alone at sea, 500 miles from base. *Liberty Lad* kept on sinking. All the pull was on the left side, and to counteract that, the twin tail rudders were swung left twenty degrees, as far as they would go, and held there only by the pilots' constant pedal pressure. If McFarland and Podgurski eased off their strained legs for an instant, *Liberty Lad* would twist sharply right on the live side. If she should fall off on the dead side just a fraction too much, airworthiness would vanish and the plane would fall into the Mediterranean.

McFarland ordered his men to clean out ship. They threw out oxygen bottles, fire extinguishers, the aerial camera and ammunition boxes. Although they were still well within range of fighters, out went ten machine guns and all the remaining ammo. With fire axes they chopped off and jettisoned everything in the fuselage which was not directly involved with keeping them flying, and then they threw out the axes. *Liberty Lad* continued to sink. From 15,000 feet the ship went down to 5,500. There, with her lightened burden, she found some stability in the thicker air.

Straining against the rudder pedal, McFarland broke the pilot's seat. Hayes and Sergeant John Brown, who was flying as an observer, got behind and braced their backs against his, so he could maintain leverage on the rudder. The two sergeants bolstered the pilot throughout the rest of the journey, one of them at a time crawling around front and massaging the pilots' legs.

The radioman, Oda A. Smathers, his head swathed in bloody bandages, managed to repair the shot-up radio and exchanged fixes with the Ninth Air Force station 75X in Libya. The rest of the crew sat in ditching position, with their backs to the main bulkhead. *Liberty Lad* heaved on across the sea in the fading light.

As the scattered Ploesti fleet droned over the Balkans, it was tracked by the Würzburg on Mount Cherin and the vigilant spotter was waiting on Corfu. He reported, "They are turning south from Sector Zero Zero, Zone Twenty-four East, into Sector Zero Nine, Zone Twenty-three East." The new zone was controlled from Athens, where, since morning, Leutnant Werner Stahl had been patiently plotting the progress of the B-24's. He had noted that U. S. bombers usually returned on the same route they took to the target. Now the Liberators were confirming that, and Stahl was ready. Sitting on the flight line at Kalamaki near Mégara, Greece, he had ten new Messerschmitts with auxiliary belly tanks, under the command of Leutnant Burk. Stahl had calculated that extra petrol and precise timing would give Burk a half hour of combat on the nearest point of intersection with the bomber course. He plotted the point in the Ionian Sea, west of the Island of Kephallenia, one of the kingdoms of Odysseus, the old sea rover. Up went the Messerschmitts, driving west in the midafternoon sun. They crossed the interception point and turned to get the blinding sun at their backs. Twelve Liberators walked across the German leader's gunsights exactly on time.

The first American to spot the Messerschmitts was the sharp-eyed Owen Coldiron, standing by his useless guns in the jammed top turret of *Daisy Mae.* He phoned pilot Ellis, "Fighters at three o'clock, straight into the sun." "We tightened up the formation and waited," said Ellis. "Since my top and tail guns were out, I dropped down a bit to uncover the guns of the ship on my left."

Leutnant Burk did not attack immediately. He still had a minute of gas in his auxiliary tanks and wanted to burn it and drop the tanks to streamline himself before giving battle. He took up a parallel course to the bombers, out of machine-gun range, and examined his riddled prey. Coldiron saw the Messerschmitt leader hold up his hand and the fighters shed their belly tanks. Five fighters turned in abreast in a shallow V and drove up the flanks of the Liberators. Ellis said, "It was no surprise action. It was a cool, well-planned attack. We knew the Germans would not frighten as the Macchis [Bulgarian Avias] had. We had to shoot them down, be shot down ourselves, or wait for them to run out of gas."

The American gunners waited professionally until the fighters were within a thousand yards before opening the action. The fighters replied with cannon and machine guns. An Me-109 passed through the bombers, shedding parts, and exploded on the other side, leaving a yellow parachute tacked on the sky. Leutnant Altnorthoff rained heavy blows on the Eight Ball Liberator piloted by Fred H. Jones and Elbert Dukate, Jr. It fell behind, sinking toward the sea, not far from where Flavelle had gone down nine hours before. That was the last of the Jones-Dukate crew as far as the others could see.*

* Two months later the tail gunner from Jones's ship, Michael Sigle, reported for duty in Benghazi. He said that his entire crew of nine had

The Messerschmitts gathered again and Burk waved six machines in for another flank attack. A Viennese cadet sergeant named Phillip picked a bomber with two engines smoking and knocked Ned McCarty's mangled Liberator out of the convoy. It shed five parachutes before it hit the sea. The jumpers didn't have a chance. They were going into the water far offshore and the running battle had now moved south of the operational grounds of Italian boats. It happened that the Royal Navy was bombarding Crotone that day and the next zone on the south was unhealthy for Italians. The fighters lost no craft on the second pass.

The sounds of the Ionian Sea engagement were heard by ships far out of sight. The radio was thick with calls: "Fighters everywhere! . . . All the ships are gone but us—don't see how we can last through these attacks. . . . Bailing out—ship on fire." Philip Ardery, leading seven B-24's home, said, "These words we heard would wrench the heart of a man of stone."

As the third assault shaped up, the bombardier of *Daisy Mae,* Guido Gioana, yielded his forward gun to the more experienced radioman, Carl A. Alfredson. The German leader changed his tactics. The Messerschmitts dissolved and came in singly from various directions. Leutnant Flor destroyed a Circus Liberator, *Here's to Ya,* piloted by Ralph McBride. No parachutes came out of it. After this assault, Gioana and flight engineer James W. Ayers lay wounded in *Daisy Mae,* and the tail gunner, Nick Hunt, was picking himself up and looking at a cracked armor glass and jammed turret tracks. Hunt took over a waist gun. *Daisy Mae* now had only her waist weapons in action. The other gunners passed their unused ammunition belts to these positions.

---

survived the ditching and were picked up from life rafts by an Italian launch. Sigle had escaped from Italy with the help of anti-Fascists. Ten months later, as General Mark Clark stood at the gates of Rome, a picturesque Italian partisan leader sneaked through the enemy lines with detailed information on the city's defenses. His name was "Duke" and he spoke American with a New Orleans accent. Co-pilot Elbert Dukate, Jr., had escaped from POW camp, joined Italian guerrillas, and helped organize the underground railway that delivered hundreds of downed Allied airmen from behind enemy lines.

The Messerschmitt leader figured that individual attack was paying off. More work could be squeezed out of the petrol that way. The fighters did not reassemble, but drove in from many angles. Two fell upon *Daisy Mae*, holing the left rudder and tearing strips off the elevator surfaces. Two 20-mm. shells exploded in the flight deck, wounding Gioana again. The shells cut inner control cables and *Daisy Mae's* nose went down, turning into a shallow bank to the left. Co-pilot Fager said, "Let's move back up to the formation. We're wide open to them." Ellis said, "Can't do it, Cal. The controls are gone." He demonstrated it by pulling the unresisting control column back into his lap. He reached for the elevator trim. It was completely loose, revolving freely, out of contact with the tab.

"Then I remembered the automatic pilot," said Ellis. "Fortunately, I always kept it warmed up. I flipped to 'ON' and it was working. We were six hundred feet below the formation, drawing Messerschmitts like honey. I adjusted the elevator settings and the autopilot and the nose came up slowly."

A Messerschmitt exploded and its pilot, Sergeant Graf, fell out. The battle had now rolled along for about eighty miles and the Germans were close to fuel warnings. Some broke off and departed for base. On the last pass of the engagement, Sergeant Hackl cannoned his Messerschmitt through the B-24's and destroyed a second engine on the ship piloted by Reginald L. Carpenter.

Carpenter continued on two engines, his craft receding from the others. When she was down to 5,000 feet, west of Crete, Carpenter called his crew to ditching positions in the front of the plane. Just above the water he feathered all the propellers. His replacement navigator, John E. Powell,* was completely unfamiliar with water-landing procedure. He chose the most perilous position he could, his feet dangling in the bomb bay and hands grasping the ladder to the top turret. The turret usually came unshipped and fell in crash-landings, and water impacts were much heavier.

Carpenter said, "We hit the sea easily, and skipped into the

* Powell's regular crew died at the target.

air, smacking in harder the second time. The tail section was torn off, just after the wing. Walter Brown, right waist gunner, and Frederick Durand, tail gunner, were pinned and never came to the surface." The pilot and six others swam out of the floating wreck and inflated their life vests. Inside, still, was navigator Powell. Providentially, the turret had not fallen upon him. Powell struggled under water and wriggled out of the swamping plane. (He doesn't remember how.) On the surface he found that his life vest was damaged and would not inflate. He swam back to the wreck and pulled out two rubber dinghies just before the ship went down. Seven of the crew got into the five-man dinghy and Powell helped the most heavily injured of them, co-pilot Edward Rumsey, into the one-man boat, and splinted his broken leg with the paddle. While the plane was falling, Powell had had the presence of mind to stick a first-aid kit in his shirt. He now produced it and gave morphine injections to Rumsey and the radioman, Joseph Manquen, who had a flak wound in his knee. "Then," said Powell, "we settled down for a night without food or water."

At dawn the men in the dinghies heard airplane engines. The Royal Air Force Air-Sea Rescue unit at Cyprus was out sweeping for ditched air crews. A Wellington came over low and dropped fresh water, concentrated food and cigarets to the raftsmen. It circled them for five hours, protecting them from German search boats out of Crete. When the Wellington's fuel gauges approached the point of no return, a sister ship arrived and took up the picket. The following night, after they had been adrift for thirty hours, an Air-Sea Rescue launch picked up the Americans. Powell's Silver Star citation mentioned his cheerfulness as well as his resourcefulness.

The Stahl-Burk Messerschmitt ambush in the Ionian Sea was the last fighter engagement in the Battle of Ploesti. The Germans claimed five bombers destroyed. Actually they had shot down only McCarty, Jones and McBride, although damaging Carpenter so that he was forced to ditch later. Apparently the Me-109's claimed Ellis when he went out of control temporarily. U. S. gunners were allowed five enemy aircraft destroyed, when only two were actually downed. The death toll was two German pilots and 22 Americans.

Ellis came out of the Battle of the Ionian Sea still flying tortured *Daisy Mae*. The unconscious Gioana had 35 wounds. The three lacerated sergeants bandaged themselves and helped look after him. As if refreshed by the new flak hits on the top cylinders and dangling sparkplug wires, *Daisy Mae*'s No. 3 motor began to revive. The Canadian engineer, Blase Dillman, spliced the severed control cables, measured the gas, and reported, "I figure we have enough to last until seven o'clock," The navigator, Julius K. Klenkbell said, "We'll never make land by then." The men in the torn Liberator dwelt on their thoughts as night came.

One of them had found an extra measure of heroism. Several weeks before, after taking off on his second mission, he had gone forward to Ellis and said, "Take me back." The pilot said, "Are you sick?" The man said, "No, just scared." Ellis said, "Hell, we're all scared. What difference does that make? If I take you back we'll never catch up with the formation." The frightened man said, "Well, I'm going to jump." Dillman grabbed the man by the collar and announced, "I'll knock your teeth in if you don't get back to your job." The flier resumed his post and reported to Ellis every half hour. Now the quaking man was flying with his comrades in complete acceptance and common praying fear.

Ellis placed his power at lowest setting to milk more miles out of *Daisy Mae*. At the fuel-exhaustion deadline he was still airborne at 155 mph, 1700 rpm and 25 inches manifold pressure. "I could not decide for sure what was best to do," the pilot remembered. "I knew that ditching at night was a very hazardous undertaking, even if we still had power. Bailing out in individual dinghies would have been O.K. for everyone but Lieutenant Gioana, who was still unconscious.

Over the Adriatic several planes found they were too low on fuel to reach Benghazi. They turned off for Sicily or Malta. One of them, *K for King*, with its electrical system shot out and all instruments dead, was navigated to the Sicilian beachhead by Leroy E. Zaruba. Pilots Miller and Hodge landed her safely without an altimeter. The Fravega brothers landed on a fighter strip at Syracuse with three other planes, one of which blew a tire and ground-looped. Anthony Fravega said, "Nobody would believe us when we told them what we had done." The returning heroes had to sleep in their planes that night.*

Lucky, Ramsay Potts's surviving wingman, proved to be aptly named. Pilot Harold Kendall was groping for Sicily with a 20-mm. hole in his bomb bay tanks which had let out most of the gas before the crew could plug it. Kendall, down to his last gallons and his crew in parachutes, waiting for the jump gong, spotted a fighter strip in southern Sicily and landed halfway up the short runway without hydraulic fluid to set his brakes. *Lucky* ate up the runway, ran over a hill, picked up some unoccupied British bell tents, and was halted by crashing into seven P-40 fighters. Kendall's men tumbled out and kissed the ground. The top turret man, James Goodgion, stroked the lucky live lizard that he carried on missions. He saw the P-40 ground crews approaching and got ready for a big welcome. A mechanic greeted him with "Jesus Christ! We just got finished taking fifteen crackups apart to make these good airplanes and you guys come along and smash 'em all up." Captain Kendall, a lifelong teetotaler, went to a village wine shop and drank two liters of *vino rosso*.

Charles Porter Henderson of the Eight Balls stretched his flight on to Malta, landing on the Luqa fighter runway high on the rock. As his thankful men dismounted, an R.A.F. man pointed to the brink of a quarry 150 feet ahead of the plane. "Bloody good landing, sir," he said. "We've had lots of chaps go in there."

Forlorn *Utah Man*, far behind the general decampment, reached the Adriatic slope. Stewart called, "Connolly, give me a fuel check." The engineer replied, "Number Three is clear out and has been since the target. One, Two and Four are dipping empty." The pilot asked, "How much time does this give us?" The sergeant answered, "I don't know, Walt. I've never been in a ship regis-

---

* Four months later the Fravega brothers were shot down over Solingen, Germany. Anthony lived. Thomas died with engineer McWhirter and tunnel gunner George Parramore, who had been with them over Ploesti. After the war Anthony became the first sergeant of an Army Engineer group building air bases, and the new youngsters in Air Force blues did not understand how a muddy "dogface" could wear the Distinguished Flying Cross.

tering this low before." Stewart said, "Well, fellows, shall we set down here on the shore and give ourselves up, or do you want to try to make it? We've got five hundred miles of water ahead." Bartlett chimed in, "Before we vote, let me make a speech. Do you call this a sea? Why, we have rivers in Montana wider than this two-bit pond. Let's go! If we have to set down, I could pull this tub with one hand and swim with the other." The Paul Bunyanesque address produced a ten-nothing vote to carry on.

In a ship nearer home, Alva J. Geron gave control to his co-pilot and went aft to give morphine to gunner Paul T. Daugherty, who had a gaping flak wound in his chest. "Kill me, Lieutenant," said the gunner. "You know I won't live. Put me out of my misery." Geron injected more anesthetic. "Lieutenant, can you pray?" asked Daugherty. "Yes, I can," said the pilot. "Will you say a prayer for me?" Geron took him in his arms and prayed. The gunner squeezed the pilot's hand and slumped in death.

One of Geron's engines had been shot out. Now another failed. The crew threw guns, ammunition, everything loose out the waist bays. The pilot called a conference on the intercom and asked if all agreed on a water-landing. One of the gunners said, "No, sir. Not with Daugherty here. We oughtn't to let him sink in the sea." To bear the pall, the crew stayed with the airplane.*

On the dusty Libyan bases it had been a long, silent, corrosive day. Despite General Ent's "Mission Successful" signal, the camps were full of sick longing to know what had happened and who would return. The R.A.F. was relaying distress calls from an appalling number of Liberators. Outside the command radio shack Gerald Geerlings, the mission draftsman, played a distracted game of horseshoes with Jacob Smart, Ted Timberlake and Leander Schmid, the leaders who had been pulled out of the planes before take-off. Inside sat General Brereton, silently fretting, growing more and more annoyed at the cheerful telephone conversations of the duty officer who affected R.A.F. slang. Late in the afternoon Brereton heard one "Bang-on, ruddy good show"

---

* They landed in Libya with five minutes of gas left. The gunner was buried in the desert and the pilot and several of the crew went missing in action over Germany three weeks later.

too many. He went over to the junior and snarled, "You're a moron!" The surprised officer was trying to shape an apology when the phone rang again. He said, "Sir, General Ent's plane has just landed at Berka Two." Brereton ran to his car to meet the first plane home.

Norman Appold landed soon afterward at Berka Two without flaps or brakes. In the interrogation shack he and George Barwell found Brereton, Ent and K. K. Compton huddled in a low, gloomy discussion. Barwell said, "Norm, I am really quite sorry for General Ent. He's one of the best of your chaps I've met, a nice man, a very unusual man." Appold said, "Let's find A-Two and tell the sad story." Ent's decision to break off the target run in the face of Gerstenberg's flak had preserved all but two of the 26 Liberando ships that had reached the target area.

Barwell found that a clerk had put his name on the mission sortie list for the first time in his many unauthorized flights with the Americans. Cross and bone-weary, the master air gunner went to his tent and flopped on a cot. One of the Yacht Club boys thrust his head through the flaps and said, "You had a hard day, pal? Want a drink?" Barwell said, "Ghastly. Thanks." He got up and joined the artists. Next day he was summoned to Cairo by a very senior Royal Air Force officer, who reprimanded him for flying without permission and packed him off for England. Barwell was the only man on Tidal Wave who never received a decoration for it.

Russell Longnecker's spectral day in *Thundermug*, his first as the commander of an airship, had been splotched with somber shades of the deaths of many comrades and rainbows of luck for him. Now, nearing Africa, the picture would be ending, black or bright. Sergeant Pinson said, "The sight gauges are empty." Longnecker sang out with a confidence that had no substance, "We ought to be hitting land any minute now." In the miasma ahead there was a yellow flash, followed by a heavy crump. Longnecker's heart leaped. "We're home!" he cried. "The British ack-ack boys are saying hello." He queued up on another Liberator to land and recognized Ramsay Potts's ship, *Duchess*. He told himself, "At least somebody else got back almost as late as me." As the Circus base spread in front of his glide, he did not see a single B-24 on the ground. Longnecker was in the Intelligence shed before he realized what had happened at Ploesti. Eleven more crews reported in after him. Addison Baker had left that morning with 39 bombers.

Timberlake and Geerlings jeeped out to meet Ramsay Potts's ship. The ashen-faced B Force Leader came out from under the bomb bay with blazing eyes, shaking with fury. "A torrent of words tumbled out of him about what had gone wrong with the mission," said Geerlings.

A ship reached Benina Main in the twilight, firing red flares. The controllers stacked the others in the air to let it in first. Chaplain Patterson went in the ambulance to meet it. Through the waist window the gunners passed out a litter upon which lay a wounded comrade, numbed with morphine, but wearing a crooked smile. He said to Patterson, "I made it back from Ploesti, Chappie. See you later." The Chaplain looked at him again and drew a blanket over a dead face. The top turret gunner watched, shakily lighting a cigaret with a kitchen match. He held the stem in front of his eyes, watching it burn in yellow sap-flame, curl over black, and die. "Is life like that, Chappie?" he asked. Patterson said, "Yes, Sergeant, life is like that." Top turret trampled the ember in the dust and walked to interrogation.

Reginald Phillips, leader of the second wave over Blue Target, sat in the shack, dog-tired and thick of tongue. An Intelligence officer asked, "What was your overall impression of the mission?" Phillips' jaw worked. He said, "We—were—dragged through the mouth of—hell."

Waist gunner Ernest V. Martin, a young Sky Scorpion man lent to Kane's force, was brought home mortally wounded. Fellow crewmen said he had stood his guns throughout the day. He died 48 hours later.

Earl Hurd landed *Tarfu* and helped lift out a wounded gunner, Thomas D. Gilbert, back from his first war mission. Gilbert asked his pilot, "Are they all like this?" Hurd, a 22-mission man, joked, "No, some of them get pretty rough." He saw the spirit ebb from the youngster, as he thought of 24 more missions worse than Ploesti. The pilot said, "Look, I'm just kidding. This was my roughest one. The good Lord had his hand on our shoulders today."

Sergeant William Nelson got out of *Valiant Virgin* and lay down on the sand. A mechanic asked, "What was it like?" After some thought Nelson said, "Well, we started out today comparatively inexperienced. Right now I'd say we are one of the most experienced and oldest crews in the Air Force."

Ben Kuroki, the Japanese-American top turret gunner, shouldered his parachute and got down from *Tupelo Lass*. He and pilot K. O. Dessert walked to interrogations in the fading daylight, passing shadowy, dejected groups of ground crewmen waiting at empty stands. Ben wept. "The fools! Don't they know they'll never come back!"

As the distracted airman sat for questioning, night settled on the desert. The interrogators did not get much from men in shock and deep fatigue and released them to stumble off to sleep. As the bomber camps sank into torpor, out in the Mediterranean night three Homeric Liberator crews were still in the air with dead radios, yearning for home.

One of them was *Utah Man* with 13 hours and 45 minutes on the flight log. The Mormon pilot took up a glide path on the Circus base and quipped on the interphone, "We're going over our tent. Watch the vultures run out. The boys are probably dividing up our junk." (The next day, sheepish people returned their belongings.) Stewart rolled to a stop in the sands and dropped out of the plane into a welter of greeters—his ground crew, truck drivers, cooks, Red Cross girls, Chaplain James Burris, Brutus Hamilton and Ted Timberlake, laughing and weeping and embracing the crew of *Utah Man*. They told him of the cloud collision, in which he had lost his friend Hugh Roper of *Exterminator*. Stewart and his fellow officers went to their tent, knelt together, and "thanked God for hearing our prayer of just twenty-four hours before." The crew chief of *Utah Man*, Master Sergeant Scott, entered and said, "Walt, I know you're beat and don't want to talk to anybody, but I got to tell you something. I just went over our plane with seventeen crew chiefs from ships that didn't get back. Did you smell gas over the target?" Stewart said, "I sure did. But it stopped about twenty-five minutes later and the gauge showed empty." Scott said, "It follows. You have a flak hole the size of a baseball under the wing tank and you got one as big as a basketball where it went out the top. The bottom one got sealed off and the only gas you lost went out the top a while. I don't know how much you have left, but the way she sits on the oleo struts, I'd say you are now out of gas."

When Stewart brought his miracle to earth, Lewis Ellis was still out in the night with *Daisy Mae*, trying to work another. Dillman reported, "All fuel gauges showing zero, sir." Coldiron, slumping tired and wounded in the turret slings, announced, "Red flares ahead. It's got to be land." Dillman spun the handcranks, letting the wheels down, to save the last hydraulic fluid for the flaps. "We need only a few more minutes," Ellis told the crew. *Daisy Mae* was chewing the air, near to stalling.

Ellis set power as low as he dared to suck the last pints of gasoline, Fager pumped the flaps half down as *Daisy Mae* settled into the dust blanket over her home port. The pilot revved up to 2,100 rpm, ears cocked for failing engines, and turned the elevator knob on the automatic pilot. He was committed to land without a nosewheel, at night, inside a bed of dust—the same turbidity that had taken the Nespor-Riley ship on the Tidal Wave take-off fifteen hours before. "We can never circle again if we miss this one," said Ellis. Fager switched on the landing beams and pistoled red flares out his window.

Daisy Mae submerged in the dust sea, touched earth at stalling speed, and bounced. Ellis shoved the throttles to the bulkhead, demanding all power to maintain horizontal progress. The engines cut out. But *Daisy Mae*'s wheels were running on the earth. She coasted on swiftly and silently through the gritty fog and ploughed her nose gently into the sand. An ambulance crew took out the twice-wounded bombardier from the bloody flight deck. Gioana lifted a hand from the litter and said, "Sure glad to be back." That night flight surgeons, employing four blood transfusions, preserved his life.

At interrogations Ellis came upon a memorable scene: the man who had been scared on his second mission was sitting with Generals Brereton and Ent, "telling them just how it happened."

In the glum Liberando encampment, hours after the ships were all home and the dust was settled, yawning towermen saw red flares arching into the night off the end of the main runway and ordered landing lights on the strip.

It was *Liberty Lad*, the last Tidal Wave bomber still in the air, with both engines dead on one wing. McFarland and Podgurski were giving the last of their tortured legs to bring their wounded to Berka Two, where the hospital was located, instead of their own Circus field. The pilots approached at 2,000 feet with half flaps, the rudders fixed grotesquely to the right, held there by their stone legs for four hours. John H. Hayes manually lowered the wheels. As McFarland made his commitment to land, his instrument panel lights blew out. John Brown held a flashlight on the air-speed indicator. It read 120 mph. If it increased, *Liberty Lad* would crash in. If it decreased, the plane would stall in.

With brakes gone, *Liberty Lad* hit hard and bounced into an uncontrollable run. The ship coasted more than a mile before it stopped, sixteen hours after take-off, completing one of the most extraordinary flights in aviation history. McFarland's bombardier, Master Sergeant Robert W. Slade, grasped his hand and cried, "Landing this heap was really something! And, man, the way you dodged those balloon cables over the target!" McFarland said, "What balloon cables? I never saw any." The pilots' legs gave way, and they were in bed several days suffering exhaustion.

During the night Joseph Tate's neighbors were awakened by yells from his tent. He was stumbling around in his sleep, ripping up mosquito netting and underwear, crying, "Bandages! Tourniquets! Take care of these men!"

A fortnight after the mission, the Ninth Air Force closed the casualty books on Tidal Wave and President Roosevelt gave the figures to Congress, saying that the losses may have seemed disastrously high, "but I am certain that the German or Japanese High Commands would cheerfully sacrifice tens of thousands of men to do the same amount of damage to us, if they could."

The price was 53 Liberators, including eight interned in Turkey. Twenty-three ships reached Allied bases on Cyprus, Sicily and Malta. Eighty-eight returned to Benghazi, including 55 with battle damage.

The official report said that 446 airmen were killed or missing, 79 were interned in Turkey, and 54 were wounded.

At least one writer about Tidal Wave has alleged that the official War Department casualties were minimized. The authors of this book, on the basis of research among survivors, checked against "201" files (the individual war records), found that 310 Americans were killed on Tidal Wave, about one in five of the approximately 1,620 men who attained the target area, including those lost on the Nespor-Riley take-off crash and in *Wingo-Wango*'s fall at Corfu.

However, many more than 54 men were wounded. The official report, coming on 17 August, accounted for only the injured who had returned to Allied or neutral bases. There were 70 more wounded in Romanian captivity, whose condition was not then known, and a half dozen in Bulgarian hands, making a total of 130.

Although the casualties were far lower than General Ent had feared, he had lost the services of 579 effectives, plus 300 "retired" airmen, who now had to be actually retired. The day after Tidal Wave he had little more than half his men left and only 33 Liberators fit to fly, out of the 178 he had dispatched to Ploesti. Killer Kane returned from Cyprus that day and found 17 B-24's listed on the Pyramider strength, but only three were in condition for a mission.

Tidal Wave was the end of the Ninth Air Force as a heavy bomber command, although it participated minimally in several more joint raids with the Twelfth Air Force, out of Tunisia. The Circus, Eight Ball and Scorpion survivors flew back to their nests in England, and the desert rats and their pink ships were absorbed into the Fifteenth Air Force in Italy, where preparations were under way for a gigantic and prolonged bombing campaign against Gerstenberg's fortress. As Sir Charles Portal had guessed, the Protector was building up a greater furniture of arms to meet it.

With a clatter of mimeograph machines, the Ninth Air Force, General Brereton and his staff, were transmogrified into a British-based fighter-bomber and infantry support command for the coming invasion of France.

Meanwhile, 108 Tidal Wave men were alive in Romania, entering one of the most extraordinary experiences that befell captured soldiers in World War II.

13

BLACK SUNDAY

When the Liberators left Ploesti they had altered a landscape and begun the transformation of a people. Around the Wallachian plain they left pillars of smoke, the epitaphs of aircraft and men, of refineries and tank farms. In the ripe fields they left smudges of burned haycocks and wheat stooks and long skid smears of planes, like those of insects squashed on a windshield. The hot ground guns were still, but the battle tympanum was pounding to a crescendo of delayed explosions in the refineries.

In *der Mordkessel* (the cauldron of death), from Câmpina to the Danube, the dead and wounded lay. The fields and woods abounded with hunting parties of soldiery, litter bearers and sightseers. On the roads to Ploesti marched battalions of slave laborers, the Russian *corvée*, to begin salvage and reconstruction. A hundred Americans were dying and another hundred, staggering with pain, with red-blind eyes from the shock of crashes and parachute falls—many to be deaf for days from the overwhelming sound of battle—were dispersing from the wrecks in the hope of getting away.

The first one to touch Romanian soil, Jack Warner, out of Enoch Porter's *Euroclydon*, awakened in a shallow creek with a shattered collarbone, and ladled water over his burns with his good hand. German soldiers hauled him out, stripped him "naked as a jay bird," and marched him away. Farm women and children pointed to Warner and shrieked, "Amerikani!" The Germans took

224

him to a room full of injured comrades, lying on parachute packs and moaning for water. Warner heard a voice say in broken English, "Put those in the dead corner." He fainted into sleep and awakened in a hospital ward of wounded Germans. One, with a fifty-caliber shell through his neck, gave Warner a cigaret. Two Germans died and their beds were taken by more wounded, one of whom yelled at the American, "Get up, you gangster! I'll wipe the floor with you." The German tried to get out of bed and fell back dead.

The young flak gunner, Erich Hanfland, got down from the hot seat of his 20-mm. battery. He had passed 1,450 rounds through the gun and burned out two barrels while shooting down two bombers. Battery Sergeant Bichler threatened to punish him for ruining the gun. Hanfland took off across the fields to see the wrecks of the B-24's he had destroyed. He came upon a tall, thin American in a leather flying jacket, who was badly burned. The American said to him in "perfect" German, "What is the damage to the refineries? You know, I worked here in Ploesti before the war." Hanfland took his escape kit and began examining the curiosities inside. The American said, "Give me back the gold piece. I can use it." Hanfland returned it. Sergeant Bichler arrived and pummeled the American. Hanfland cried to his sergeant, "You hate yourself! You hate life!" Bichler turned from the airman and said to the young gunner, "That finishes you, Hanfland." * The thin American who spoke perfect German and claimed to have worked at Ploesti was taken off to the hospital.**

* Hanfland was sent to Germany and punished with parachute training. That autumn he was dropped behind Allied lines in Italy and was captured unhurt by Americans. Battery Sergeant Bichler and most of Hanfland's Ploesti comrades were killed in Romania the following year.

** The authors have not been able to identify this intriguing thin man. Charles Cavit remembers an American sergeant in the Bucharest jail who asked the guards to let the pilot go to the toilet. "The sergeant spoke real good German," said Cavit. "They told us later that he died from a piece of flak, but some of the boys saw him in Germany." The latter were eight POW's sent to Frankfurt for interrogation. One of them remembers a ninth man who spoke both American and German idiomatically. They had never seen him before. The ninth man had special privileges, including parole from the interrogation center, and did not return with them to Romania. Was he a German spy? If so, he was a very thorough worker to have himself "badly

Elmer Reinhart, the last man to jump from his failing Liberator, was alone in a cornfield eighty miles southwest of Ploesti. He fitted his compass buttons together and set off along a creek, on the theory that it emptied into the Danube. His escape instructions favored two routes out of Romania. If the downed man was loose considerably west of the target, he was to search for Yugoslav partisan areas. If he was too deep inside Romania, as was the case with Reinhart, the breezy advice was to "hop a log or a raft across the Danube" and "jump" a Turkish ship at Constanta.

Reinhart trekked along the creek all afternoon, avoiding people. Toward evening he saw an elderly shepherd on a hilltop and decided to take a chance on him. The old man gazed at Reinhart with frightened eyes. The pilot pantomimed that he was unarmed and handed over his pocket knife. This won a timid smile. Reinhart gave him a dollar bill. The shepherd studied George Washington's portrait and cried, "President Roosevelt!" He led Reinhart to his cottage, left him there, and returned with policemen. The populace followed Reinhart to a dirt-floored village jail and gave him cheese, bread and melons.

The reception turned ugly. A Romanian officer arrived, chained Reinhart's hands and feet, and threw him into a horse cart. The pilot was delivered to a town police station, where a man questioned him in English. On a desk Reinhart saw a hunting knife and pistol belonging to his co-pilot Charles L. Starr. The interrogator could not tell him where Starr was. Reinhart was taken in a 1929 Ford to Slatina, where he met five of his parachuted sergeants. They had puffed eyes and bruises from beatings by peasants. "They probably took us for Russians," said Sergeant Alfred Mash. "Where is Lieutenant Starr?" Reinhart asked. Russell Huntley said, "We never did hook up with any of the officers.

---

burned" or struck with flak before taking up his masquerade. Ninth Air Force Intelligence officers doubt very much that anyone who had lived in Ploesti flew the great mission; Tidal Wave planners had scoured Britain and the United States for people with prewar experience there, and it is unlikely that they would have overlooked one on the air bases. Was the thin man a defector? Did he invent a story for Hanfland about working in Ploesti, thinking it would get him preferred treatment, or even a trip to Germany?

The story is that the peasants killed Lieutenant Starr. His chute didn't open and they put him out of his misery."

Near burning and exploding White Five the Catholic missioner, Corporal Ewald Wegener, and a Dr. Kauter worked all Sunday afternoon on a gravely burned Romanian soldier, who had been brought in naked wrapped in newspapers. They sent him to the hospital, where, thanks to their early work, his life was saved. As they removed their wrist watches to scrub up, the medical men noticed the hour. It was five hours since the bombing. "Wegener, there must be many other wounded," said the doctor. They went seeking them through the smoke and came to a schoolhouse in the city, where airmen were being carried. In the main hall, upon a straw-littered floor, lay thirty Americans, burned and broken, naked and dying. Wegener saw a man with "C" for Catholic on his identification tags and said in clumsy English, "I am a priest." The airman looked up through his pain at the sooty enemy, groaned and waved him away. The next man with a "C" touched the corporal's hand and received the last rites in Latin before he died. Wegener administered them to several others.

As Dr. Kauter began organizing the impromptu dressing station, there was a clatter of boots and snarls; in came Wegener's CO, the Mad Prussian, yelling, "*Sie sollten umgebracht werden, diese Mörder!*" (These murderers should be killed.) Corporal Wegener said, "They are only soldiers, *mein Kommandant*. They were only doing their duty." The CO shouted, "You will go to the Russian front!" and clomped out of the schoolhouse.

Other wounded men were brought to Bucharest in carts and trucks, with people peering in, the women bursting into tears, seeing in their mind's eye their young men going to mound graves in Russia. Disaster-followers thronged the amphitheater of the Queen's Hospital, watching masked surgeons and their white-robed courtiers perform emergency operations on the blackened airmen. When the doctors lost Maurice Peterson of *Jersey Bounce*, women in the gallery keened the *doina*, the ancient Gypsy lament.

General Gerstenberg sent officers around the collecting points for American wounded to see that they had proper medical care.

Leutnant Scheiffele found several B-24 crews laid out in a flak battery barracks and phoned, "Herr General, none of them are conscious. They all have heavy burns and dreadful wounds. They are beyond help, but the doctors are administering morphine to ease their last hours." In a field dressing station, Scheiffele found German medics picking flak splinters from the heads of a dozen Americans. He reported, "It is hard to believe, Herr General. They came here without helmets! Most are in severe shock. They cannot believe what they have experienced. I find it hard to believe myself. Our soldiers, to the last man, are astonished that anyone would dare such a low-level attack. They do not understand how anyone could underestimate our defenses so badly."

Only a dozen Americans were in condition to be interrogated. An English-speaking Intelligence officer sat alone in a room and the fliers were admitted one by one. The officer had orders to be courteous and not try to force answers. He offered the men cigarets, but they declined and smoked their own. The airmen gave only the minimum personal identification required by the Geneva Convention on Prisoners of War. However, many of them could not help unburdening themselves to the sympathetic German on the great disillusion of Ploesti: "They told us before the mission that the flak would never get us if we flew low!"

Those Americans able to walk were collected in the Bucharest city jail. There Elmer Reinhart and his five parachutists met pilot Jerome Savaria, who lay in shock from a heavy scalp wound. He had fallen among country folk who had not observed Allied Intelligence advices that "the peasants are honest, friendly, kindly and hospitable to strangers." They had mobbed Savaria, one swinging an axe. He ducked the fatal stroke but took a glancing blow on his head. The peasants put a rope around his neck and marched him to a tree. A German patrol arrived and stopped the lynching.

John Palm lay in a barrage balloon shack near Bratulesti, holding onto his nearly severed leg. He pantomimed to his captors how to construct a litter. They made one of saplings and carried him on it to a truck. After a jolting, excruciating ride to a Bucharest gynecological hospital, Palm was sent in a pushcart on another hard ride to Spital Shuler, a first-class private clinic run by Dr. Georg Petrescu. Palm said, "I could tell right away that Dr. Petrescu was a wheel and an Allied sympathizer." The surgeon removed his dangling leg, sutured the stump, and put Palm to bed.

That night the Texan was awakened by a crowd of thuglike types in long leather overcoats, cradling machine guns in their arms. In front of them stood a small fox-faced man wearing a black homburg, a pin-striped Savile Row suit and suède shoes. In English he said, "So you are an American?" Palm admitted it. The little man scowled and walked out with the gunmen. Dr. Petrescu said, "Do you know who that was? General Antonescu." The dictator of Romania had come to see one of the creatures for himself, after a day of absurd frustration. At his villa on Lake Znagov, he had heard the aerial noise and assumed that it was merely Woldenga running another surprise mock attack on Ploesti.

In the morning Palm received friendly visitors, with an unarmed escort—a slender, pleasant lady, her arm held by a hulking teen-aged boy. She said, "I am Helen and this is the king." Palm said, "It's sure nice to make your acquaintance," looking at the first king he'd ever laid eyes on. Palm remembered a newspaper item about Michael running away with a tank on army maneuvers, and engaged him in a discussion about planes, guns, cars, tanks and motocycles, for such was their mutual passion. The queen mother found a chance to whisper to Palm, out of earshot of her retinue, "You know, we are not free to speak. Do the Americans understand that our sympathies are with you?" Palm gave the queen a big secret wink and a Lucky Strike. He was now American ambassador to Romania.

The queen bade Dr. Petrescu move Palm into a private room, where she could come incognito without spying courtiers. She was the wife that Carol II had put away in favor of his famous baggage, Magda Lupescu. On the days that Helen did not come to the hospital Palm received anonymous perfumed notes on crested writing paper. The Texan began to form the impression that if one had to lose a leg and languish in foreign durance, this was not a bad way to take it.

During the long hot afternoon and night after the raid Bernard Traudt, the seventeen-year-old gunner who had bailed out of the flaming orange ship, slept blissfully under a bush, undetected by search parties. He awoke refreshed at dawn Monday and saw a farmer walking toward a privy. Traudt selected from his escape kit a mimeographed form letter in Romanian asking help for an American aviator. With an extra-sunny smile the lad stepped out and presented it. The peasant studied it from all angles, including upside down. He was illiterate. From behind, another rustic came up stealthily and clouted Traudt on the head with a pitchfork handle. The boy awakened in an oxcart on the way to captivity.

That Monday morning the Bucharest stock exchange opened for ten minutes, then shut its doors to assess the economic impact of the bombing.

Princess Caradja had been very busy since the bombers crossed her house. Hearing that American prisoners were being detained by her countrymen instead of the Germans, she advised "her boys," as she had begun to call O'Reilly's crew, to surrender to Romanians and arranged a discreet rendezvous for them. Poulsen collected their dollars and gave them to the princess to hold. She sent her field hands with a winch to the wrecked plane to lift the turret off the dead flight engineer, Frank Kees, and started the orphans' carpentry shop to constructing his coffin. Women washed the body and repaired the ripped suntans in which he would be buried next day.

The princess sped to Bucharest to pursue her main purpose, to hold the Americans in Romania and not let them be sent to Germany. She persuaded her social circle, which included several wives of cabinet ministers, to exert conjugal politics on their husbands. Colonel Sarbu, an old family friend, implored her to go to the ruins of the Women's Prison and try to identify the body of his sister, Elena. He was a member of the Iron Guard and Mademoiselle Sarbu had been sentenced to prison as a leftist Allied sympathizer. The princess identified the charred body of Elena Sarbu,* and drove to a café rendezvous to see how the campaign

* Today, on the rebuilt Women's Prison, according to Princess Caradja, there is a memorial tablet to Elena Sarbu, saying that she was "treacherously

to hold the Americans was coming. The cabinet ladies had good news. Their husbands had bucked up Antonescu to go see Gerstenberg and claim the Americans. The Iron Guard leader had approached the Protector with deep misgivings; Hitler's captives, wherever apprehended, were always sent to German stalags. Antonescu said, "The Americans have been captured in battle here, therefore Romania should be the detaining power." Gerstenberg pondered the question. It occurred to him that this was an elegant solution. Instead of carting the rambunctious, high-calorie-consuming Americans off to tax the rations and billets of the Reich, why not leave them in Romania and win a point for his generosity? He said, "My dear General Antonescu, they were shot down here. Of course they are your prisoners! I shall hand over all those we have arrested and will give you the ones we have sent to Frankfurt for interrogation." It was Antonescu's second victory of the war, the other being his refusal to adopt Wehrmacht time.

The princess heard the good news in a café which was otherwise buzzing with talk about the fantastic accuracy of the bombing and the patent fact that the Americans had tried to avoid hurting civilians. Except for the tragedy in the prison, few Ploesti dwellers had been harmed.

She drove back home to conclude arrangements for burying O'Reilly's top turret man. Her major-domo said, "The parish priest refuses to conduct the funeral. He says this man bombed our people." The princess phoned a bishop in Bucharest, "My fool of a priest won't bury one of the American boys." The parish priest was on hand in the morning, leading a procession of villagers and orphans behind Kees's body to the Cantacuzene private cemetery on the estate. To the sound of chants in an alien tongue, a boy from Kentucky was laid among the bones of princes who had fought the Saracen. Women covered the grave with flowers. The priest said to a grandmother, "You fools! They shoot your sons and you decorate their graves." The old woman replied, "Our

---

murdered." This perversion ignores the fact that she died in the crash of a Liberator crippled by a Romanian pilot who disobeyed orders not to fight over the city. The ten Americans in the plane were as helpless as the women in the jail. The plane was a prison too.

sons are falling in Russia. We hope that other mothers are doing this for them."

King Michael drove to the princess' manor in his sports car to see O'Reilly's Liberator, which was among the best preserved of the crashed ships. Michael saw gasoline trickling out of the wing tanks and collected several liters for his car. He leaped in and roared away. Down the road a way, his motor failed. U. S. aviation gas was too rich for it.

Hitler telephoned congratulations to Gerstenberg, and then Goering thanked the Protector for brilliantly justifying the arms and men he had sent to the quiet theater, sometimes at the expense of the Reichsmarschal's dwindling prestige in Berlin. Gerstenberg and Woldenga inspected the damaged refineries with their petroleum production engineer and economist, Frau Gramach, a feminine doctoral engineer from Hanover. She told Gerstenberg that it would be only a matter of days before she could give him full shipment quotas of oil. Ten thousand Slav captives were at work clearing rubble and connecting by-pass pipelines in the quick recovery system the Protector had devised.

Woldenga told Gerstenberg that he thought the American bombs were too small for the job. Many had not exploded. But the fighter controller's opinion was: "The deep-level attack was a good idea. I myself have seen the effect of total surprise at zero altitude. In October 1940 I took forty Messerschmitts over London at roof-top level. We took off from the French coast, went up the Thames, and swept the city from end to end without losing a plane.* It was only a forty-minute flight. One can attain surprise on such short missions, but the American voyage was much too long. The risk of detection is too great on a six-hour flight."

Woldenga remarked on the high proportion of Liberators with Eighth Air Force colors and markings. Gerstenberg said, "Yes, we have punished two American air forces." Woldenga gave him one of Geerlings' perspective route charts found in one of the

---

* This may have been the fighter bomber sweep of 7 October which hit Lambeth Palace, or that of 10 October which destroyed the high altar of St. Paul's Cathedral.

wrecks.* "Extraordinary," said the general. "It shows a very special effort. Excellent planning." He added, "I am certain the Americans will come again, despite what happened to them. Their bases are moving closer. They have a foothold in Sicily; southern Italy may be next. I reminded Goering of the Me-110's he promised. We must have more aircraft, more guns, more troops. We lost about a hundred flak people yesterday."

Woldenga said, "That is unfortunate, sir. I have the pleasure to report that we lost only two German pilots.** I believe three Romanians were killed."

Ever since he had made his fortunate guess on which threaded part disarmed the American bombs, Armament Inspector Egon Schantz had been continuously rendering them harmless. In the first 24 hours his men dealt with "more than a hundred," according to Adjutant Scheiffele. Of course many of them were duds to begin with, but some of the sleeping monsters, with tardy detonators, were still exploding on the second day.

---

* German Intelligence assumed that the prewar postcards and snapshots were photographs from a recent Allied reconnaissance flight. The Luftwaffe warning system was reprimanded for not detecting it. Of course there had been no photo-reconnaissance prior to Tidal Wave.

** The authors received this same remarkable assertion in separate interviews with eleven Luftwaffe officers in the battle, including four fighter pilots of I-JG 4 at Mizil. The Air Ministry in London opened its captured Luftwaffe documents for southeastern Europe, which bore out Woldenga. They state that IV-NJG 6, the night-fighter group at Zilistea, lost two Me-110's and five were damaged, while two Mizil Me-109's were destroyed and two damaged. Presumably the Mizil fatalities were from Captain Toma's integrated Romanian wing. The Air Ministry documents do not include Royal Romanian Air Force figures, which the writers were unable to find. The Athenian Me-109's lost two planes of record in the Kephallenia ambush. Apparently the Bulgarian Air Force lost none of the fighters that attacked the B-24's during the withdrawal. The ascertainable facts shed a revealing light on wartime allowances for enemy aircraft destroyed. Tidal Wave gunners were credited with 51. A cautious estimate of German evidence would scarcely show two dozen fighters actually downed in the general mêlée around Ploesti, the Bulgarian border fray, and the Ionian Sea ambuscade. The Luftwaffe officially credited eighteen Liberators to Romanian-based fighters, after examining the crashes. Two B-24's were definitely shot down in Bulgaria and four in the battle of the Ionian Sea. Human losses in the intra-aerial engagements of Tidal Wave would appear to total approximately: Americans—150; Axis—15.

There was an unexploded 500-pounder hanging in the top of a fractionating column, and the defenders wanted to save this vital unit. Fireman Schütz volunteered to climb the column and disarm the bomb. Trailing a phone cable to Schantz in a bomb shelter, the fireman went up the tower. He phoned to the ground, "The first screw is bent and I can't get it off with my bare hands. I'm going to use a wrench." Schantz replied, "I don't think you should. If there is too much force, it might turn the second screw." Schütz said, "No, I think it will work." A huge explosion rocked the shelter. They didn't even find Schütz's belt buckle.

Gerstenberg ordered that the American dead be buried with full military honors. There were several mass funerals of Americans and Germans together, with trumpets, parade standards and honor guards firing the final volleys.

The Protector analyzed the event for which he had prepared for three years. He was clearly the victor of the day, but he did not warm himself with that or the encomiums from Berlin. The American wrecks around the target and a projection of that figure for damage, death and wounds, in the bombers that got away, convinced him that the Ninth Air Force would be unable to send a follow-up mission. Perhaps it had effectively lost its bomber command. Yet the enemy's great daring, the evidence of long and shrewd planning, and the combining of two air forces for the raid, told Gerstenberg that the Americans valued Ploesti as highly as he did. Never one to underestimate the enemy, the Protector imagined himself in Brereton's brown study: What could he do, without planes, to try to finish the destruction of the refineries? While the fires were still burning and the bombs exploding— sabotage! Gerstenberg thought that if hundreds of Americans had come suicidally as bomber crews, others could parachute in to finish the job. He ordered his entire command on alert against parachutists.

Axis Sally, in her English-language broadcasts from Berlin, said, "Good show, Brereton, but you lost too many." Oddly enough, Goebbels made little of the fact that the Americans had missed the Standard Oil refinery, while destroying British and French-built plants. Café wits in Bucharest did not overlook it.

They were saying, "Now we may expect British bombers to hit the American plant." The Germans sent inspired rumors by neutral businessmen headed for Turkey, greatly exaggerating the damage to the refineries—a ploy wistfully designed to make the Americans think they need not come back. However, Brereton soon knew exactly what had happened to the White Targets. Two days after Tidal Wave, a Mosquito photo-reconnaissance plane from Sixty Squadron, South African Air Force, appeared 28,000 feet over Ploesti in perfect weather. In it were Lieutenants A. M. Miller, pilot, and W. R. Allison, navigator, busy photographing the refineries. The plywood Mosquito was the only aircraft in the world, other than the Liberator, that could duplicate the round trip from Benghazi. Amidst intense flak the bold South Africans made stereo-pairs of the White Targets and returned safely. They did not have the fuel to cover Red and Blue Targets, and the damage dealt them was not known until two weeks later when another Mosquito picked them off with a camera.

In a Bucharest hospital lay Charles T. Bridges, the only crewman alive from *Porky II* in the last Eight Ball wave. The battered gunner was smarting over an incident after the crash. As he had staggered away, half blind and drenched with blood, a German sergeant seized his escape kit and knocked him down. Bridges counterattacked and was knocked down again. Now at his bedside there appeared a jovial Roman Catholic priest, who said, "There you are, my son! I'm glad to see you're alive. You know, after I pulled you out of the plane, you sent me to get help for the others, and when I returned you were gone and they were dead."

Bridges said, "*You* pulled me out of the plane, Padre? Why, I crawled out by myself. I don't remember seeing you at all. Some Jerries worked me over, and a big Romanian soldier charged me, trying to throw the bolt on his rifle. I yelled, 'Kamerad!' and he took me to a hut. Next day I woke up here."

"Nevertheless, we are old friends, Sergeant," said the holy man. "After I pulled you from the plane, you spoke to me in Latin." Bridges said, "I haven't spoken Latin since high school. I doubt if I know ten words." The priest said, "You asked me to send word to your mother in Andersonville, Indiana, that you were all right." This was Bridges' home town. The cleric said, "I sent her a cable through the Vatican."

Mrs. Bridges had received the cable via the Roman Catholic diocese in Fort Wayne. Two days later she received a War Department telegram announcing that her son was missing in action. The poor mother was prostrated by these conflicting messages, but the diocese could furnish no further information; it had simply forwarded the cable sent through hierarchal channels. Nor could the War Department add anything. It was going to be months before some of the folks at home knew whether their men were alive or dead in Romania.

A week after the raid the wounded B-24 men were removed from Bucharest for convalescence at the King's Hospital at Sinaia in the Transylvanian Alps above Ploesti. Its quarters, food and medical care were excellent. One day the Americans were taken to a huge white building near the hospital and helped and carried up an imposing staircase into a great hall. A well-dressed woman and a strapping teen-aged boy entered and a major-domo yelled, "His Majesty, Mihai the First!" The G.I.'s were in the royal summer palace at Peleş. An airman remarked, "The kid looks like good college football material." The king addressed them, "We say to you American airmen that you will be well treated in our country. Our people are favorably impressed by the fact that you did not bomb civilians. We are personally writing letters to your families, saying that you are safe." A voice from the back of the hall hollered, "How about cabling!"

The Archbishop of Bucharest visited the hospital and distributed gifts of *tsuica,* or plum brandy. The livelier wounded began dicing on the beds and romancing the nurses and female sightseers. The next time His Beatitude came to the hospital he passed out New Testaments. Romanian society girls, whose previous diversions had been tea-dancing with German officers at the hotels in Mamaia, now flocked to Sinaia, bringing comforts for the Americans, including books from the shuttered British Council Library in Bucharest. The titles included, *The Sheik, I Carried a Gun for Al Capone,* and *The Happy Prisoner.* However, patients Charles Bridges and Donald Wright were not happy prisoners. One night they slipped out of the hospital and struck out for the woods. Their hospital robes attracted attention and the pair were apprehended and sent back. The hospital staff was hurt. The chief physician lectured them: "You are guests of this country and should behave yourselves accordingly."

A friendly English-speaking Romanian lieutenant visited the forty airmen in the Bucharest city jail and told them, "There are seventy of your men in hospital. They are receiving the best medical attention. We have counted thirty-two wrecked bombers. Here in Bucharest we have buried two hundred fourteen of your men. Only sixty-five bodies could be identified."

The jailed men were removed to a schoolyard and left there without explanation. A police van came and put in with them four men in ragged civilian clothes. The Americans suspected they were spies and made disparaging remarks about them. The newcomers said nothing. They had never seen an American soldier before. They gaped at the wide selection of uniforms permitted to the fliers—fleece-lined leather jackets, singlets, overalls, cotton shirts and woolen shirts of different colors, British battle jackets, desert shorts, and, it seemed, ten styles of long pants. They were shod in laced boots, ornamented Brazilian cowboy boots, British hard-bashers, basketball shoes and Arab sandals. On their heads they wore steel helmets, plastic helmet liners, peaked caps, cork topees, unshorn sheepskins, brimmed dress caps with the top ring removed, forage caps—both olive drab and suntan— and a jaunty Afrika Korps bonnet. One of the strangers muttered under his voice to another, "I never thought I'd live to see the day." The other said, "S-s-s-sh, don't talk. Let's listen to them slanging us."

The strangers were Britons, captured three summers before during the German transgression in western Europe. The ragged band consisted of a courtly London *Times* correspondent named Jerome Caminada, trapped in the fall of France; an eagle-beaked Yorkshireman named Robert Johnson, bagged in Denmark while practicing as a swine veterinarian; a rugged soldier from Nottinghamshire, Platoon Sergeant Edward Lancaster of the Sherwood Foresters, taken at Narvik, Norway; and a tall, vivacious youth with snapping brown eyes, Platoon Sergeant Douglas Collins of the Gloucestershire Regiment, overrun at Dunkirk while holding the perimeter as the last boats left for England. They were the British Vanishers, the inner circle of the elite prison-camp escapers on the eastern front, with a collective total of 21 departures from enemy cages, including stalags, maximum security fortresses and secret police cells. Collins and Lancaster had seen more of Hitler's Europe than one of his inspectors general. The lion-hearted sergeants had left a trail of empty cells, knotted ropes, teetering gangplanks and boot leather from the Arctic Ocean to Poland, to Chetnik regions of Yugoslavia—almost to the Black Sea. They had spent several sybaritic months at large in Budapest, maintained in luxury by Allied sympathizers, but had not forgotten their burning goal—to get back into the fight. They came to Romania, where they had been taken while trying to cross the broad Danube. While being questioned in the cellar of a Bucharest secret police headquarters, they escaped through a sewer and emerged from a manhole on Calea Victoriei, the main street of the capital. Amidst sirens and street-corner loud-speaker announcements of the escape, they legged it forty miles to the river again. The Danube, which prospective American escapees had been instructed to paddle across on a log, once again brooked the British Vanishers. This time the captors put them in a cage manned by a battalion of guards who had no other inmates to look after. Collins said their strolls in the compound "followed by four hundred pairs of eyes, was rather like playing in the center court at Wimbledon." When the Americans dropped in, the Romanians decided to mix the bothersome Britons in with them. Here they were in the schoolyard, temporarily down on their luck, much intrigued with an ally they had never seen, and listening to his scurrilous remarks in their mother tongue.

Buses arrived and took them all aboard. Collins and Lancaster selected a seat behind radioman Russell Huntley, whom they had heard the others calling "Limey." (The nickname was merely inspired by the fact that Huntley had served in the Canadian Army before his own country went to war.) Lancaster leaned over to Huntley and spoke the first words to come from the unprepossessing quartet: "I say, give us a light, mate." Huntley jumped. The allied parties began to talk. Collins' sharp eyes scanned the Americans for potential escapee material.

The buses went north on the Ploesti highway, on a route that happened to provide a sight-seeing tour of the stricken refineries. As the buses neared Blue Target at Brazi, the guards primly drew the blinds, which tipped off the airmen that there was something worth looking at. They rolled up the blinds and saw Creditul Minier in total and desolate ruin. The guards ran back and forth in the aisles jerking down the blinds. At Ploesti the airmen saw the Russian *corvée* toiling in the wreckage of White Four and White Five, which had cost them many comrades and their own freedom. Passing Red Target at Câmpina, there was an approving hum and elbows in neighboring ribs: "Boy, that one is hammered but good!"

The convoy climbed the winding Predeal Pass from the heat of the valley to cool breezes scented with balsams. Halfway up the Transylvanian spur of the Carpathians, the buses stopped at Sinaia and took aboard the walking wounded from the King's Hospital. The journey took up again, higher and higher, toward the domain of Count Dracula and the werewolves. Near the summit, at a resort called Timisul de Jos, where Gerstenberg had taken his ease on the morning of Tidal Wave, Lancaster spotted barbed wire across the parallel railroad and said to Collins and Huntley, "This is it."

The buses turned across the tracks into Prisonaire de Lagurel No. 18, as it was called. Nothing like it befell other captives in World War II. The officers' new home was a three-story resort hotel. The enlisted men drew two buildings of a neighboring private school for girls. The gunners inspected the girls' dorms, scowling at the tiled wood-burning stoves, the ample washroom and kitchen, and the outside toilets which had French-style footprint offices. A sergeant moaned, "Jeez, are these people ever behind the times!" Collins said, "This is absolutely marvelous. You should see what you get in Germany." He recognized the compound at Timisul as by far the best prisoner-of-war establishment in Axis territory. It resembled the princely aviation-officer detention centers of the First World War. The Liberator gunners had no basis of comparison, and, in the fashion of traveling Americans, proceeded to knock the foreign plumbing.

The officers' hotel was superior to air base quarters in the States. It had a spacious dining room, two baths, four lavatories and fourteen bedrooms, each with a hot-water basin, individual lockers and goose-down mattresses. On the pleasant grounds there were graveled walks, a fine view of the Alps, a small gymnasium with showers, and tennis courts. The officers had nothing to cavil about, so patently luxurious was their lot. They found some empty fish pools which a co-pilot promptly learned to fill from a mountain stream, and they began to amuse themselves by flooding and emptying the ponds.

Both compounds had Russian prisoner cooks, kitchen hands, cleaners and orderlies. The officers had a hearty Ukrainian cook named Ivan. There was no kitchen police or any sort of work detail for the prisoners. Romania was doing well by its uninvited guests. However, the barbed wire was serious. The adjoining camps of the officers and men were separated by guarded gates and a wire-lined connecting track. The whole was surrounded by double lines of wire interconnected by barbed entanglements, and in some places there were four outer strands.

The British Vanishers were delighted with the food. They had nearly starved in the stalags, while "here there was always enough to eat," said Collins. "True, it was beans, bread, bits of meat, cabbage and potatoes, but there was no hunger." The Americans did not like the fare, although it was no worse than the grub at Benghazi. Their culinary comparison overlooked that and went back to steaks and ice cream in the Big PX across the Atlantic.

Red Cross parcels arrived in the gunners' compound and the men crowded around Master Sergeant Frank Garrett, who called off the lucky recipients: "Sergeant Edward Lancaster. [*Three cheers for the Limey.*] Sergeant Douglas Collins. [*That a boy, Doug.*] Sergeant Douglas Collins. [*Lucky bastard.*] Sergeant Douglas Collins. [*Hey, what goes on?*] Sergeant Edward Lancaster. [*He gets two?*] Sergeant Edward Lancaster . . ." All thirty parcels from the British Red Cross were for the embarrassed British decampers. They had never received any before, due to their unavailability at mail call much of the time. Now three years' accumulation of parcels had caught up with them. Lancaster said, "Just a minute there, Yanks. This lot is for all of us." Collins recalled, "We pooled the loot. It would have been unthinkable to sit apart and nibble at our parcels. In POW camps nothing leads to strife quicker than having a favored few around."

American officers received the equivalent pay of their rank in the Romanian Army—in the case of a first lieutenant, 22,400 lei (about $22.50 U. S.) a month, a large salary in Romania. A hardworking peasant was lucky to earn two dollars a month in Hitler's protectorate. Two hundred lei per day was deducted from each officer's salary for rations. Although that amounted to twenty cents, it bought plenty of good food.

When the word got out in the countryside that Timisul was full of rich Americans, farm wives arrived at the wire with a small harvest fair: juicy peaches and plums, squealing piglets, chicken and geese, apples, slabs of bacon and pungent sausages, goose liver salami, and two veritable marvels—ripe watermelons and roasting ears of corn. The officers quickly learned the word for beer—the famous brand name "Bragadir"; *tsuica,* pronounced "sweeka," for plum brandy; and "Monopol" for champagne.

Romania held in escrow from the officers' wages all but the allowance for rations and comforts. The depositors figured their growing bank accounts and plunged heavily at craps and poker, using I.O.U.'s. Caminada and Johnson received captains' salaries, which the veterinarian said "were of little use to us. We could not always compete with the 'Damn Yanks' at poker. We poor 'Limeys' were easy prey." One officer won $3,000 from his cagemates. Some of the shouting card-slappers and pot-rakers had "appalling wounds and burns, which really should have been attended to in hospital," said Johnson. There came a shipment of medications from the British Red Cross and the "Limey Pig-Doctor" looked after the "Damn Yanks." "I worried each time I dressed the burns, because it was inevitable that I had to take off more layers of flesh," said Johnson. "The only way I managed to get any cure was to expose the wounds and put the men out to sunbathe."

Seventy-nine other Tidal Wave men were interned in the first-class Yeni Hotel in Ankara, Turkey. General William D. Tindall, the U. S. military attaché, paid their full salaries, obtained parole for them from morning to night, and shipped the disabled men to the States. The fliers walked in Captain Mooney's funeral procession. As it passed the German Embassy, a drooping swastika banner almost brushed the Stars and Stripes on Mooney's catafalque. When the Turkish honor guard fired the last volley, storks flew out of their nests in the trees. Franz von Papen, the Nazi ambassador, protested to the Turkish Government over the insult done his banner by permitting the American flag to parade past it.

Tindall got the men credits to buy civilian clothes. Earl Zimmerman said, "As Uncle Sam was paying the bill, we wore nothing but the best." They played chess with interned Russian airmen, who inquired after the health of previous American chess opponents, the Halpro men. They dined at the best restaurant in the capital, Pop Karpic's. He sent gifts of caviar to their tables, particularly when von Papen was sitting nearby. One of the bored B-24 men went on a spree and was jailed for striking a policeman. Karpic sent him caviar and champagne.

The military attaché evacuated them piecemeal. Sergeant Zimmerman departed via Syria and arrived in Prestwick, Scotland, in General Sir Bernard Montgomery's private plane. Charles Hughes, Sylvester Hunn and two brother officers were taking an apéritif on the waterfront at Izmir when a smiling Greek named Thorgarous Christopholis invited them to inspect his little fishing caïque. As the airmen recoiled from the cramped, reeking and verminous forecastle, Captain Christopholis said, "This is where you will stay." His lone seaman was casting off lines. During four miserable days the Americans remained belowdecks as German patrol planes buzzed the boat, sighting nothing but a sailor toiling and a skipper squatting on the afterdeck, arm over the tiller, mouth sucking on a hubble-bubble pipe. Christopholis landed the airmen in Cyprus, and the R.A.F. returned them to their squadrons.

Three weeks after Tidal Wave, Washington target analysts held a convention to "reach agreement" on the damage inflicted on Ploesti. They concluded that "the most important effect was to eliminate the cushion between production and capacity." It was tantamount to admitting that the unprecedented effort and sacrifice had not taken any oil from Hitler.

However, the European war was no longer static. The Allies were going over to the land offensive on two fronts in Italy and the U.S.S.R., forcing Hitler to find more fuel than before. Just when he needed the Ploesti cushion, it had disappeared. The German drive to seize the Soviet oil centers had been defeated, and the Reich was now obliged to divert labor and capital to synthetic oil production. The Ploesti raid hastened German retreat in Italy, where the Allies were marching on Foggia and Bari to build bases much closer to Ploesti than Benghazi. Although Tidal Wave had fallen short of expectation, it made a pivotal contribution to the crisis of the Third Reich.

The most telling effect of the mission was to inaugurate the downfall of the German Air Force. The Reich was expanding fighter production at an astonishing rate to meet the ever-growing, round-the-clock bomber offensive. More than enough eager youths came forward to fly the new German fighters, but there was not enough extra oil to give them proper training. The Luftwaffe began to eat itself. A pilot parachuting from a disabled plane was immediately given a new one, but a pilot lost in battle could not be as readily replaced. There was no such thing as retirement of an able-bodied flier in Goering's command. The fighter pilots in Romania faced nothing but overwork, fatigue and death.

Tidal Wave was a pronounced moral victory for the Allies, a desideratum of the great plan, which was realized to a greater degree than had been hoped for. Romanian eyewitnesses spoke admiringly of the accuracy of the strikes, "like a postman dropping a letter in the box." Europe is a community, even when divided by war, and this sort of talk spread from country to coun-

try. In Britain the U. S. Office of War Information produced a
Tidal Wave booklet in French, which showed the extraordinary
photographs of Liberators flying in the target flames and smoke.
It was airdropped in France and Belgium and passed from hand
to hand around Europe, which despised the inaccurate Allied
high-level bombings that killed many innocent and friendly people. To Europeans Tidal Wave was evidence that U. S. bomber
men were brave enough to fight on the ground amidst their own
explosions, and that they could deliver bombs accurately on military objectives with a minimum toll of civilians. The mission was
the last act of chivalry in aerial bombing.

There was probably no other urban air raid of the war in which
more airmen died than civilians. Excluding German military
casualties, 116 Romanian military and civilians were killed,
against 310 U. S. airmen. One hundred fifty Romanians were
wounded, against a comparable number of Liberator men.

In the target kingdom respect for Allied power, not Soviet
might alone, leaped in a day. In power psychology—the only
terms by which abused Romania could judge friend or foe—the
United States suddenly became as highly regarded as Germany
and the Soviet. The First of August aroused stirrings of national
spirit, and Romania began a slow upturn from resignation to active resistance toward the Nazis.

Although Tidal Wave was not a strategic success, it bore out
Jacob Smart's contention that a zero strike would be more efficient
than the orthodox high-altitude approach. Damage surveys after
the war found that the low-level mission produced a greater rate
of destruction per ton of bombs against tons of oil than any of the
mighty high-altitude raids that were to follow it.

These assaults were now being planned. The Ploesti file was
left open in Washington, although it was being closed in the
desert. In his Tidal Wave summation to the Chiefs of Staff, General Brereton ticked off the mission leader for the wrong turn
into the bomb run and the Circus commander for striking out on
his own from the erroneous course. However, he did not reprimand
these officers. "Combined operations of this nature," Brereton
said, "require extreme precision and are most difficult to control

. . . when navigation must be conducted over great distances. Hindsight suggests that a decision to break radio silence and reassemble the entire formation at the Danube might have resulted in greater success and fewer losses." Brereton apparently did not think of the consequences had all the groups followed the mission leader on the wrong turn toward Bucharest.

Subsequent official U. S. Air Force historians have attributed the disappointing results of Tidal Wave to the error at Targoviste, which they thought had alerted the defenses and spoiled the surprise. Neither Brereton nor the historians knew that the enemy had detected the take-off and tracked the bombers most of the way to the target.

Soon after the battle Leon Johnson and Killer Kane were gazetted for the Medal of Honor for bombing their briefed targets, although they were already burning and exploding. General Brereton hung the starry blue ribbon around Kane's neck on the cricket pitch of the Gezira Sporting Club in Cairo before a fashionable audience, and pinned Silver Stars and Distinguished Service Crosses on fourteen other Ploesti warriors. Leon Johnson received the highest U. S. award for valor one gray mizzling day on an airdrome in England in front of rank after rank of great-coated Liberator men.

It took months before the remaining three Medals of Honor for Tidal Wave were announced, the laurels of one of the most intense battles in history. Lloyd Hughes's posthumous medal for driving into flaming Red Target with his ship streaming gasoline was won for him by the O.W.I. man, but there was an inner-circle dispute over recognizing a similar deed by Addison Baker and John Jerstad, who had flown their flaming lead ship to the Circus target. A conservative faction in the award councils held that men who had broken formation discipline could not be honored. Officers who had served on Tidal Wave disputed this view with great vehemence and won for Baker and Jerstad the first paramount award given to both pilots of an aircraft for a mutual act of valor.

All over the United States, relatives and friends of the men who did not return from Ploesti had had no word of them other than the War Department telegram announcing that they were missing. One little town, Belvidere, Illinois (population 8,000), had given four inseparable high school companions to Tidal Wave, and two of them, Lieutenant Jack Lanning and Sergeant Arthur White, were missing. The Belvidere *Republican* tried to strike a note of hope for Lanning by publishing a letter he had posted to his bride the day before take-off. Under a headline, JACK LANNING AND PALS HAD A NEW PLANE ON PLOESTI RAID, the story said, "It is called *Wingo-Wango,* which is supposed to be some kind of a bird."

Brian Flavelle's *Wingo-Wango* was 3,000 feet down in the Ionian Sea. Belvidere did not learn that until several weeks later when a letter arrived from another of its Ploesti men, Sergeant George K. Holroyd, telling of seeing his friend's ship go down. The letter barely arrived before a telegram announcing that Holroyd had been killed in an air crash in England. The town held a memorial service, at which Lanning's and Holroyd's Distinguished Flying Crosses and Purple Hearts were given to next of kin. Two unexpected waves of emotion came over the gathering. The chairman was handed an announcement that the fourth local lad, Lieutenant Lon Bryan, had been killed over Germany. And then he read a letter from Sergeant White, alive in Romania!

It was one of the first letters to reach home from the fantastic prison camp of the Ploesti men.

And make each prisoner pent

Unwillingly represent

A source of innocent merriment,

Of innocent merriment.

W. S. GILBERT, *The Mikado*

14

THE GILDED CAGE

As the fallen Americans settled into the Timisul de Jos camp, the Romanians brought the rest of their western Allied detainees to the new foreign colony in the Alps. There were not many of them, but they were unusual men. There were a stately Dutch admiral, L. A. C. Doorman, and his aide, Baron van Lyndon, a young esthete, who had refused to swear they would not take up arms again when the Germans smashed into Holland. Carried off to a stalag, they broke out and walked southeast, employing the admiral's five languages, but were recaptured in Romania. There were two Yugoslav pilots who had run out of gas in Romania while trying to reach the British lines as the Wehrmacht crashed into their country.

Soon the oddest cage bird of them all arrived in the officers' stockade—a slender man with a broken leg in a cast. He was wearing a Royal Air Force uniform, and his papers identified him as Flight Lieutenant Marcus Jacobson. In heavily accented English he explained that he had broken his leg in a parachute jump. The inmates thought everything about him was queer. There had been no R.A.F. raids on Romania. Americans who had served in the R.A.F. quickly ascertained that Jacobson knew nothing about that service. In fact, he was highly ignorant of airplanes. Furthermore, he spoke perfect Romanian. They concluded that the new man was a spy and shunned him.

Jacobson took from his pocket two easel snapshots of young women and placed them on his bedside table. He got into bed and began knitting a sweater. His roommates waited expectantly for him to begin prying into military secrets, but he remained silent, sticking to his knitting. Clay Ferguson happened into the room and glanced at the snapshots. He left quickly for the game room and announced to the officers, "Jacobson's got a picture of my wife beside his bed." Nobody believed it. Ferguson said, "I'm absolutely sure of it. Why, I left the picture behind in Benghazi. Some of you guys saw it there." Suddenly there was a stream of visitors passing the bedside of the pariah. It was Mrs. Ferguson all right. A bombardier recognized his sister in the other photograph. They confronted the R.A.F. man.

Jacobson said, "I have never met these beautiful ladies. These pictures were my visas to come to Romania and find you." He took off his mask and told them who he was. His real name was Lyova Gukovsky. He was a native of Bessarabia, the province that Queen Marie had mulcted for Greater Romania in 1920. Her rule was hard on Jews. Gukovsky emigrated to Palestine and became a goatherd and schoolteacher in a large communal farm, Kibbutz Yagour, where he found peace until the new war came.

British Intelligence asked the Jewish Agency in Palestine for former Romanians to be parachuted into their native land to organize escape systems for Jews, politicals, and Allied airmen who would be raining down on the country when the next big bombing offensive came on Ploesti. Gukovsky volunteered and took parachute training. One night, carrying a bag of gold, he stepped into the air from a black plane over Romania and had the bad luck to land on the roof of a police station and break his leg.

He ditched the gold before the police seized him. Because of his correct uniform and credentials they did not suspect the nature of his mission and passed him routinely into Timisul, sentenced to a life of ease instead of death in a Gestapo torture chamber, which was the fate of other Palestinian parachute agents. Thus did Antonescu, leader of the Legion of the Archangel Michael for the Christian and Racial Renovation of Romania, roll out the red carpet for a runaway Romanian Jew.

The parachutist was fortunate in having a stout uniform. Most of the Americans had lost theirs in crackups and hospitals and were wearing parts of castoff Romanian uniforms and canvas underwear. The Red Cross shipped in some U. S. Army pants and blouses and an assortment of gaudy checkered shirts, which restored the individuality of costume essential to the morale of the American fighting man.

With no camp labors to be performed, the captives amused themselves with bridge, poker, cribbage, torturing musical instruments, exercising in the gym, playing volleyball, and making fudge and wine. They taught their guards the game of craps and cleaned them out. A Bucharest professor came and offered Romanian language lessons. He opened his first class with a nostalgic description of Boston, Massachusetts, where he had spent some time as a young man. "I wish I had never come back here," he said. The pupils chorused, "You can say that again, Doc!"

There was a farmhouse next to the camp. The men spent patient hours coaching a chicken to stick its neck through the wire. All evidence of the bird disappeared in prestidigious time. Lawrence Lancashire found a book on butchering and the boys went after big game outside the wire. During the weekly church parade to a chapel outside the camp the neat column passed close to a pig. When it was gone the pig was too. They were great churchgoers; Catholics and Protestants used the chapel on alternate Sundays. Many POW's professed to both creeds in order to march outside each week.

The enlisted men did not fare as well as the officers in procuring spirits. They remedied the situation by stealing the gun of a guard and locking him in a room until he promised to deliver plum brandy.

As their vigor returned the airmen related themselves to the war as best they could. On the railroad just outside the wire they saw long strings of tank cars running north from Ploesti and knew their work at the refineries had not succeeded. They longed for the bombers to come again. The railroad ran through the Predeal Pass over the Transylvanian Alps, and over it passed most of the German troops and supplies for the Ukrainian front and the Ploesti oil moving north. A spy could not have picked a better place to observe enemy movements. One of the caged birdmen professed a keen love of nature and sat long days by the wire counting troop, freight and tanker trains and German road convoys. He noted that Germans rode coaches and Romanian troops rode cattle cars. From Bucharest came a man in a green coat— the identification Antonescu forced Jews to wear—and gained admission to the compound as a dentist, volunteering to look after the prisoners' teeth. He brought a jar of powdered porcelain manufactured in Philadelphia, which gave a twinge of homesickness to the co-pilot of *Pudgy*, Wilmer Bassett, who came from there. (Bassett still has a stout front tooth of this material.) The man in the green coat actually was a dentist—and more. He regularly collected the nature lover's tallies of German traffic and passed them on to a British Intelligence contact. It was probably the only instance in the history of espionage in which a prisoner of war continuously transmitted top-rated logistical reports.

One day the guards announced, "No prisoner must go near the wire on pain of being shot by the Germans." The nature lover made himself small, until an American officer induced the commandant to give the reason: "The Germans complain of a prisoner who shouts terrible things at their troop carriages." It was Douglas Collins, humoring himself by yelling in German, "Bad luck for you! The Russians will kill you all. *Auf Wiedersehen*." Collins was induced to stop taunting the foe. The heat died down and nature loving and dentistry resumed.

The wealthy American market attracted two thieving Romanian

officers, who opened a canteen in the camp, chased the farm women away, and doubled prices down the line. The Americans called them "Minnie the Moocher" and "Red the Thief." The pair levied rent on the POW billets and forced payment for firewood. They even charged for gasoline used in a wheezy chore truck. It was a rather galling note for men who came to destroy Romanian gasoline, not to purchase it.

Princess Caterina Caradja visited the camp to look after "her boys." She was not a Red Cross official and had no claim to enter, but she persuaded the commandant to admit her to indoctrinate the Americans against the Russians. This was not a subterfuge: she brain-washed them constantly while looking after their comfort. She brought in a console radio and the fliers put up a map beflagged with the latest war fronts according to the British Broadcasting System's Overseas Service. Romanian officers dropped in to study and discuss the daily situation. Sometimes they heatedly disputed eastern front positions. A navigator caught on. He told his comrades, "Don't argue with them. They're getting the frontline situation from secret enemy reports. Don't ask for proof, just milk it out of them." After that, when differences arose, the prisoners let the Romanians move the pins. Timisul de Jos became one of the most accurately informed war rooms in Europe, although its generals commanded nothing.

Prominent Romanians visited Timisul from mixed motives of sympathy, curiosity and a desire to court the nationals of what could be the winning side. They spoke to the Americans as though the Soviet were a common foe. Most of the prisoners remembered that the United States was at war with Romania and allied with the Soviet Union. The split concept of the war at Timisul was typified by a colloquy between a Romanian officer and a naughty U. S. sergeant. The jailor said, "If you are not a good boy, the Russians will get you." The prisoner replied, "Watch how you're talkin', you grafter, or we'll send *you* to the Russian front."

As the months passed with no Allied raids on Ploesti the prisoners began to wonder if their sacrifices had gone for nothing. They did not know what was happening in Italy. The Allies had captured the Puglia Valley, under the spur of the Italian boot, and were laying out bomber bases 500 miles nearer to Ploesti than were the plains of Benghazi.

Norman Appold and the Liberators were based at San Pancrazio near Bari. Again the low-level experimentalist became bored with routine high-level missions and began solo depredations in a weird fighter assembled by his service squadron from wrecks of five aircraft. It was nominally a Curtiss Warhawk (P-40), a type that had given its best service with the American Volunteer Group in China four years earlier. The name of the private Appold air force was *Bon-Bon*. Without putting himself on record, he began racing across the Adriatic on the wave tops and shooting up German road convoys in Yugoslavia.

One day three spray-walking Spitfires nearly potted *Bon-Bon*, which had a silhouette resembling the Me-109. U. S. Brigadier Charles ("Muzzle Blast") Bourne "suggested" that Appold surrender *Bon-Bon* to a fighter outfit at Foggia. Appold obediently delivered the Warhawk, but the fighter people were getting racy new Mustangs and scorned the shopworn gift. The little pilot parked *Bon-Bon* at Foggia until Muzzle Blast's attentions were diverted elsewhere, and then sneaked her back to an inconspicuous corner at San Pancrazio.

The third generation of air crews thronged in from the United States, inculcated with realistic gunnery theory. At General Ent's behest Squadron Leader George Barwell had been borrowed from the R.A.F. to instruct air gunners in the United States. (In Colorado, Barwell won a half ton of prizes in rodeo marksmanship contests.) The Italian bases were filling up with silvery, unpainted B-24's and B-17's. Appold took over as master of ceremonies on their practice missions. He would climb *Bon-Bon* over the gathering fleet and radiophone, "Number Two, tuck in closer to your lead man and I'll make a fighter pass at six o'clock high." The petrel would dart through the frigate birds calling, "White Leader. Alert your crews. I am making a low attack at three o'clock." The new gunners silently tracked *Bon-Bon*. "Next will be a frontal attack on Red Leader Two. Now, let's not accidentally fire your guns." Buzzing through Red Force, *Bon-Bon* called, "Number Two and Number Three not tucked in. You let me through. You should've got me." Appold was preparing them for the next assault on the deadliest target in Europe.

In the mountain camp above the target the POW's felt homesick as the trees turned red and gold against the blue Carpathians. Russell Huntley accosted Collins and Lancaster. "Look," said he, "I figure you guys are planning a getaway. I want in on it. Some of the other guys will come in too." Collins said, "Okay, Limey, bring them to a meeting in the main barracks after lights out."

Thirty Americans came. Collins put it to them bluntly: "There is precious little chance of getting clean away. We are deep in enemy territory. The Russian front is five hundred miles away, and patrols from both sides will be looking for strangers mucking about in no man's land. Another direction is Yugoslavia. Now, Teddy and I were in Yugoslavia and the people nearly had heart attacks when they learned we were British. They were as scared of Mikhailovitch and the Chetniks as they were of the Germans. The third route is cross-country through Bulgaria, trying to make the European part of Turkey. It's a long way, but I think it's the best." Fourteen airmen volunteered. Afterward Lancaster opined that sixteen men were enough for a tunneling operation. Collins said, "Yes, I give the Yanks good marks. We got one out of five men in the ruddy compound. Not bad at all."

They started tunneling through the floor of main barracks, aiming to clear the wire after digging forty feet. Getting rid of the dirt was the hardest part. They carried it upstairs in pillow cases and hid it in nooks and crannies. They used bed boards for pit props and a homemade oil lamp that gave off poisonous fumes. After fifteen feet of excavation the lamp would go out from lack of oxygen, and some of the diggers blacked out.

Collins wanted candles. One Sunday he marched out to the Roman Catholic service and braced the priest. "I'm not a Catholic," he said, "but we Anglicans have a custom of burning tapers on Saint George's Day." Tears sprang to the cleric's eyes and he thrust an armload of candles on the pious soldier. "The priest never checked up on that Saint George's Day rot," said Collins.

Soon tunneling had to stop again. The barracks were sagging from the earth hidden upstairs. Lancaster had been surveying the heavy, padlocked outside door to the barracks basement and noted that nobody went in and out of it. He started another hole through the barracks floor in to the disused cellar to use it as a dump. It took him a week to breach the foot-thick foundation slab. Then tunneling resumed at a great rate. Occasionally men dropped into the cellar to spread out the mound of dirt. Jack Ross and a friend were down there one day shoveling when a pair of guards entered through the outside door. The Romanians had sneaked in to steal potatoes from a storage bin. Their flashlight happened to shine on the two frozen Americans. The guards and the prisoners looked at each other without saying a word. The guards went out the door and locked it. "They didn't squeal on us and we didn't squeal on them," said Ross.

As the shaft neared the wire, men began to have second thoughts about the ordeal ahead. Collins said, "It was always understood that a man could drop out any time he had the slightest doubt about the deal. No one thought there was anything cowardly about it. In fact, Lancaster and I encouraged drop-outs among the guys we thought didn't stand much chance of making it. The fewer that got out, the better our prospects were." As they came to the last feet of excavation, there were eight men left of the original sixteen.

The British Vanishers' experience had been that dusk was the best time for emerging from escape tunnels. Then the guards' vision was adjusting to floodlights. Accordingly the breakout was scheduled for 6 P.M., which gave the party three hours before roll call. A man went into the tunnel and broke through the last inches to the surface. He came back and announced, "Christ. It's like daylight out there." The floodlights were on.

Collins went down to lead the escape. "In a jump of this sort," he said, "one always feels nervous, like a jockey before the gate goes up. It was so bright outside the hole, it seemed impossible that one could stick one's head up and not be seen. But for national pride, I most certainly would have gone back. I foolishly put my hat up on a stick to see whether it would be shot at. I was under the influence of American movies. To my secret disappointment, nothing occurred. I heaved a sigh and pushed my face out."

He slithered to the surface and crawled for a stockade fence outside the wire. The floodlights were so placed that they cast a long, deep shadow under the fence. Collins intended to employ the shadow to hide his men until they reached a sentry box at the high corner of the stockade. If they could get past the sentry undetected, they were free in the nearby woods. He paused momentarily in the shadow and saw Lancaster crawling toward him. Behind were Limey Huntley, Harry Baughn, Philip Rurak, James Brittain and Joseph Brown.* When the British Vanishers were together, they scrambled past the sentry, got safely into the wooded mountain slope, and started running.

As they reached the top of a ridge, firing started in the camp. Collins said, "Teddy and I crossed the hill and ran down the other side like a couple of Jesse Owenses." About a mile away there was a road intersection with a clearing a hundred feet wide, which they had to cross. It would be the first interception point for patrols pursuing the tunnelers. The moon came out and lighted up the road crossing. Collins and Lancaster dashed across. A truckload of guards arrived, set up machine guns, and began raking the trees into which they had disappeared. Bullets sprinkled twigs on their heads as they hurled themselves up the slope. The fire came so low they had to stop and huddle to the ground. Lancaster said, "I can hear your bloody heart beating." "So can I," said his partner. "I just hope the Romanians don't hear it."

Back near the fence, five of the escapers were being rounded up. Their chances of freedom had been lost when the eighth man imagined a guard had seen him crawling along the fence. He got up and ran, which did attract the guard. Baughn was the only man other than the two Britons who remained at large. He had to sacrifice his heavy pack of food to make it over the first hill. Without provisions, alone in a strange forest, he thought of the Tidal Wave escape instructions warning of wolves and bears in the Carpathians, but he kept on going.

Collins and Lancaster lay low in the hills for two days and then walked twenty miles north to Brasov. There, using the German

* The escapees did not remember the identity of the eighth man.

they had learned in the stalags, the British Vanishers bought tickets and boarded the Trans-European Express for Bucharest. They passed the POW camp on the way. The guards were beating up the recaptured men. They dragged Rurak around by his beard. Baughn had been picked up when he had had to beg for food.

From Bucharest the British sergeants took a train for Constanta. They did not intend to try boarding a Turkish ship at that port, as the U. S. escape plans advised. Instead, they got off at the first stop beyond the Danube and hiked to the Romano-Bulgarian border, intending to cross Bulgaria to Turkey. They felt immensely confident after negotiating the big river that had twice foiled them. They found the border thick with guards on both sides. They reconnoitered for a weak spot and started running. Romanian guards opened fire and captured them again. They were taken to Constanta for interrogation. Lancaster had now come from the Arctic Ocean to the Black Sea, a unique escape journey among Allied prisoners of war.

The eight escapers were sent to a punishment camp at Slobozia, which means "freedom" in Romanian. It held two thousand hard-case Soviet officers and paratroopers. The compound was dotted with "sweat boxes" in which Russians were kept for days, unable to sit or stand. The Timisul party was put into a dark, unheated room, and each man was fed a piece of bread and two watered soups a day. They talked in low voices with Russians in the next room. Collins said, "They asked when the western Allies were going to get off their backsides and start a second front. We pointed out our enormous successes in North Africa and Italy. The Russians smuggled food to us—pieces of sausage and salami."

After a month the escapees were sent back to Timisul. They arrived on a snowy night with bright moonlight gleaming on a picture postcard setting. As the guards came to admit them Collins roared, "Rotten Romanian bastards!" and the mountain echoed it hollowly back. They began laughing hysterically. The camp awoke, yelling and laughing. The party marched smartly into the compound singing "Tipperary." The first American Red Cross parcels had just arrived. Collins said, "We stuffed on Spam and other riches, were violently ill and very happy."

The British Vanishers were unhappy about the snow, however. It made escape impossible. "But we needed a period of quiet to lull the guards," said Collins. "We laid plans for another break in the spring."

The last of the wounded were brought to camp from the Sinaia hospital. Among them were the ranking U. S. officer and NCO, who became prisoner-commandants of the respective compounds —Captain Wallace C. Taylor, only survivor of the plane he had piloted in the last wave at White Four, and Master Sergeant Edmond Terry, who had crashed in with Lindley Hussey. The new leaders came under the expert appraisal of Douglas Collins, who pronounced them "first-class chaps." A Romanian guard officer complained to Terry, "Is it correct in your army for soldiers to curse an officer the way your men are abusing me?" Terry replied, "Sir, how can you expect enlisted men to respect an officer who begs cigarets from them?" The Romanian said, "Yes. You are right, Sergeant."

Now, with the wounded in camp, all 108 of the living deposited in Romania on Tidal Wave were together, except for John Palm. The crippled pilot of *Brewery Wagon* remained at large in Bucharest, punching his peg leg into the carpets of the best salons as Queen Helen showed off her personal hostage. Palm was not a defector or a collaborator. No one had suggested imprisonment for the queen's friend and the Texan saw no reason why he should request it.

In the mountain camp above, brother officers yearned for the fleshpots, and several found that if they were nice boys they could obtain week-end paroles in Bucharest with casual escort. If they made their guards drunk early, they could enjoy the overnight freedom of the capital. One of them, "Officer Z," as he will be called here (his real name is not among the Tidal Wave fliers mentioned in the chronicle) felt called upon to spread cheer in a society growing more depressed by Russian advances and the threat of new American bombings from Italy. Officer Z accepted an invitation to address the Rotary Club of Bucharest. He said, "I have traveled the whole world in an airplane and I have fought on all the fronts. I have made over one hundred missions in Japanese territory and was shot down three times in the Philippines, where our army lost twenty thousand men. Each time I have been unharmed. I have made many missions over the Atlantic, in Africa and Germany, and last of all Romania.

"I have heard only good things about Romania, about the heroic battle the Romanian Army has been fighting in Russia and how they repelled the Russians. I commanded a group of heavy bombers on the low-level raid on Ploesti. With the wish not to bomb civilians, I took over the controls myself. Never before have I seen such well-organized antiaircraft fire. There were also Romanian fighters in this sector. Your fliers must be proud of their work. They are well trained.

"I was taken prisoner. Life is good. The attitude of the people is very humane. We have everything we need. We are treated as if we were in our own country. If my wife and children were near me, I could never say that I was a prisoner of war."

The speech was published in a Bucharest newspaper. In the camp, Sergeant Louis Medeiros, a printer from New Bedford, Massachusetts, who had learned Romanian in six weeks, translated it for the gunners. An auditor said, "After that load of stuff, all they can do is send for his family." Another mused, "I don't get it. Aren't the Romanians our enemies?" Most of them laughed it off. Officer Z was the biggest bag of wind in the camp. The Rotary Club speaker returned to the officers' mess and described his triumph to a stony-faced audience. Norman Adams followed it with a fable: "A little sparrow sat on a telephone line, cold and hungry. A horse passed below and the little sparrow flew down and consumed a great amount of fresh warm droppings. He flew back up and opened his mouth wide in song. A hawk swooped down and devoured the sparrow. The moral of the story is: If you are full of the stuff, keep your mouth shut." Officer Z got up and went to his room. After that he was served his meals there by the Russian orderlies.

All these months ten Tidal Wave men were in Bulgarian custody —the survivors of *The Witch*, *Prince Charming* and *Let 'Er Rip* —under Lieutenant Darlington. At first they were treated humanely. Then, in November 1943, U. S. bombers from the new bases in Italy, warming up for the all-out offensive on Ploesti, raided Sofia twice. The Bulgarians reacted primitively by abusing their captives. They force-marched Darlington's men to a mountain camp along with parachuted fliers from the Sofia raids. The stockade had no running water and no medical attention for the newly wounded. It was lice-ridden, and the rotten food gave the men dysentery. Clifford Keon said, "It was rough as hell." More downed fliers arrived, including a Yugoslav crew and a Greek who had been dropped with money for the Bulgarian underground. The camp overflowed and the Bulgarians built a larger and worse one at Choumen and herded the prisoners there in an all-day mountain march.

In contrast to the Bulgarian misery, the men in Romanian detention enjoyed a "Christmas that must have been one of the most extraordinary ever spent by prisoners of war," said Collins. "We were being paid salaries, more money was coming from the Red Cross, and the Pope sent seventy-two thousand lei. We bought beer, wine and champagne. We were permitted to do anything we liked except dig holes," he added. They listened on the radio to a speech by President Roosevelt and to Bing Crosby singing "White Christmas." The wealthy captives exchanged gifts. John Lockhart gave two bottles of beer to each Russian cook and orderly. The enlisted men entertained the officers at a steak dinner, followed by a concert from an imported Russian POW orchestra and comedy skits by the internees. The British Vanishers were the stars of the show. With nearly four years' experience in prison theatricals, they easily outshone the American amateurs.

The winter social season reached its acme on New Year's Eve, with the officers returning the hospitality of the enlisted men. The Romanian commandant made a fine speech, and one of his lieutenants got drunk with the captives and came out on the losing end of a beer-slinging match. The officers served the men champagne and hot dogs.

The first mail from home arrived after six long months of imprisonment—a bounty of letters that the Timisul inmates rationed to themselves over the days to stretch the pleasure as long as possible. Lawrence Lancashire received the news that he was a father—the baby was already seven months old. It had been born ten days before he took off on Tidal Wave.

Romanian ladies lent them skis and skates. The winter of waiting went as well as could be hoped, except for an incident involving a sentry box on a slope outside the sergeants' compound. In cold weather the guard liked to stay in the box as long as possible. One day he heard a mass howl from the cage and stuck his head out. Seventy snowballs whizzed by, several scoring direct hits. As punishment for the prank the prisoners ate rejected potatoes for a week.

Folded in the deep February snows, the sleepers were awakened one night at the thud of distant guns, fumbled into boots and overcoats, and went out to look. To the south, over Ploesti, there were firefly winks in the sky and delayed reports of flak bursting high in the air. "The boys are back!" "They're hitting Ploesti again!" went the cries. But they heard no bombs, just the remote tattoo of shrapnel. They stood in the snow for an hour while the puzzling aerial show went on.

It was Norman Appold over Ploesti again, not to bomb, but to take radar photos from 24,000 feet in a lone special Liberator, the APS-15, out of Italy. He was making radar plots of the refineries to use later for high-altitude bombing through clouds. While Appold flew back and forth, methodically bounding the city, Colonel Woldenga sent three M-110's into their own flak to destroy the impudent B-24. Appold spent an hour over the deadly target, eluding the night fighters, and completed his maps before he put his nose down and dived out of the mess.

One day Captain Taylor ordered all the POW's to smarten up and make a formation in the officers' compound, where the sergeants were admitted on special occasions. Six limousines entered the gate, and two small figures, surrounded by a swarm of plug-uglies in long leather coats, approached the men. Dictator Antonescu and his wife were calling. The general walked down the ranks asking if anyone had any complaints. Douglas Collins gave him an exaggerated salute and said, "Why aren't the other ranks permitted contact with the officers? We're all in the same camp."

Antonescu said, "I will look into the matter." Soon afterward the barriers between the two compounds were removed.

Collins had made the dictator an unwitting accomplice of the new escape operation he was planning. In the officers' camp there was a lot of Romanian money, and Caminada and Johnson were secreting an ample stock of compasses and maps. The four British Vanishers were now reunited and could start a full-scale escape academy of officers and men.

Skyward in air a sudden muffled

sound, the dalliance of the eagles,

The rushing amorous contact high in

space together,

The clinching interlocking claws, a

living, fierce, gyrating wheel . . .

WALT WHITMAN, "The Dalliance of the Eagles," 1881

15

THE HIGH ROAD TO PLOESTI

During the long peace after Tidal Wave, General Gerstenberg
obtained more guns, more radar, and thousands of smoke generators to conceal the refineries. He barely held his fighter strength,
but his antiaircraft became the heaviest concentration in the
world. The build-up in Romania was matched by the swelling
power of the Mediterranean Allied Air Force. The Fifteenth
U.S.A.A.F. in Italy was stacking up hundreds of gleaming Liberators and Fortresses with new smartly trained crews. Officer discipline was improved; gone was the individualist of the Libyan
period. The new leaders were formation keepers, and they carried

bigger bombs that exploded more often than those carried on Tidal Wave.

Norman Appold, who had rehearsed them to cope with fighter attacks, attended a briefing on 4 April 1944 in which the new men faced the opening stroke of the final offensive on Romanian oil. He offered to check out the gunners as they left for the real thing. "Today we have complete radio silence," said Appold. "You will not hear me announcing attacks. I'm going in without warning. So, all you flexible gunners and turret gunners—on your toes!" As 230 four-engined bombers assembled in the sky, little *Bon-Bon* darted through, stitching them up tight. The silvery school set out across the Adriatic for the second round with Alfred Gerstenberg. Appold waggled his wings for bon voyage, and dropped back to Bari. The bomber force carried a blizzard of metalized paper strips to confuse the German radar.

The force bombed Bucharest. In one of the target areas, the railway marshaling yards, there happened to be several trainloads of Romanian refugees from the east. Many were killed and wounded. At Timisul, peasants shook their fists at the Tidal Wave men behind the wire. Sergeant Francis Doll wrote in his diary, "The Romanians definitely don't like us now." The ugly atmosphere was offset, however, by the arrival of a new camp commandant, a plump, affable colonel named Saulescu, who was openly an Allied sympathizer. At each new setback for Hitler he brought a case of champagne to the American officers and joined them in toasting Allied victory. Their eyes popped when the colonel brought his daughter, Carma, to the compound. She was a beautiful twenty-two-year-old who spoke excellent English. A sergeant cut out the officers and won the maiden's favor. Carma and her mother made pastries and sweets and gave them to the POW's. To the canteen directors, Minnie the Moocher and Red the Thief, interfering with Romanian business enterprise was worse than fraternizing with the enemy. They began pulling strings to remove Colonel Saulescu and his shocking womenfolk.

The second high-level raid struck Brasov. The POW's could see smoke rising from a target set aflame by two hundred bombers. "We jumped up and down with joy," said Sergeant Francis Doll.

As yet Ploesti had not been hit. However, when the sirens sounded there, the citizens of the shelterless city no longer yawned. Thousands of shrewd ones ran east to the Romana Americana refinery area, in the conceit that the American bombers would deliberately spare the U. S.-built plant.

The spring thaw was working in the earth and escape weather was returning. Caminada, Johnson, Gukovsky and three Americans, including Lawrence Lancashire, holed the floor of the officers' hotel and started a short shaft under the wire. A Romanian sergeant unexpectedly walked in and caught Lancashire in the hole. "The guards went stark, raving mad," said John Lockhart. "They drove the rest of us into our rooms at bayonet point and beat the escape party with hobnailed boots and rifle butts." The beaten men were sent to Slobozia. There the prisoner in the next room was a Russian girl paratrooper named Antonina, who had just spent ten days stooped in the punishment box, where one could not sit or stand. Through the barbed wire on an adjoining veranda she relayed their messages to Russian officers in the cubicle on the other side of hers. The Russian men sent the Americans bits of food and tobacco by Antonina's hands. Two more Russian girl soldiers moved in with her and the Timisul men heard some sort of machine running in their cell. One morning the girls came out on the veranda transformed. Gone were their uniforms and boots. They had scrounged a sewing machine and cloth and made themselves pretty frocks.

Early in May 1944 the long-awaited high-level offensive on Ploesti began, with 485 Liberators and Flying Fortresses smashing at the refineries and railway yards. It was well-executed bombing. Few civilians were harmed. Romanians took the Tidal Wave men back into favor. Nineteen U. S. bombers were shot down, but none of the parachutists were brought to Timisul. They were incarcerated in Bucharest.

A few days afterward the Fifteenth Air Force went in force to Wiener Neustadt to bomb the Daimler-Messerschmitt factories. The lead Flying Fortress of the 97th Bomb Group took a direct flak hit over the target and exploded in the air. No parachutes were seen to open. The pilot was Colonel Jacob E. Smart, the principal planner of Tidal Wave. His loss was immediately classified top secret. In high Allied military circles it laid an icy finger on many hearts. Smart was privy to world-wide Allied strategy and capabilities, and he knew the biggest secret of the war—that a nuclear chain reaction had been achieved and the Allies were building an atomic bomb.

If Smart had somehow survived the mid-air explosion—well, no sensible person undervalued the talking inducements of Gestapo torture. Washington made no public or private announcement that he was missing. A month later, in an exchange of crippled prisoners of war, an American airman came home from Austria with grave news. He had seen Colonel Smart alive in a German hospital.

In mid-May the Italian-based bombers hit Bucharest three times in one day. Soon they came to Ploesti again. The lead bombardier was Boyden Supiano, who had been wounded over the target on Tidal Wave. After the raid Colonel Saulescu shook hands with the Timisul men and gave them permission to walk outside the compound for an hour a day. It proved to be his last fraternization. He was replaced by a tough major named Matiescu, who put a stop to Saulescu's coddling policies.

Captain Wallace Taylor, the POW commandant, sent for the British Vanishers and said, "If you are planning another escape, I'd like to offer some suggestions. We are now in touch with friends on the outside. They want three of us to escape, including a radio operator. You will be taken to a secure post in the mountains, where Romanians will bring the men being shot down on these high-level jobs." Collins said, "We'll think it over, sir." Back in their billet, he said to Lancaster, "That's an odd request. Why do they want POW's to run the show, when parachute agents would be better? Maybe it's a blind and he has something else for us to do when we get out." Lancaster said, "I've got the radioman. Did you know Huntley was a radio operator in the Canadian Army?" Collins said, "Fair enough. I'd go anywhere with old Limey." Lancaster reached under his mattress and said, "Feast your eyes on this." It was a pair of wire cutters. "Pinched 'em off the camp electrician," he explained. They gathered up Huntley and went back to see Captain Taylor, who gave them the pseudonym of his underground contact in a village near the camp.

The new effort was to be a breakout through the wire from a privy a few yards away. There were two sentry boxes near the spot, but the British Vanishers intended to leave on a rainy night when the guards would be taking shelter in them. Sergeant Garrett was in charge of the inside arrangements. He had discovered how to short-circuit the lights and put the camp in darkness. When Collins attacked the wire, Garrett would blow the lights and the rest of the men would start yelling and singing in the barracks. Some of them would be lookouts, to warn the escape party of movements of guards during the uproar. The lookouts could yell in plain English, which none of the sentries understood.

On the first rainy afternoon Collins set the break for dusk, and Garrett extinguished the lights at 1845. While his two companions sheltered in the privy, Collins dashed to the inner strand of barbed wire and began snipping. The sound of the shears was muffled by the rain. He had to cut through the inner double strand, a thick entanglement between it and the outer wire, and go through four strands there before Lancaster and Huntley could leave the privy and join him in the bolt for freedom. The camp guards were confused by the darkness and the howling in the barracks and did not spot Collins laboring in the open. He passed through the entanglement and cut three of the outside wires. As he was attacking the last strand a lookout yelled, "Keep quiet. The guard is moving up on you."

The sentry passed ten feet from Collins without seeing the silent, unmoving escaper. Lancaster called, "Pull back, Doug. The lights are going on any second and they're beginning a roll call in the main barrack." Collins kept his head. He did not run for the barrack to get there before the roll call. That would leave the gap in the wire, followed by a major Romanian offensive to get the wire cutter. Methodically he began twisting the severed wires together again, thinking, "There's some compensation in getting your brains blown out on the way out of prison, but I'm going to look funny if they pot me while I'm trying to get back in." Praying the blackout would hold, he backed out, hooking up the wires. When the lights went on in the barracks and the roll call began, Collins was there, standing at rigid attention, panting somewhat.

The rain continued next day and the Romanians did not discover Collins' wire hookup. In the evening the three escapers took positions as before, and the lights went out. Collins parted the wires and was cutting the last one when a voice called, "Come back, Doug! The guard is on top of Ted and Limey and they can't make it out of the can." Collins decided he was too far out to return, and there was not enough time to replace the wires. He cut the last wire and took off alone. The decision was sound. A moment later the floodlights came on and machine guns began spraying the gap in the fence.

Collins prowled into a back yard in the underground man's village. The populace was outdoors, talking about the prisoner's escape. Entering the village would endanger both himself and the contact man. Collins departed north through the rainy forests.

He was caught near Brasov six days later. "It was a sad sort of balls-up," said he, "but we had showed willing." He told his interrogators that he was an American Air Force officer shot down a few days before, a ruse designed to get himself sent to Bucharest to join the high-level prisoners. He figured his chances for the next escape were better in Bucharest. The tale was going over well when Major Matiescu arrived from Timisul and claimed his runaway. He dragged Collins back to the camp and turned him over to the guards for a thorough beating. Admiral Doorman and Captain Taylor vigorously protested, and Matiescu gave Collins a week in isolation, after which he would be sent to the Slobozia punishment camp for a month.

The sixth of June "was the day of all days!" said Sergeant Doll. "The bombers hit Brasov and we had a short glimpse of aerial fighting. We saw a Focke-Wulf 190 crash into the mountain. Our gunners were on the ball." Romanian officers ran into the compound yelling, "The British and Americans have landed in France!" Doll thought, "They're as happy as we are."

The POW's saw a strange and exciting new type of plane in the battle sky, a fork-tailed speedster that flew big arcs around the

Messerschmitts. The twin-engine Lightning (P-38) had entered the Ploesti campaign. The new American fighter-bomber was now escorting the heavies all the way, and it sometimes swooped down and strafed the refineries.

As the offensive grew in power and intensity, Gerstenberg sent Colonel Woldenga to Belgrade to manage fighter interception on the bomber streams going to and fro. The lethal game wore on— bombers up from Italy, fighters up from the Balkans, flak most of the way. The adversaries got to know each other. As they attacked, German pilots radiophoned greetings to U. S. commanders by name. The Ploesti campaign became gladiatorial. The contesting airmen felt a queer sort of comradeship, like slaves of a mad emperor sent forth in the accursed arena to slay each other with swords versus nets and tridents.

An impulsive act by an American pilot brought heavy retribution to his group. The Messerschmitts shot him out of formation with a crippled engine. As his ship fell behind, shaking with hits, he lowered his landing gear, the classic act of surrender in the air, but one rarely used by the American bomber army. The Me-109's ceased fire and formed a diamond around the B-17 to escort it to their base. Then the American flight engineer phoned his pilot that he could recover the engine and give nearly maximum power. The pilot told his gunners to aim at the fighters, and, upon command, they shot down the Messerschmitts. The B-17 pulled up its wheels and returned to base.

The next mission of its group brought a day of terror. Every fighter in the air attacked the group, virtually ignoring the other bombers. Before the following mission, the U. S. commander painted out the group symbol on his rudders, but the fighters ganged up on him as before, calling his pilots by name and littering the air with burning planes and parachutes. Throughout the high war on Ploesti the fighters unerringly picked out the group, exacting heavy revenge.

Norman Appold flew two high-level missions to the refineries. To him Ploesti was a crusade. Some new men went to the deadliest target more often than his four times. On every mission

Gerstenberg took installments on his price for the refineries—a 3.6 percent average American loss per raid. The Fifteenth Air Force paid it from the minting of new planes and men rolling out of the fully geared production lines and air schools in the States.

Hundreds of white parachutes dotted the bomber courses, overtaxing camp facilities in Romania. None of the high-level men were brought to Timisul, however. They were kept in Bucharest. The high strikes could not help hitting civilians. The petulant Romanians talked of the low-level captives as the "Africans," and complained to them about the unmannerly "Italians"—the high-level Americans. The "Africans" grew in esteem as more "Italians" fell into harsher confinement in Bucharest. The offensive went on, wider attacks on the whole Romanian oil system—refineries at Ploesti, rail tanker yards at Brasov and Bucharest, and water transshipping points at Giurgiu and Constanta.

On 24 June the popular former commandant at Timisul, Colonel Saulescu, and his beautiful daughter drove into the POW compound and spread a picnic for their American friends. Carma brought them news of the throngs of comrades in prison in Bucharest, where she had volunteered as an interpreter. She said the boys there were not as gentlemanly as her low-level favorites. During the bucolic afternoon the bombers struck Ploesti, Craiova and Brasov. Sergeant Doll saw some P-38's flying low and noted, "It looks like a Lightning reconnaissance."

It was not a reconnaisance. It was an American defeat, proportionately heavier than the low-level mission. By now the resilient Gerstenberg was gaining on the bombers, and oil production was rising, due to extensive use of smoke screens. He had had two thousand smoke generators placed in patterns to take advantage of prevailing winds. It took twenty minutes to raise a smoke blanket over Ploesti, and his radar gave him plenty of time to prepare for high attacks. The Fifteenth Air Force on this day tried to circumvent the smoke screens and radar by sending 46 twin-engined Lightnings with thousand-pound bombs slung on their bellies to attack under the smoke. The overburdened P-38's were surprised by Messerschmitts before they reached the target. The second low-level mission on Ploesti cost 26 Lightnings, more than half the force.

Yet this bad day was the turning point of the Ploesti campaign. Escorting Lightnings destroyed ten fighters, and not long after that the Luftwaffe was a negligible factor. This was due principally to U. S. Mustang (P-51) and Lightning escorts that were now able to go all the way to the target with the bombers. Gerstenberg's hoarded fighter strength was vanishing and he could not get replacements from Goering. In fact, Romanian defense squadrons were being pulled out to defend northern Italy and Germany.

Soon after its day of ignominy the Lightning became the dictator of Ploesti. The Fifteenth Air Force took a leaf from the British textbook and sent out, in advance of the bombers, a Master Bomber in a Lightning. He sat high over the target, inspecting Ploesti for holes in the smoke screen. Despite Gerstenberg's concealment, winds usually exposed a refinery or two. The Master Bomber openly radiophoned the oncoming destructive force, directing it to the openings. He was quarterbacking the defense posture just before the play. The bomb force no longer went in with a pattern set by side-line coaches in Italy. In the end the formula for destroying the refineries, which had begun with the ponderous Tidal Wave instructions, was found in fewer briefings at base and more improvisation over the target. Gerstenberg could not shift fast enough for the Master Bomber.

At last, in early summer, bombs found Romana Americana, and the deluded civilians who ran there for sanctuary painfully learned that the United States was not sparing Standard Oil property.*

During the ferocious June battles the air-raid alert sounded on the Liberator base at Bari, Italy. Radar had picked up a lone, unidentified aircraft approaching. Three Spitfires scrambled to meet it. The plane was a new Focke-Wulf 190, with its wheels down.

---

* When the U. S. Strategic Bomb Survey team inspected Ploesti after the Red Army captured Romania, its Russian hosts were amazed at the proof that capitalism had destroyed its own property.

The German machine waggled its wings and landed. The pilot was resigning from the Ploesti campaign. German aviation fuel was so low that none could be spared for training new pilots. What there was went to the front, where the old pilots kept on fighting and dying hopelessly against giant swarms of fresh Allied planes. The Tidal Wave fighter pilots were all gone from Romania. Werner Gerhartz had been shot down twice in Italy, once by a Liberator, once by an R.A.F. Kittyhawk, and was going to his last rendezvous at Berlin. Gamecock Hahn had been shot down and killed over Rome. Sixty U. S. Mustangs jumped Hans Schopper's eight Me-109's at Fulda and shot off his arm. Hans Eder was killed in Italy. Manfred Spenner was hunting U. S. artillery liaison planes in Italy when he was hit in German and American crossfire. He parachuted and was captured in no man's land by Americans. Uncle Willie Steinmann succeeded Gamecock Hahn in Italy. He was to be the only Mizil pilot still fighting at the end of the war.

Bulgarian interceptors were punished severely. Just after Tidal Wave, Germany had presented 120 French Dewoitine 520 pursuits to the Sixth Bulgarian Air Polk. The Dew-520 was a good fighter in 1938, but this was 1944. With this inferior equipment the unfortunate Bulgarians threw the first blocks on the invading air armies. The bombers and P-38's knocked them out of the sky. By the time the Bulgarians were traded up to Me-109's, the invaders had the superior Mustang. When there were four pilots left in the Wraschdebna strength, the regiment was regrouped at Karlovo and given thirty Me-109's from battle-repair shops. While new pilots were being trained, the R.A.F. clobbered the Karlovo field, killing 82 airmen and destroying or damaging all aircraft, including a hundred Me-109's in the repair shops.

At the start of July the Timisul POW's who were counting German military movements outside the wire noticed a convoy of half-tracks and armored trucks going north. Gerstenberg was beginning the final phase of his plans, the creation of *Festung Ploesti* to stop the Red Army and the national rising. Big changes were at hand. The Royal Air Force now appeared in force in Romania, bombing Bucharest by night, while American heavies struck Brasov and Ploesti by day. The Russian cooks and servants in the POW camp were removed, and the noncommissioned officer prisoners had to work for the first time. They squawked to Major Matiescu about cleaning toilets. Food deliveries became uncertain. Uncollected garbage piled up at the camp gates. The idyl was over.

They grumbled among themselves about another infliction. Officer Z, the luncheon speaker at the Bucharest Rotary Club, wore out his welcome in the officers' camp and came to live with the gunners. Top Sergeant Terry was equal to the occasion. He called Officer Z before a meeting of the enlisted men, explained that all duties were shared among them, and put the officer on latrine duty. Officer Z bought a lamb and butchered and ate it himself, without sharing the food. The sergeants bleached the lamb's skull and surreptitiously strung a line on pulleys between the barracks. At night they put a candle in the skull. Garrett doused the lights, and they hauled the candlelit skull between the buildings. The guards poured out, yelling and shooting. They saw the ghostly death's-head in the sky and fell on their knees in prayer.

The deteriorating situation offered no such relief to German soldiers below at the target city. Werner Horn, a radio operator at H.Q., Flak Regiment 180, stationed five miles north of Ploesti, lived with two gnawing anxieties. His fiancée, airwoman Liesel Droge, was in a plotting center under the American salvoes, and a *Soldatenklau*, one who steals soldiers, was prowling among the Luftwaffe technicians. His name was General Unruh, which means "unrest," and he was causing plenty of it. Hitler had sent the *Soldatenklau* to impress rear echelon men for front-line military duty. Horn was in danger of being torn from his intended wife into a death mill grinding harder than Ploesti—the Red front. By now the Soviets had hurled the last German from their soil and were gathering a swift and shattering blow for Gerstenberg and Antonescu.

Horn said, "The U. S. Air Force put us under a test of nerves. Every day that God made, the attackers swept over. Shortly after sunrise, the Master Bomber appeared in the sky at great heights, and a few hours later the bomber formation came. Our troops became unnerved under constant attack. Daylight was hardly ever seen in Ploesti as the black clouds rolled over it. And night never really came, as the refineries blazed away. Everybody felt things were going backward. The supply lines broke down. Prospects of victory diminished by the hour. The Romanians turned anti-German. The situation was hopeless, but we had to obey."

Horn's regimental commander was a great morale asset to the bedeviled men. Then, late in July, the spirit suddenly went out of him. An unsuccessful attempt had been made on Hitler's life and the plotters were being rounded up. The commander listlessly obeyed an order to report in Bucharest, where the Gestapo pushed him out a high window, as a suspected member of the assassination ring. Sergeant Horn decided he had to disobey. He trumped up medical grounds for sending his fiancée home to Germany, and she left before the debacle of Romania.

At Timisul the Romanians took away the sheets and blankets from the POW's. Matiescu separated the officers and men, confiscated the radios, and took up the rule of an uneasy tyrant. The bomber hordes came stronger and more often. On 15 July, 607 planes bombed Ploesti. An FW-190 fell toward the camp, shedding its wings, but crashed beyond the wire. John Palm, finding the bombing rather hazardous for a chap with a peg leg, took a vacation in the Alps and brought along to Timisul a high-level officer named John Cune. Cune gave the Rip Van Winkles of Tidal Wave a year's news from home; he described the awesome B-29 Superfortress and the new hot Liberator and the Black Widow fighter. The POW's learned for the first time that they had all been awarded the Distinguished Flying Cross.

Francis Doll spent his twenty-first birthday remembering his lost connections with home. "I'm eligible to vote," he wrote in his diary, "but God only knows when I'll get a chance. Good old F.D.R., stick in there. Most of us are with you. The R.A.F. bombed Bucharest, Ploesti and Craiova last night and we hit Ploesti today. Songs we sing: 'Darling, It's All Over Now'; 'When the World Has Turned You Down'; 'Dear, I Dreamed I Held You in My Arms.' These songs make me either homesick or sick." The first of August, the first anniversary of Tidal Wave, the POW's spent in somber contemplation of life, thanking God for deliverance, or getting happily drunk.

For some months the Romanian paymaster, who was known as "Jesse James," had been stealing part of their salaries. Major Matiescu, who was suspected of getting some of the loot, would not listen to complaints. Sergeant Doll wrote a letter of protest to the Romanian Minister of War and gave it to "Jesse James" for transmittal to Bucharest. The thief was thunderstruck. In his army an ill-humored glance from an enlisted man entitled an officer to thrash the soldier on the spot. The puzzled officer alternately threatened Doll and whined to him, but the soldier stood his ground. The complaint actually reached the minister. He settled it in Romanian fashion, by ordering Doll and three fellow protestors, including Lieutenant Henry Lasco, to imprisonment in Bucharest with the high-level captives, under the bombs. During the slow rail journey Doll got a good look at the high-level depredations at Ploesti. "All the marshaling yards and refineries that we could see were nearly flat," he said. Among Romanian passengers he noted a healthy increase in the national spirit kindled a year before by Tidal Wave. "The Romanians are fed up with the Germans," he wrote in his diary.

Princess Caradja visited Timisul and was accosted by Sergeant Robert Locky, who, she said, was "a boy who could get anything out of me." Locky asked her for electrical wire, sockets and bulbs for a big camp show. "Copper wire is just about the last thing you can find in Romania," she told him, "but I'll try." Locky said, "If you have any old ladies' dresses lying around, we could use them to dress up in—I mean for the show." She left in a pensive mood, suspecting he wanted the electrical gear to light a tunnel, and the dresses for getaway disguises. During her visits to the camp she had scrupulously avoided involvement in military matters. Antonescu's fascist crowd had indulged her as an anti-Soviet brain-washer, but if she were inculpated in an escape plot, the Iron Guard would surely try to hang her. Nonetheless, she scrounged the lighting equipment and rummaged in her attic for female costumes. She heaved open a mildewed trunk and gazed inside with a wicked grin. It contained camphored layers of ball gowns worn by her mother, Princess Irene Cantacuzene, at galas in Vienna and Budapest in the halcyon days of the Second Hapsburg Empire. Here were enough watered silks and lace, swags and bangles, bugle beads and boas for the camp show! Runaway G.I.'s scuttling cross-country in this *fin-de-siècle* attire would attract crowds in no time. She took the stuff to the camp. When Locky saw the lighting gear, he smiled covetously. "And now, dear boy," she said, "here are some perfectly marvelous costumes for your show." Locky's smile faded, and she knew they were tunneling.

It was no mean tunnel that Edward Lancaster had designed. It was an eighty-foot subway, to pass beyond the wire and under the adjacent highway. "It will certainly allow everyone involved to get quite clear of the camp," pronounced Collins. With the princess' lighting system and "air conditioning"—forced ventilation devised by Larry Yates and James Barker—eager shifts of sandhogs drove the tunnel forward. Collins, aching from his beatings, set pit props. "For me, time was of the essence," he said. "I was due to be sent to Slobozia any day. I wanted to look out of that magnificent tunnel, and felt absolutely confident that when I did I was going to make Turkey."

After weeks of digging around the clock, the miners struck water. They stopped up the irruption and started a detour six feet back. More maddening water came from the sky, heavy rains that caved in the tunnel, closing off thirty feet of it. The Romanians did not seem to notice the depression in the prison yard and the POW's started a new parallel shaft a few feet from the starting point. Lancaster contracted blood poisoning from handling pit props and was taken to a Bucharest hospital, borne away from the major escape enterprise of his distinguished career.

Collins took over as construction superintendent. One day, while on watch at a barracks window, he noticed the Romanian guards rolling their eyes and pantomiming to each other. The moles in the tunnel were making too much noise and the guards were on to it. "The tunnel was hopeless now," said Collins, "but we couldn't resist milking it for laughs." The prisoners lined the windows and Collins sent men into the shaft to make noise. When the guards began their miming, the barracks exploded with laughter and catcalls. The game was broken up by the entrance of what looked like a Romanian cavalry regiment. Major Matiescu formed the POW's for a roll call and held them there while the cavalrymen shook down the camp and found the tunnel. Matiescu lined up the prime suspects, Douglas Collins at the head of the queue. "What do you know about the tunnel?" the Major asked. Collins said, "What tunnel, sir?" The Romanian said, "You know very well there is a tunnel under your barracks." Collins said, "Imagine that, sir! Did you keep prisoners here in the First World War?" Matiescu leaped up, kicked Collins, and stormed away. The commandant announced the punishment for the Timisul subway: the camp was to be liquidated and its inmates mixed in with the high-level captives in Bucharest, imperiled by their own bombs.

This gave Collins the idea for a fake escape. He and Limey Huntley took packs of food, climbed into the eaves of the barrack, and were boarded up. They planned to stay up there until the camp was evacuated and then move on. Garrett short-circuited the lights. The guards heard the dread hubbub of the traditional Timisul jail break. Matiescu threw his full force out to kill Collins on sight. Off-duty guards in their underwear came out firing at anything. Officers ran up hill and down dale, cursing, slapping and kicking their men. In the meantime a survey of the camp turned up no tunnel or breach in the wire. Matiescu pitted his fevered brain against the British Vanisher, searched the barrack three times, and finally spotted Huntley's coat showing through a crack in the boards.

Collins said, "Huntley, poor brave fighter, was first out. They smashed the hard-boiled eggs, our iron ration, on his head and rubbed them in his hair. They dragged him outside and beat him up. My turn came next. I got it badly and was knocked out. They shipped me to Slobozia that night."

The final raid on Ploesti was flown by 78 Wellingtons, Liberators and Halifaxes of the Royal Air Force on the night of 17-18 August 1944. Once again a dying bomber streaked across Princess

Caradja's estate. In the glow of the burning targets she saw two parachutes coming down. One of the airmen was on fire. She ran toward him and found a middle-aged man, terribly burned. She drove him to a physician. On the way the airman held his peeling arms away from his body and blinded eyes and conversed calmly. He had three children and was trying to win the war. The doctor worked fifteen hours but could not save him. The Princess buried him in the family cemetery next to the low-level gunner from Kentucky.*

The aerial campaign at Ploesti and associated oil targets in Romania came to a close as the Red Army stormed west in an irruption of men and armor that flooded half the country in ten days.

At the end Gerstenberg's bill was 286 U. S. heavy bombers and 2,829 men killed or captured. The Royal Air Force lost 38 heavy bombers on 924 sorties at night. Thirty-six R.A.F. men were prisoners of war.

Bucharest trembled with fear and hope as the Red Army clanked toward the city in the summer heat.

* There the warriors of the first and last strikes on Ploesti lay until an Allied disinterment party sent them home. Coming upon the open graves, the Red Army laid two of its fallen in them, punched wooden stars into the mounds where crosses had once stood, and hurried on toward Berlin.

Yonder a maid and her wight

Come whispering by

War's annals will cloud into night

Ere their story die.

THOMAS HARDY, "In Time of 'The Breaking of Nations' "

16

"LIBERATION, GLORY BE!"*

In Bucharest, hidden arms passed out of Romanian Army hoards to patriots as the Army dissolved in apathy. Antonescu was out of touch with the front. He did not know that the Red Army had placed the same value on Bucharest as the Protector had—not worth fighting for. Soviet tanks and motorized columns were bypassing the fleshpots of Bucharest on the south, keeping up momentum for a northern hook to cut off the German retreat through the mountain passes above Ploesti.

Russian detachments came sniffing into Bucharest and contacted liberal politicians who had escaped Iron Guard assassination. The Allied sympathizer, Queen Helen, encouraged her son to treat with the liberals. The king secretly appointed a new cabinet under General Senatescu and summoned Antonescu to the

* Gertrude Stein.

city palace on Place Roi Carol. The dictator left his befuddled G.H.Q. to attend what he expected would be a council of war. But the young king was alone, talked only of his stamp collection, and invited Antonescu into the large vault where he kept his specimens. Michael stepped out, shut the ponderous door, and locked his deposed Prime Minister in the vault.

Michael sent for Gerstenberg. The Protector knew what was up as soon as he saw that Antonescu was not present and that the king was surrounded by Romanian generals who he knew had been storing arms. The two parties reached a *modus vivendi:* in return for respecting Bucharest as an open city, the Romanians would permit Gerstenberg to remove his people, unmolested, through certain mountain passes, including the Predeal route past the Timisul POW camp. Michael accepted a Russian armistice offer and called on his subjects to receive the Red Army without hostility.

To Douglas Collins, just settling into his third term in the punishment camp at Slobozia, came "the moment I had waited on for four years!" The Romanian sergeant major who had brought him from Timisul opened the cell with a big smile, embraced Collins, and cried, "Comrade!" Collins said, "Comrade, indeed! Yesterday you were booting me in the guts." But he accepted the Romanian's offer to drive him back to Timisul.

The roads were choked with German convoys retreating to the north. The sight gave Collins "a childish feeling of elation I have not been able to match since." Sensible civilians kept to their shuttered houses in those chaotic days, but not Princess Caterina. She roared around the roads, hauling orphans out of harm's way, taking care to avoid Russians. On one of her journeys her car trunk was full of bundles of clothing she was distributing to the orphans. The clothing had been looted in the Ukraine and bore tags in Russian. Unexpectedly a Red Army officer popped out and halted her. He spoke the same fashionable English-inflected Romanian that she used. She thought he was probably a Romanian captive of the Russians who had defected to them. The officer instructed her chauffeur to drive to his command post and got into the car. At the command post a colonel came out beaming at the wonderful Plymouth. With him was a booted Red Army woman, fingering a lacy peignoir she wore over a grimy campaign uniform.

The colonel gestured for Caterina's party to come out. She yelled to the Romanian-speaking officer, "Tell him this car is used on vital social services!" The colonel reflected on the term, "social services," undecided what to do. He grinned and said, "We'll simply trade cars." He indicated a rusty 1926 Chrysler sitting in the courtyard. Caterina's chauffeur wailed, "*That* for my Plymouth!" The princess snapped "Get in," and her party piled into the wreck. She coolly opened the trunk of her car and threw the looted Russian clothing in to the orphans. She went to the glove compartment and palmed her papers. She was fishing in the trunk for an inner tube when the colonel noticed it and cuffed her across the face. With a wheedling smile, she said, "No harm in trying." The colonel clumped her on the back in a pally fashion, one looter to another.

The Chrysler had no starter. Caterina pantomimed, "Push" to the Russian onlookers. Still the motor would not fire. The colonel lent mechanical assistance with his prize trade-in and the Chrysler took off. Down the road she came upon the rear of a plodding Russian supply column. "Bad news," she thought. "It means their armor is up ahead, nearing the orphanages and the American camp." The Red Army rear consisted of horse-drawn victorias and farm wagons laden with happy souls drinking brandy. Some wore opera hats. "Make this car sound like hell," she ordered her chauffeur. He did, without half trying, and holding their noses and gesturing toward their clattering car, they passed the supply train. The Russians laughed so hard they forgot to seize the Chrysler. She detoured the tank column on country lanes, beat it to a village of foster homes, and hid the girls in the woods. The princess pushed the old car up the pass for the Timisul camp.

She found the G.I.'s in full charge. Although the gates were open and the guards gone, Captain Taylor had decided to keep the POW's together until some reasonable move materialized. Two days before, a German armored train had enfiladed the camp while passing north. Perhaps there were men on the train who remembered a prisoner mocking them as they rode south in the days of their glory. No one was hit in the spiteful volley.

The princess told Taylor, "We've got to get you out before the Russians come." It is doubtful whether the Russians would have done worse than leave them with hangovers, but the POW's were restless. They scrounged seven farm trucks, covered themselves with blankets, and Romanians drove them west across forest tracks to a valley that Gerstenberg had agreed not to use for evacuation. In a downpour of rain they arrived in Pietrosita, a hamlet spared the cruelty of war, and were billeted in private homes, where they found refugee girls from Bucharest. Morale took a leap. They awakened to sunlight and joyful stirrings: a peace festival in the town park, to which they were conducted by smiling people. They sat down at tables with corn on the cob, roast meats, melons, milk, fresh loaves and kegs of wine. A year before they had fallen in Hitler's black harvest. Now the victory yield was in.

Maidens with whirling skirts danced the *hora* to strumming balalaikas and guitars. A fallen Sky Scorpion, Sergeant James Sedlak, took to the band pavilion with his trumpet and lined out a screaming chorus of "Flat-Foot Floogey." Village strings and faltering voices of youths who had heard the tune on the illegal radio took up the nonsense words of Pietrosita's liberation paean. Princess Caradja said, "Those boys had all the fun there is in this world." In the middle of it a bleak convoy of disarmed Germans passed through, clutching their ears.

Collins returned to Timisul and found the camp deserted. A peasant told him his friends were in Pietrosita. Collins joined them there. "Those were riotous days," said the escaper, "but Captain Taylor did not let it get out of hand. He was the kind of officer no one wanted to let down."

Into the victory gala came an old acquaintance, the bully, Major Matiescu, now a most humble and sincere friend of the Americans. Huntley and Collins started for the camp commandant to pay him back for the whippings he had given them. Captain Taylor said, "Hold on, you guys! Be sensible. You don't want to lower yourself to the level of a Romanian officer, do you?" Collins hesitated and said, "Limey, he's right. There's too much at stake here for petty revenge." Huntley said, "I'd like to take just one crack at him, but what the hell." They turned away from Matiescu.

In Bucharest, the American high-level officers were holding on in their compound. They had heard the news of the Romano-Russian armistice late at night, and awakened the Romanian commandant, their spokesman saying, "What happens now?" He replied angrily, "What is the meaning of this?" The American said, "Your outfit is out of the war. Kaputt." The commandant made a phone call. He dropped the phone in the cradle. Without further remark he belted on his dress sword over his pajamas, saluted them, and handed over the blade in ceremonial surrender.

Rifle shots were crackling outside the compound. The Romanians returned the Americans' side arms. A high-level captive, Lieutenant Martin Roth, said, "Well, I guess we're allowed to leave." Another said, "I don't want to mess in it. It's between the Romanians and the Germans." Most of the officers agreed they wanted no part of the shooting. Henry Lasco, the low-level pilot, was smoking a cigaret. His face wounds had healed, leaving an open hole in one cheek, and in order to take a puff, he had to plug the fistula with a finger tip. He said, "Well, speaking for myself, I'd like to take a crack at the krauts before it's over," and started for the gate. Roth said, "Hold on a minute, Hank. I'm going with you." The two-man patrol ventured into the dark, empty streets reverberating with spang of rifles, distant cries and pounding boots. The fusillades thickened and the airmen espaliered themselves against buildings, moving cautiously into this unfamiliar type of war. Hands came out of a doorway and hauled them in. The captors were Romanian patriots who embraced them and rained kisses on Lasco's shattered cheeks, crying, "The Americans are with us!" The Romano-American band went into the night to round up Germans. Lasco felt a knock on the head. He had walked into the boot of a German soldier hanged by the neck from a lamppost.

Toward morning they understood what was happening in

Bucharest. Roth said, "There was a tight Romanian ring around the city. The Germans could not get through it. Outside the Romanians the Germans were milling around, trapped by the third ring—a powerful Russian encirclement with big tanks. After two days Hank and I decided to let them settle it among themselves and went back to the compound."

General Gerstenberg was trapped in the double encirclement north of Bucharest, trying to remove some of his forces pinched between the Russians and Romanians. The last movement he was able to control was the evacuation of 1,200 Luftwaffe airwomen through the Russian ring. Their colonel was killed defending the rear of the female convoy. The Protector, who had placed such a high end-game value on *Festung Ploesti,* was unable to get into the city when the crisis came. The redoubt was now just another devastated place on the map, instead of the key defense of *Südostraum.* Gerstenberg's command was shattered. The Danubian plain was flooded with about 100,000 German troops in hopeless flight, paced by the fastest runners from the broken eastern front army. In addition, there was a fantastic rabble of German civilians crossing Romania, trying to bring home loot from farms they had been awarded in the Ukraine. Heinz Schultz was carting his farm implements in eight wagons drawn by sixteen oxen and sixteen horses, with twelve Ukrainian peasants aboard. He was threading through the battle lines on back roads and river fords. Other displaced German agriculturists plodded home with their plunder packed on Caucasian camels.

Flak man Werner Horn said, "With the Russians moving in, our fate was sealed. We had no equipment to defend ourselves against tanks." The last hopes of Gerstenberg's people touched the extremes of illusion. "We expected American airborne troops to occupy Romania," said Horn, "rather than relinquish her to the Russians. But nothing happened. Thus came the inglorious end of the German Air Force in Romania. We went into Russian captivity."

Even in the *Oberkommando* in Berlin it was now evident that both the eastern and western fronts were broken and Bucharest and Paris were being delivered. Hitler reacted in perfect Hitlerian

form. He ordered the Luftwaffe to bomb both disloyal capitals.
His commanding air generals in Bucharest and Paris, Alfred Gerstenberg and Otto Dessloch, were old comrades from World War
I days. Dessloch had taken over in Paris only a few days before,
direct from a post with Gerstenberg as commander of Air Fleet
Four, Balkans. Looking at Hitler's wanton order, Dessloch faced
the moral crisis of his career. He told Berlin he did not have the
planes to bomb Paris. This statement was substantially true after
the massive destruction of the Luftwaffe in France since D-day.
Hitler's order was obeyed, however, by a Luftwaffe general in
eastern France who sent planes that set fire to wine storehouses
in the Paris produce market, Les Halles.

In Romania, nobody could find Alfred Gerstenberg to deliver
the order to bomb Bucharest. The phones rang in his empty H.Q.
at Pepira. Signals went to the fighter control center at Otopenii.
There was no acknowledgment. Several days before, a Romanian
partisan band had taken Gerstenberg in his last post in the field
and was holding him and his staff to hand over to the Russians.

Hitler's order to bomb Bucharest was heard by Luftwaffe officers still left on the bases at Mizil and Zilistea, in the northeast
sector, out of the path of the Soviet advance. They had about
thirty Junkers 88's and Stuka dive bombers. Without hesitation
the new German pilots flew to punish defenseless Bucharest.

At Pepira, the Romanian pilots refused to fly, either to bomb or
defend their capital, and that was the end of the playboys of the
Royal Romanian Air Force. The bombing of the open city began.
A few Romanian flak crews resisted it with light guns.

The bombing turned the precarious German situation into a
complete debacle. The nation rose against the Germans. King
Michael declared war on Hitler immediately. A handful of Romanian pilots took to the air and fought the Luftwaffe. Romanians
captured heavier flak guns and turned them on the bombers. But
explosives continued to fall on Bucharest. An American POW
was killed when he ran from a shelter to the hospital to rescue
a Romanian nurse. The bombers flattened the POW compound
and started on the hospital. A Ju-88 hit a prosthetics shop and
destroyed an articulated wooden leg that was being made for

John Palm. The Texan filled his old hollow leg with mementos of his halcyon days, including a small pistol. A Bucharest heiress importuned him to store her jewels in his leg, but, upon reflection, Palm declined.

A Stuka hit the POW hospital and the ceiling fell on Francis Doll. He dragged himself out and helped carry wounded through the empty streets to a new shelter. As the Germans buzzed overhead, he felt his "nerves going to pieces." He and a buddy decided to leave Bucharest. On the edge of the city two girls took them home, fed them, and let the grimy sergeants wash up. Another raid alert sounded. "The whistle of those bombs!" said Doll. "We took off in nothing flat out of Bucharest." A mile out of town a woman advised them to go no farther. There was a German machine gunner around the next corner. A man across the street hurled a grenade at them. Doll and his friend ran away from the burst and were not hit. They entered a Romanian garrison, where the guards gave them helmets and guns. Doll remembers, "I was scared at the idea of fighting seasoned troops—me, of the Air Force—with a foreign rifle. But we got brave and said we were going out to hunt Germans." A guard said, "Americans, stay in safe place," and introduced them to an old man who had a son in America. He took the sergeants into his home and his neighbors came with gifts of food and wine and patted them on the back.

Up in the mountain, out of the war, the low-level men still frolicked in Pietrosita. Robert Johnson, the veterinarian, left the village, and Collins, Caminada and Gukovsky, the Palestinian parachutist, asked Captain Taylor's permission to depart for Bucharest. The American commander said he had no objection but intended to keep his own men in Pietrosita until he could safely move them. A chauffeur-driven limousine arrived in the village and out stepped Johnson. He had liberated Antonescu's car and driver. He took the British party in style to Bucharest, where the Swiss consul, in charge of United Kingdom affairs, put them up in suites in the Hotel Ambassador, recently vacated by the German general staff.

Collins took a stroll, curbing an impulse to start running when he saw policemen. He encountered Lancaster in the street and the comrades yelled for joy. Lancaster said, "Let's make for Constanta and take a ship for Turkey." He couldn't quit escaping. Collins said, "I think we ought to sit tight and see what happens here." His partner agreed.

A day or so later, after the bombing had ceased, Captain Taylor brought the low-level men to Bucharest. He and Top Sergeant Edmond Terry were appalled to find wounded Americans lying around the city, uncared for. The bombing had killed five POW's. Four others died when a German stepped into a restaurant with a machine gun and cut down the diners. Dozens had been wounded in the Luftwaffe attacks and there were dozens more with untended wounds from the final air battles at Ploesti. Terry took a gang of POW's to the bombed hospital and cleaned up several wards. He collected a hundred wounded men and started looking after them. But since the departure of the Romanian jailers there was no money for food or medication. Terry asked John Palm to raise some money. The pilot of *Brewery Wagon* stumped away and applied to one of his useful acquaintances, Arieh Fichman, another Palestinian agent who had been parachuted into Romania by British Intelligence. Fichman was carrying a fortune in operational funds. He peeled off several million lei for the starving Americans.

Francis Doll drifted back from his refuge on the outskirts of town and reported to his favorite topkick. Terry handed him a stack of lei and said, "You're the hospital cook. Don't give these men anything but the best." Doll's first menu consisted of roast beef and gravy, mashed potatoes, milk, coffee, apples, cakes and all the beer they could drink.

The senior U. S. prisoner of war was Lieutenant Colonel James A. Gunn (not related to Captain James A. Gunn III, lost on the low-level mission), who had been shot down on one of the last American raids. With some of his men dead and others dying, Gunn undertook to save the rest. He got permission from the new Romanian government to radio the 15th Air Force in Italy about the plight of the 1,274 American and Allied personnel trapped in Bucharest. The 15th did not want to discuss it on the open radio and requested Gunn to report personally to Italy. He borrowed an ancient Savoia-Marchetti, was checked out briefly on the Italian instrument panel, and took off. The plane was incapable of the long flight and Gunn was forced to return. Princess Caradja's cousin, a big, resourceful pilot, Captain Constantine Cantacuzene, volunteered to fly Gunn to Foggia in an Me-109 single-seater. This entailed painting an American flag on the craft, folding the lanky colonel into the empty radio compartment, and screwing the entry panel shut on him.

Cantacuzene alighted at Foggia and announced, "I have somebody here you will be pleased to see." He removed the panel and a soldier said, "Get a load of those G.I. boots," as Gunn uncoiled from his cramped nest. The Fifteenth Air Force sent a fighter reconnaissance to Bucharest to determine if Popestii airport was safe for aerial evacuation of the POW's. Cantacuzene led the flight in a Mustang, a machine he had recently opposed in the air but had never piloted. The scouts reported that the airport seemed secure, although there were German machines still in the air.

A flight of Fortresses went to Bucharest with a liaison party, including medical officers, to round up the men and prepare history's first large-scale air evacuation from a point 550 miles inside enemy lines. At Foggia, ground crews fitted fifty Fortresses with bomb-bay seats and litters in the fuselage to accommodate twenty men in each ship. Many of the mechanics had sat out long nights waiting for men who did not return; now they cried and cursed with joy and fatigue as they rigged the bombers for deliverance instead of death.

A special B-17 flew to Bucharest with an Office of Strategic Services party to pick up German records and survey damage to the Ploesti refineries. It was led by Sergeant Philip Coombs, a former economics professor, who brought a ton of C-rations to see his people through the hardships of the field. At the Bucharest airport Coombs was surprised to find another O.S.S. man, a Washington journalist named Beverly Bowie, in a U. S. Navy uniform. Bowie had hitchhiked from Italy some days earlier. He ushered Coombs's people into a fleet of Buicks and Packards given to him by Romanians who wished to keep them from the Germans and Russians. Bowie howled when he saw Coombs's field rations. He took them to lunch in an outdoor restaurant called Mon Jardin, where the buffet consisted of pâté de foie gras, Black Sea caviar, roasts of beef, ham and goose, a six-foot sturgeon and pheasants in paper pantaloons. As the waiter captain uncorked a magnum of champagne, Bowie said, "Welcome to operation bughouse."

Bowie was sitting in by invitation on Liberation cabinet sessions. He explained to Coombs, "Before they vote on anything, they ask me what I think. I go into a trance and figure out what Franklin D. Roosevelt would do, then give 'em the answer. They pass all my laws unanimously. I never thought running a country was so easy."

Bowie drove the field team to the Hotel Athenée Palace, in front of which a Red Army band was playing. A haggard youth in rags came through the crowd, calling, "Professor Coombs! Don't you remember me? Irving Fisher? I took Economics One under you at Williams." Coombs took his former pupil, a high-level POW, into the hotel for a square meal. The O.S.S. men drove to Ploesti. Along the road they came upon an emergency hospital full of airmen shot down on the last raids. The place stank of gangrene. The Romanian physician in charge said, "We can do nothing. We have heard of penicillin, but we haven't got any." The O.S.S. radioman cranked out a message to Italy, and a B-17 took off with drugs and doctors.

Coombs's party found Ploesti seemingly in utter ruin. However, during three days of detailed inspection and interviews, they found that the remains of five plants, linked by Gerstenberg's pipeline web, were still producing 20 percent of capacity. This was the residuum of the resistance put up by the defensive genius, Alfred Gerstenberg, against 23 heavy bombing raids, totaling 9,173 individual bomber and fighter sorties, which had dropped 13,709 tons of explosives.

The statistic is Gerstenberg's only note in the official military history of World War II. By then the Protector was in O.G.P.U. H.Q., Moscow, chatting with secret police chief Lavrenti Beria, who passed on praises of Gerstenberg from Marshal Klimenti Voroshilov, who had been his commander at the clandestine German air school in the U.S.S.R. fifteen years earlier. Beria promised to use Gerstenberg again. Instead, the Protector was sent to Lefort Prison to solitary confinement for two years. He was to be in Soviet prisons for twelve years.

In Bucharest, Coombs's O.S.S. men found Gerstenberg's H.Q. untouched. They sent two tons of his archives by air to Italy, and began looking for the German espionage center for southeast Europe, which Coombs had reason to believe was located in Bucharest. He could not find any live Germans to help him, but he heard there were two dead ones in the German Embassy. The Nazi ambassador, Baron von Buch-Killinger, who had purchased Antonescu to begin the tragedy of Romania, and his counselor had committed suicide. Coombs thought there might be some living Germans in the building, which was guarded by Red Army men.

Coombs procured a hearse and two pick-up coffins. In one he placed O.S.S. man Fred Burkhart, a philosophy professor in civilian life, who spoke German. Coombs figured to get the hearse down a basement ramp entry to the embassy on the pretext of removing the corpses, and smuggle out a live German and Professor Burkhart in the boxes. Coombs drove circumspectly behind the hearse. As it turned into the ramp, a Red Army officer halted it. The driver explained his mission in Romanian, which the Russian did not understand. Coombs showed himself in U. S. uniform and tried English, but the Russian could not understand that either. The lid of the pick-up coffin opened and Professor Burkhart joined the argument in German. A second Red Army officer approached and said in English, "What is it you wish?" Coombs said, "We have come to pick up the bodies of the ambassador and the counselor." The Russian said, "There are no Germans here, living or dead. We took them all away yesterday." Coombs drew himself up and said sternly, "Don't you know that it is a violation of international law to seize an embassy?" The Russian apologetically replied, "We only came for our furniture." Coombs began to understand why Bowie had called it operation bughouse. The Russian explained, "You see, when Germany attacked us in 1941, Buch-Killinger looted our furniture from the Soviet Embassy here. We are only making an inventory to get our state property back."

Coombs found the German espionage center through a tip by a Romanian: "Why not look in at von Schenker?" The O.S.S. man said, "What's that?" The informant said, "A German travel agency, the largest in the world, bigger than Cook's or the American Express." In von Schenker's Bucharest office Coombs found business going on as usual, as though German tourists were still visiting the Acropolis and booking freight home from the Ukraine. Von Schenker's was the spy center. A week after Bucharest was in Allied hands, the clerks of the German espionage apparatus continued to process reports.

From the high-level POW's, Coombs picked a German-speaking Jewish sergeant and put him in charge at von Schenker's to sift its files for important papers. The German clerks worked industriously for the new management and completed the research in three days. The sergeant brought Coombs the gem of finds: the paybook of Nazi secret agents in southeast Europe, giving their real names and addresses.

Coombs and the spy archives were flown to Washington, where General Arnold personally congratulated the sergeant. Afterward Coombs lunched at the Cosmos Club with President James Baxter of Williams College, where he had been an instructor. Hearing the tale of Ploesti, Dr. Baxter said, "Our alumnus, Irv Fisher, lost his son there." Coombs said, "Irving Fisher, Junior? He's alive! I saw him in Bucharest." Baxter hastened to phone the father.

In the Romanian capital, young Fisher and more than a thousand other Allied airmen, many of whose kin did not know they were alive, were drifting around the streets. In the midst of a monstrous war, they were free far inside hostile territory, enjoying the fulsome hospitality of a nation that had been their enemy the day before. Douglas Collins noted "small bands of Romanian communists trudging through the streets with banners proclaiming that the millennium had arrived, but there were more Americans than Russians to puzzle over the slogans." Collins ran into a few Royal Air Force men. Waiting, the occupational disease of soldiering, settled on them all.

In Italy, the Fifteenth Air Force was now ready for the risky airlift of the POW's from Romania. It would be a 1,100-mile round trip by Fortresses virtually stripped of arms to make room for men. About 1,500 airmen, including the B-17 crews, would be in the air—a tempting target for German fighters, of which quite a few were still operating. The rescue force, therefore, could not broadcast any formal order to the POW's that might be intercepted by the enemy. A courier went to Bucharest and started the news by word of mouth among the POW's. Collins was approached in the street by an American he had never seen before who muttered, "Tomorrow morning. Nine o'clock at the airport. We're all getting out of this sonofabitching country."

Next morning at Popestii airport the liberated men stood around the perimeter in groups of twenty to board the planes quickly during the short turnaround. The British Vanishers arrived promptly at the rendezvous of their last escape. They, who had marveled at American military costume when they first saw it a year before, now descried it in the bloom of victory. The airmen were attired in rags and grimy bandages, wearing German helmets and Russian caps and sagging under the weight of wine bottles, captured dress swords, riding crops, balalaikas and cabinet photos of Romanian beauties. Some had sewn upon their tatters the large, resplendent insignia of the Royal Romanian Air Force and Parachute Corps. The better-dressed element sported Army pants newly distributed by the Red Cross. All the trousers in the shipment were size 40, and not one of the emaciated men could fill such a waistband. They had gathered them at the waist in pleats reaching the knee, and, to mock the current "zoot-suit" style of boys at home, had draped their identity necklaces across the belly like the watch chains the zoots wore there.

John Palm was there, stumping around on his loaded artificial leg, exchanging adieux with sobbing lady friends. Fichman, the rich Palestinian parachutist, tapped him on the back and asked for the balance of the emergency fund he had lent the Americans. Palm returned a wad of lei and the Palestinian and the Texan, on behalf of the Chancellor of the Exchequer and the Secretary of the Treasury, traded penciled receipts to square Anglo-American joint accounts for Romania.

It was a sultry morning on the Wallachian plain. Collins and

Lancaster took shade under the wing of an old Heinkel, lay down, and dozed. At noon they were awakened by "a royal buzz" of P-51's, which swept up high and circled to cover the B-17 landings. The first two Fortresses rolled up to Collins, Lancaster, Caminada, Gukovsky, Johnson, Admiral Doorman, Baron van Lyndon, and 36 men of 205 Group, Royal Air Force. "We took off and circled," said Collins, "waited for the others to come into formation, and then we headed west, over the Danube that had beaten us, and over Yugoslavia where we had not been able to find Tito. Never had we dreamed of such an end to our efforts to escape from Europe."

At Camp Choumen, in the wilds of Bulgaria, there were still 257 men who had fallen along the low road and the high to Ploesti. They lived in lice, mud, misery and abuse, licking their wounds, shut off from the jubilee at Bucharest. On the eighth of September Soviet planes flew over Bulgaria, dropping leaflets announcing that the Red Army was coming and calling upon Bulgarians to lay down arms and release prisoners of war. Within a day Julian Darlington, his nine Tidal Wave men and the rest were aboard a train for Turkey. Six weeks later they arrived in an Army transport ship at Newport News, Virginia.

The Ploesti men were the first of democracy's warriors to be redeemed en masse from world fascism, which lived briefly by killing forty million people.

The British Vanishers returned to England, where Edward Lancaster was discharged as medically unfit. Douglas Collins rejoined his regiment and led a platoon through the liberation of Belgium and Holland. He was in Germany again, with a machine gun in his hand, at the end of Hitler's Thousand-Year Reich.

As it fell, tanks of the U. S. Third Army liberated a prisoner-of-war camp at Moosberg, near Munich. A tall U. S. Air Force officer greeted the tankers with "Colonel Smart. Glad to see you." The planner of the low-level attack on Ploesti, the possessor of the atomic bomb secret, had survived nearly a year in Nazi hands.

The Allied chiefs, who had been living in dread that the secret had been tortured from Jacob Smart, brought him immediately to Washington to report on what had happened to him. "When my aircraft came apart in the air at Wiener Neustadt," he said, "I found myself falling among the debris. My parachute opened. I landed in a meadow and took cover in a woods. I had body and face wounds that were not serious, but they were painful, and I was losing considerable blood. I fell asleep and was awakened by soldiers out looking for prisoners.

"I was in German hospitals for two months, wearing my dog tags and insignia, and no doubt my right name on laundry marks. My co-pilot survived but died later. The tail gunner is still living. The tail snapped off in the explosion and he rode it to within a few hundred feet of the ground before bailing out. I was at Stalag Three in eastern Germany until the Russians came near it in January 1944. The Germans then marched us west and put us on a train for Moosberg, where I was liberated."

Smart had been delivered from German hands four months before the first atomic bomb was to fall on Hiroshima. Now, in Washington, he realized what the anxious audience of generals and colonels wanted to know. He concluded his report with it. He smiled and said, "At no time did the Germans ever question me about nuclear fission."

To the Fallen of Ploesti

To you who fly on forever I send that part of me which cannot be separated and is bound to you for all time. I send to you those of our hopes and dreams that never quite came true, the joyous laughter and showery tears of our boyhood, the marvelous mysteries of our adolescence, the glorious strength and tragic illusions of our young manhood, all these that were and perhaps would have been, I leave in your care, out there in the Blue.

John Riley Kane, Colonel, U.S.A.F. (Ret.)

BIBLIOGRAPHY AND CREDITS

First, the authors wish to thank those listed below for making available unpublished personal diaries and narratives of Tidal Wave:

David W. Alexander, Norman C. Appold, Philip P. Ardery, Charles Deane Cavit, Charles P. Decreval, Francis W. Doll, Lewis N. Ellis, Gerald K. Geerlings, Brutus K. Hamilton, Charles E. Hughes, Lindley P. Hussey, John Riley Kane, Joseph F. Kill, Clifford E. Koen, Jr., Lawrence H. Lancashire, Henry A. Lasco, Jr., Robert J. Lehnhausen, Robert T. Locky, John O. Lockhart, Worthy A. Long, Russell D. Longnecker, Stefan Marinopolsky (Sixth Bulgarian Fighter Regiment), James H. McClain, Dwight D. Patch, Douglas Pitcairn, Jack W. Preble, Jr., Elmer H. Reinhart, Hermann Scheiffele, Walter T. Stewart, Raymond P. Warner, Worden L. Weaver, Earl L. Zimmerman, and Douglas Collins for his prisoner-of-war chronicle.

Books

Anon. *The Official Guide to the Army Air Forces*. New York, 1944.

Anon. *389th Bombardment Group: A Pictorial Review of Operations in the ETO*. San Angelo, Texas, n.d.

Anon. *The Story of the 93rd Bomb. Group*. San Angelo, Texas, n.d.

Butcher, Harry C. *My Three Years with Eisenhower*. New York, 1946.

Caminada, Jerome. *My Purpose Holds*. London, 1952.

Churchill, Winston S. *The Second World War*. New York, 1950.

Dmitri, Ivan. *Flight to Everywhere*. New York, 1944.

Eighth Air Force Staff Writers. *Target: Germany*. New York, 1943.

Green, William. *Famous Fighters of the Second World War*. New York, 1958.

Harris, Arthur. *Bomber Offensive*. London, 1947.

Harvel, Ursel P. *Liberators Over Europe* (44th Bomb Group history). San Angelo, Texas, n.d.

Historical Office of the Army Air Forces. *The Official Picture History of the AAF*. New York, 1947.

Martin, Ralph G. *The Boy from Nebraska* (Ben Kuroki). New York, 1945.

McCrary, Tex (John R.) and David E. Scherman. *The First of the Many.* New York, 1943.

Owen, Roderick. *Tedder.* London, 1952.

Wolff, Leon. *Low Level Mission.* New York, 1957.

Reports and Articles

Anon. *Report on Enemy Air Attacks on German Centres of Fuel Production and German Counter-Measures* (Aug. 1943-June 1944). (Translation of a captured Luftwaffe document.)

Anon. *Reports of German Air Force Interrogations of Prisoners of War Following Ploesti Raid 1 August 1943.* (Translation of a captured Luftwaffe document.)

Anon. *United States Strategic Bombing Survey,* 109—Oil Division (Final Report); 110—Oil Division (Appendix); 113—The German Oil Industry (Report Team 78).

Bachmann, L. P. "Operation Reunion," *Air Force* magazine, Nov. 1944.

Crichton, Kyle. "A Texan in King Michael's Court," *Collier's,* 25 Nov. 1944.

Cruickshank, Earl. *The Ploesti Mission 1 August 1943 (AAFRH-3).* (Unpublished operational intelligence study for the War Department.)

Gervasi, Frank. "Hitting Hitler's Oil Barrel," *Collier's,* 18 Sept. 1943.

———— "Flying Through Hell," *Collier's,* 2 Oct. 1943.

McFarland, Kenton D. and Arturo F. Gonzales, Jr. "Hell at Fifty Feet," *Argosy,* Feb. 1960.

Smart, Jacob E. "Planning the Mission," *Air Force* magazine, Nov. 1943.

Suchenwirth, Richard. *Historical Turning Points in the German Air Force War Effort,* U.S.A.F. Historical Studies No. 189.

Sulzberger, Cyrus L. "Life and Death of an American Bomber," *New York Times Magazine,* 16 July 1944.

Young, John S. "Over the Target," *Air Force* magazine, Nov. 1943.

Other articles in *Air Force* and *Impact* magazines, U.S.A.F. publications, were consulted, as well as the *Prisoner of War Bulletin* of the American Red Cross. Among newspapers furnishing file information were the *Akron Beacon-Journal,* the *Belvidere Republican,* the *Broken Bow Chief,* the *Colorado Springs Gazette-Telegraph,* the *Cincinnati Post & Times-Star,* the *Columbus Commercial Dispatch,* the *Dallas Morning News,* the *Denver Post,* the

Rocky Mountain News (Denver), the *Des Moines Register-Tribune*, the Harlan Newspapers, the *Hartford Courant*, the *Hartley Sentinel*, the *Kalamazoo Gazette*, the *Lincoln Journal*, the (Little Rock) *Arkansas Gazette*, the *Times* of London, the *Moline Dispatch*, the *Murray Eagle*, the *New York Herald Tribune*, the *New York Times*, the *Omaha World-Herald*, the *Salt Lake City Tribune*, the *Sioux City Journal*, the *Spokane Spokesman-Review*, the *Stars & Stripes* (wartime London and Cairo editions), the *Toledo Blade*, the *Washington Star* and the *Waterloo Gazette*.

A score of West German Republic newspapers and the weekly *Frankfurter Illustrierte* published the authors' appeals for survivors of the Tidal Wave battle, as did many U.S.A.F. base newspapers.

The authors hope that relatives of Tidal Wave men who gave information will accept acknowledgment in the form of mention of their men in the text. Others who assisted research were Joseph Angell and David Schoen of the U.S.A.F. Historical Liaison Office, Emile J. Bourge, Jr., of the Louisiana Department of Veterans' Affairs, William G. Conley of the Arkansas Press Association, J. Alan Cramer of Wayne, Nebraska, Senator Carl T. Curtis of Nebraska, James M. Darley, chief cartographer of the National Geographic Society, Walter Feinberg of Newton Centre, Massachusetts, John Gilligan of Twentieth Century (CBS-TV), Senator Roman Hruska of Nebraska, Roland Riviere, Jr., of New Orleans, Vern Sanford of the Texas Press Association and Francis Edgar Thomas of the University of North Carolina.

The following were also particularly helpful in preparation of the book: Mrs. Henry H. Arnold, widow of General Arnold U.S.A.F., Chief of Staff; Captain Veryl Bevelacqua U.S.A.F., Intelligence officer 44BG (I-C); Major Hans Otto Boehm, Luftwaffe, secretary of Luftwaffe Fighter Pilots' Society, editor of its bulletin, archivist and historian; Richard Crone, German press liaison with H.Q. U.S.A.F. in Europe; Dr. William Deakin, colonel in British Army, Sir Winston Churchill's literary aide and member of a wartime military mission to Tito; Paul Deichmann, Luftwaffe officer, widely acquainted with Luftwaffe staff officers; Lieutenant Colonel Gordon C. Furbish U.S.A.F., Deputy Director of Information, H.Q. U.S.A.F. in Europe; Major Gerald K. Geerlings U.S.A.F. (I-C-Unp); Ion Georgescu, manager of Ploesti refinery prior to nationalization (I-C); Herr Greffrath, West German military archivist; L. A. Jackets, Squadron Leader R.A.F., chief of Air Historical Branch, Air Ministry, London (C); Marguerite K. Kennedy, Chief of Archives

Branch U.S.A.F., Historical Division, Maxwell AFB, Alabama; Evard Leb-beu, Luftwaffe pilot; Captain Marvin McFarland, Science and Technology Division, Library of Congress, Washington, D.C. (I-C); Colonel Laurence H. Macauley U.S.A.F., chief of Information Services, Air University, Max-well AFB, Alabama; Alice Martin, secretary to Major James H. Sunderman U.S.A.F. Book Program, Pentagon, Washington, D.C.; Lothar Müller, Luft-waffe pilot; F. C. Myers, archivist of U.S.A.F., Historical Division, Maxwell AFB, Alabama; Hans Ostertag, Information Directorate, H.Q. U.S.A.F. in Europe; Rev. John Popovitch, Romanian Orthodox Church of the Descent of the Holy Spirit, Phila., Pa.; Captain Jack Preble U.S.A.F., Historical officer 376BG (C-Unp); General Richard Reimann, Luftwaffe, commanded Ploesti flak forces from March '44; Hans Ring, Luftwaffe officer; Joan St. George Saunders of London, England; Major H. Schnaars, Luftwaffe; Generalmajor Karl-Heinrich Schulz, Luftwaffe, Romania (C); Captain George Y. Scriba U.S.A.F., Intelligence officer 93BG (I-C); Dr. Albert F. Simpson U.S.A.F., chief of Historical Division, Maxwell AFB, Alabama (I-C); Major James M. Sunderman U.S.A.F., Public Information Officer, Dept. of the Air Force, in charge of A.F. Book Program; Joseph Tustin, Historian of U.S.A.F. in Eu-rope; Captain Attillio Verna U.S.A.F., Photo Officer 93BG (I-C).

Picture Credits

The authors wish to thank the following for permission to use pictorial material in the book:

Philip P. Ardery, Norman C. Appold, Veryl Bevelacqua, George S. Brown, Jr., Charles T. Bridges, Paul Baetz, Douglas Collins, Richard M. Crippen, Julian T. Darlington, Lewis K. Ellis, the family of Brian W. Flavelle, the family of Jesse D. Franks, Jr., Anthony Fravega, Jack Gurnett, Werner Ger-hartz, Donald J. Grimes, Lindley P. Hussey, John Riley Kane, Robert T. Locky, Russell D. Longnecker, Erich Menge, Werner Nass, Laurence Ocamb, Russell B. Page, John D. Palm, Douglas Pitcairn, John E. Powell, Elmer H. Reinhart, Manfred Spenner, Wilhelm Steinmann, Walter T. Stewart, Attillio Verna, Raymond P. Warner, Ewald Wegener and Ray Wier.

The photos of Colonel Timberlake and of the group of Circus men by David E. Scherman, and of Colonel Kane by John Phillips, are used by permission of the photographers and *Life* magazine. Other publications clearing photos were the *Kalamazoo Gazette* and the *Rocky Mountain News.* Many pictures came from the United States Air Force, whose 1360th Photographic Flight was additionally helpful. Betty F. Geerlings made the sketch of Squadron Leader Barwell from a 1943 newspaper cut, after all attempts failed to turn up an original photo.

Special thanks go to the Convair Division of the General Dynamics Corporation, successor to the builders of the famous Consolidated B-24 Liberator, whose draftsmen prepared the end-paper map and the charts in the text.

The authors appreciate the aid of interpreters/translators who worked on the German evidence: in Wiesbaden, Anna Tolzer, Elke Seidel and Monika Meurer; in Augsburg, Colin Murley; Munich, Lisolette Thoene; and at St. Mary's Academy, O'Neill, Nebraska, Sister M. Adeltrude, OSF, and Kathe Arnold.

GENERAL INDEX

Afrika Korps 7, 9, 27, 32
Air Ministry, British 233
air-sea rescue, R.A.F. 199, 200, 213
Alanya, Turkey 199
Albania 94, 95
Alexander, Sir Harold 54
Allison, W. R., 235
Anglo-Iranian Oil Co. 180
antiaircraft (flak) 33, 43, 66, 76, 77, 102, 114, 118-121, 125, 131, 205, 225, 228
Antonescu, Ion 8, 24-29, 75, 229, 231, 249-250, 260-261, 278-279, 285
Arnold, Henry H. 4, 5, 36, 59, 68, 76, 290
Astro Romana refinery 8, 11, 13, 43, 123, 137, 165
Athens, Greece 209, 233
atomic bomb 265, 292
Augsburg, Germany 41
Avia-534, 74, 98, 201
"Axis Sally" 234

Baetz, Paul 104-105, 127
Baku, U.S.S.R. 7, 9
Balkan Mountains, Bulgaria 177, 178, 198
balloons 112, 116, 169, 174
Bari, Italy 243, 252, 270
Baxter, James 290
Beck, Gerald D. 53, 82
Belvidere, Illinois 246
Benghazi, Libya 30, 31, 32, 49,
50, 55, 61, 68, 81, 87-89, 162, 207, 222, 235
Berkovitsa, Bulgaria 98
Bessarabia 23, 26, 248
Black Sea 13, 73, 238
Black Widow 273
Bodleian Library 45
bombs 67, 80, 81, 84, 131, 180; disarming 137, 138, 233-234; accuracy 244
Bourne, Charles 252
Bowie, Beverly 287-289
Bozhurishte, Bulgaria 98
Brazi, Romania 43, 159, 239
Brasov, Romania 255, 263, 267, 269, 272
Brereton, Lewis H. 18, 30, 34, 46, 59, 61, 62, 68, 69, 76, 140, 216-217, 221, 223, 234-235, 244-245
British Broadcasting System 251
British Vanishers 238-241, 265-266, 276, 291-292
Bryan, Lon 246
Bucharest, Romania 22-25, 28, 29, 31, 75, 87, 94, 100, 103, 107, 108, 109, 110, 111, 112, 115, 128, 136, 230, 235-238, 256-257, 263-265, 269, 271, 274, 277, 278-291
Buch-Killinger, Manfred von 23, 24, 28, 289
Budapest, Hungary 238
Bukovina 23, 26
Bulgaria 26, 97, 98, 99, 106, 198, 204, 253, 258-259, 292

ABOUT THE AUTHORS

CARROLL STEWART is a Nebraska newspaperman. At fourteen he was the typesetter-reporter-editor of the *Belden Progress* and, at nineteen, editor of the prize-winning *Cedar County News* at Hartington. In 1942, as Private Stewart, radioman of the 93rd Bomb Group in England, he published *The Liberator,* the first overseas U. S. troop newspaper of World War II. Elevated to corporal, he took charge of 93rd BG public relations, which were frustrated by security bans on numerical identification of units. He made the group famous by dubbing it "The Traveling Circus" and mailing to U. S. newspapers Circus releases fresh from his mimeograph. The morale of a dozen other bomb groups was lowered by the coup, and a two-star general told Stewart, "From now on you'll work for the whole Eighth Air Force, or else." Stewart assisted Tex McCrary and David E. Scherman with a 1943 book about the Eighth U.S.A.A.F., *The First of the Many,* and at the end of the war produced a history of the Franco-American First Tactical Air Force. In order to give full time to this book he sold a successful postwar enterprise, the *O'Neill Frontier.* When *Ploesti* was completed he returned to publishing with the simultaneous launching of four *Sun* newspapers in and around Lincoln.

The late JAMES DUGAN came from Altoona, Pennsylvania, and attended The Pennsylvania State University. During World War II he served overseas for three and a half years with the Eighth Air Force Photo & Newsreel unit and as staff correspondent for *Yank,* the Army weekly. His book, *The Great Iron Ship,* was a selection of the Book-of-the-Month Club. Another, *Man Under the Sea,* is considered the standard history of underwater exploration and has appeared in six languages. He assisted Captain Jacques-Yves Cousteau with *The Silent World* and wrote the narration for Cousteau's feature movie of the same title, which won the Grand Prix at the Cannes International Film Festival in 1956 and a Hollywood Oscar the following year. He died in 1967.